PLAINTIFF BLUES

JOB DISCRIMINATION AND THE CHILLING EFFECT OF RETALIATION

JUDITH PEARSON

Also by Judith Pearson

Myths of Educational Choice
Praeger 1993

Printed in the United States of America

ISBN 13: 978-0-9795689-0-9

To our kids and grandkids,
in hopes they will always have equal opportunities.

Acknowledgments

THANKS TO THE DEDICATED school personnel, teachers, and counselors I have worked with who helped make a positive difference in the lives of children.

Thanks to my students over the years who ultimately taught me far more than I taught them.

Thanks to editor Catherine Holm for encouraging me to write in ways I didn't think I could.

Thanks to my grandparents who spoiled me at a young age and to my parents who didn't. The combination created a balance of confidence and common sense that has served me well.

Thanks to my sons and daughters-in law, Erik and Jill, Max and Julie, who are a loving and supportive family from which one can take risks.

Most of all, thanks to my husband Rick. He kept his promise, for better and for worse, for richer and for poorer. He listened and shared through the years. He's my partner, my guide and my best friend.

And God Bless The USA, where there are civil rights to exercise.

St Louis County School District

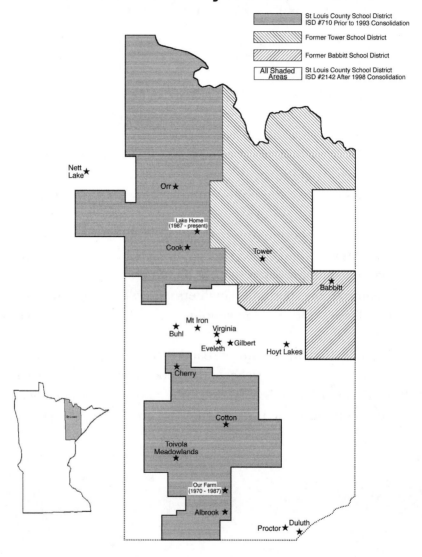

	St Louis County School District ISD #710 Prior to 1993 Consolidation
	Former Tower School District
	Former Babbitt School District
All Shaded Areas	St Louis County School District ISD #2142 After 1998 Consolidation

Nett Lake ★

Orr ★

Lake Home (1987 - present) ★

Cook ★

Tower ★

Babbitt ★

Mt Iron ★
★ Buhl
Virginia ★
★ ★ Gilbert
Eveleth ★
Hoyt Lakes ★

★ Cherry

Cotton ★

Toivola Meadowlands ★

Our Farm (1970 - 1987) ★

Albrook ★

Proctor ★ Duluth ★

St Louis

CONTENTS

PREFACE

"If you had been a man, you would have had the job."

"Hell will freeze over before we hire a woman principal at the Cook High School."

THOSE STATEMENTS AND THE hiring of a less qualified man were the responses to my 1986 application for that position in the small town of Cook, Minnesota (population 650).

Now what do you do? Fight or forfeit?

I fought back and this is my story.

It spans seventeen years of EEOC (Equal Employment Opportunity Commission) charges, civil litigation, and retaliation, including nine years as a plaintiff in two federal lawsuits. It is a story of breaking into a man's job in a man's world. The job is public school administration. The world is northeast Minnesota's Iron Range, where a mining economy and Old World provincialism have produced a distinctly macho worldview.

This is the same Iron Range described in the book, *Class Action* (Doubleday 2002) and the Warner Brothers film, *North Country*, based on that book. My story is the white-collar version of that nonfiction account of the sexual harassment women experienced after they were first hired in 1975 to work in the Iron Range mines. I experienced sexual discrimination, not sexual harassment. However, retaliation was common to both stories and is too often the response whenever someone asserts their employment rights.

In the 34 years I served in public education—16 as a teacher, 16 as a high school principal, and two as a district superintendent—no one ever questioned my competence or my superior credentials. Regardless, I lost six administrative positions to men later determined——by EEOC decision, Federal Court verdict, public exposure, or School Board action—to be less qualified or incompetent. Every one of those hiring decisions followed closed meetings or procedures that violated due process.

My experiences were unique in many ways. My challenges took place in small towns in rural northeast Minnesota, where everyone knows everyone. There were none of the protections of urban anonimity. I challenged the discrimination I experienced from both outside my employment institution and from within. Those two experiences differed significantly and the comparison provides unique insight into the plaintiff experience. In the end, it was challenging from within that left me so vulnerable to retaliation.

Retaliation is devastating for the individual and has a chilling effect on co-workers. Everyone runs for cover, no one wants to speak up. It is destructive to the productivity of the institution involved and to the progress of civil rights in general.

If you have ever been treated unfairly on the job because of sex, race, age, disability, or religion, you will relate to these experiences and the lessons I learned over the 17 years of struggle against discrimination and retaliation. If you have represented or may represent a victim of job discrimination, you will gain insights into their experience as a plaintiff and the retaliation they risk.

The civil rights pendulum continually swings back and forth on the political spectrum. My story illustrates how the fine points of civil rights laws and precedents can vary with time and place. Civil rights will never be settled law. Civil rights will always be a work in progress. People will always have to take risks to assert their rights. No one else will do it for you. Only when individuals fight for their own rights, do the rights of all advance.

That's the bedrock of civil rights.

I didn't want this fight, but it was a fight I couldn't walk away from.

This is my story.

Along the way, I've included enough autobiographical information to provide context for the events described above and some of the common sense insights about education that I gained in thirty-four years as an educator.

All material quoted in this book is cited within the text itself. All material quoted is taken from original sources: newspapers, letters, e-mail, EEOC documents, sworn depositions, affidavits, and documents that were included in trial exhibits.

When first told about the rumor that I got the interview for the principal's position because I was "sleeping with the superintendent," I started taking notes and have kept taking them ever since. In high school, our class read and loved Tale of Two Cities. In 1963, our class adopted the story as our theme throughout our senior year and has used it for our class reunions ever since. Somewhere in that process I must have identified with Madame DeFarge, keeping track and knitting names into her scarf. Many of these contemporaneous notes became part of the official court records and they form the basis for much of the dialogue included in the story.

The illustrations on the front cover were taken from artwork given to me on November 26, 1990, by Al Wilander, the official courtroom artist in Judge Alsop's Federal Court in Duluth, Minnesota.

If you have similar experiences to share, comments, or questions about the material or topics in this book, check out the website at www. plaintiffblues.com or e-mail me at jpearson@plaintiffblues.com.

Chapter 1

1968–1979
THE FIRST STING
OF DISCRIMINATION

"That's the way it's always been done."
Superintendent response to grievance, 10/23/75

WAS I BORN THIS way or did I learn to be so headstrong and stubborn? Nature or nurture? That question has bugged me many times, especially when those traits propelled me up the proverbial creek without a paddle!

Was it being the oldest of five kids, the only girl and a tomboy at that? Maybe it was growing up on Minnesota's Iron Range, where a mining economy and an Old World provincialism had produced a fierce independence and a distinctly macho worldview?

But why me? Why was I the one to challenge authority when so many others let the same issues pass? I wish I knew.

My dad had a solo law practice in Virginia, Minnesota, and was later appointed to the state district bench. My mom never worked after I was born, although she had a four-year degree in nursing. It was a pretty typical middle-class family. My parents never treated me differently or special as the only girl in the family. I was just one of the "kids."

However, I was treated special, "spoiled" in fact, by my maternal grandparents. My mom was an only child, so I was their first grandchild and only granddaughter. I was born in November 1944. My dad did not get out of the service until December 1945, so during my first year, my mother and I lived with her parents in Virginia, Minnesota. I took my first sauna at their cabin on Long Lake south of Eveleth, Minnesota, in the summer of 1945.

My dad began law school at the University of Minnesota in January 1946. During those first few winters he was in school, there was a polio scare in the Twin Cities. So again I spent time living with my grandparents up north. After my dad completed his degree, my folks moved back to Virginia and he began his law practice.

I continued to spend a lot of time at Nana and Grandpa's through most of grade school. We only lived two blocks away, so I could easily skip over to Nana's. At home, like my brothers, I had to eat what was on my plate, but Nana would fix my favorites. If I asked for a new bike, my mom would say, "we'll see." Grandpa would get it for me the next day. I even had my own bed, dresser, and closet at Nana's. Eventually my dad would put his foot down and home I went, until the next time. In retrospect, I think that early balance of the special treatment at Nana's and the down-to-earth reality checks at home gave me a strong sense of self-confidence.

Having four brothers and no sisters may explain why I was a tomboy. Being a tomboy probably contributed to my stubbornness and my competitiveness. I liked to compete whether it was marbles, ice hockey, card games, debates in senior civics, or top grades. While the girls played with paper dolls, I was out with the boys, shooting marbles with my prized cat's eyes and steelies. I loved to win, but I always felt sorry for the losers and I hated it if a game wasn't fair.

In elementary school, the same kids were always picked on and picked last for teams in gym and recess. It wasn't fair and I hated it. Whenever I was captain, I'd pick them first. I suppose that's why I wasn't made captain very often.

On Valentine's Day, I'd give them extra cards and treats because the other kids often skipped them. On Halloween, I shared extra candy with them. I didn't see myself as champion of the underdog, just trying to be fair and compensate for the hurt those kids experienced. As far back as I can remember, fairness was a big deal for me.

Fair is an interesting concept. It's hard to define in observable terms, but most of us recognize it when we see it. Equal is fair, right? Not always. A $100 fine means one thing to a rich man and something altogether different to a poor man. For me, unfair is a gut feeling, a sickening sense that something's not right.

Perhaps growing up as a tomboy, competitive, yet pigheaded about fairness, explains why as an adult, I stood my ground when faced with discrimination on the job. Why so many just accept unfairness on the job without fighting back is a nagging mystery. Do most people intuitively grasp the risks involved in taking a stand? The risks I failed to appreciate until I was in too deep? Are the accepters simply in denial, refusing to accept the idea that what happened to them was actually discrimination? Whatever the answers, I wrestled with the questions many times, mostly from the perspective of "Why me? How did I get into this mess when so many others manage to avoid it?"

Rick and I grew up a few miles apart on the Iron Range and attended Virginia Junior College the same years, but never met until we left home to attend the University of Minnesota. Even then, I attended the College of Education on the Minneapolis campus and Rick's forestry classes were on the St. Paul campus. We met on the weekend breaks back home on the Range. Our first "date" was in the fall of 1965. We hunted partridge on the Echo Trail and on the second date we deer hunted behind Pike River. That November, he gave me a pair of Irish Setter leather hunting boots for my birthday. When he attended an off-campus forestry course that winter quarter, his birch-bark Valentine read, "I love you more than a cow loves a warm hand on a cold morning!" It's been an outdoor romance ever since.

We were married in June 1967 in Virginia. Aside from the best man and the bridesmaid, the wedding party included my four brothers, Rick's two brothers and his sister. The only controversy in planning the wedding was Rick's beard. I wanted him to keep it, but his mom and my grandmother wanted it shaved off. They won, but it's been with us ever since.

In 1968, I completed my teaching degree in history and secondary social sciences from the University and Rick got his degree in forestry. That same fall, I began my first job teaching Senior Social Problems at North St. Paul High School.

I instantly loved teaching!

I loved all aspects of the teaching experience: the students, the subjects, the profession itself. I was one of the lucky ones to find work that I loved. Teaching was an intense and completely absorbing activity. Every student was a unique challenge. How do you challenge the gifted student while figuring ways to motivate the reluctant or slow learner? Although I spent more time and energy trying to reach the turned-off students, I had a couple of very unique, gifted students that I'll never forget.

For the Senior Social Problem classes, I used guest speakers, films, case studies, music, visual arts, and supplemental readings to present several approaches to the problems we were examining. The curriculum included the Vietnam War, civil rights, government, politics, poverty, and the general disciplines of economics and sociology.

As a part of the Vietnam unit, I brought in a leading anti-war activist from the University of Minnesota campus to explain the movement. For balance, I invited a colonel from the Minnesota Selective Service Office to discuss the rationale for the war and to explain the draft. The lottery system was a complicated two-step process and a particularly relevant subject for those seniors in my class who would be subject to its ramifications. After speaking and answering questions, the colonel had a confrontation with one of my students.

He was a brilliant but eccentric kid, a loner shunned by other students. He was obsessed with economics and anti-capitalism philosophy. He carried Mao's little red book in his briefcase and quoted from it regularly. Weeks after the colonel spoke to the class, the offices of the Selective Service were broken into. The offenders splattered pig's blood on the files. Shortly after that incident, two FBI agents visited my classroom. They presented an intimidating front with their crew cuts, bow ties, and khaki trench coats. As a part of their investigation into the break-in, they wanted the name of the student who had confronted Colonel Knight.

I told them I would not give out a student's name without notifying the student's parents. I worried that if they talked to the student without some representation, he would curse them out in his usual inflammatory style and end up in real trouble.

"Do you want to be listed as not cooperating with the United States government?" demanded the taller of the two agents.

"Of course not," I replied. "But I have an obligation to protect a student's rights. He needs his parents involved."

Our meeting ended in a stalemate. They left in a huff, upset with my position. To my knowledge, nothing ever came of their visit. I knew my student had nothing to do with the break-in. As I explained to them, he didn't drive, had no friends, and never left the neighborhood. But I always wondered if I made some list somewhere.

I encouraged and required students to form their own opinions and to justify them. We studied bias and propaganda. I wanted them to be skeptical, to read between the lines, so they could become independent learners and thinkers. A poster I kept in the front of my classroom summed it up. It read, "Give them a fish, they eat for a day; teach them to fish, they eat for a lifetime."

In 1993, out of the blue, I received a letter from another gifted North St. Paul student I had in 1969. Twenty-four years later, he had earned a degree in pre-med, a fellowship at the University of Pennsylvania, and his Ph.D. in clinical psychology. He wrote:

"I was a student in one of your classes, at North St. Paul High School, a long time ago. Do you remember me? I've thought about you often. You made a big impact on me. You helped me to develop my values, and you helped me learn how to think for myself. Your teaching method was very unusual and effective: basically, you gave me my ideas by showing an interest in what I thought, and by letting me explain my opinions to you. By trying to clarify to you what I thought, I also ended up clarifying my ideas to myself. I also remember that you believed in me. You thought that I had potential and you were sure that I was going to make some kind of difference. Your confidence in me helped me to believe more in myself." It was rewarding to learn that my teaching had made a difference for someone.

Regrettably, I had to leave North St. Paul after two terrific years. Rick received his second degree in teaching secondary science from the University in 1970. He decided he liked teaching more than forestry, his first degree. He accepted a science and math teaching position at the Proctor High School in the fall of 1970, so we headed north from the Twin Cities. We were glad to be closer to our families on the Iron Range and to our favorite pastimes of fishing and hunting.

While Rick began his teaching career in Proctor, I searched for a teaching position in the area. For two years, from 1970 through 1972, I did almost full-time substitute teaching and homebound instruction for area school districts. Subbing taught me about the difference between well-run and poorly run classrooms. With no seating charts and no lesson plans, a day of subbing in a junior high classroom could be pure hell.

I quickly learned to ask whom I would be subbing for and when to say no. I learned to bring my own plans for the day, just in case. Holding up a book I was reading and telling the book's story really caught students' attention. Kids might say they hate history, but they loved historical fiction. I would tell the story just to the turning point, timed just before the bell rang. They either wanted me back the next day to find out what happened or they wanted the book to finish for themselves. I used historical fiction regularly as a part of my teaching. It brought history alive for students and involved them in ways that dates and facts did not.

I also gained valuable insights doing homebound instruction. I taught students in their homes and sometimes in the hospitals. Most of my homebound students were pregnant girls. Our first son Erik was born in April of 1972, so my students and I were pregnant and first-time mothers at the same time. It gave me an advantage in teaching about prenatal care, nutrition, infant care, and other parenting issues. Teaching in the homes of twenty students provided experiences that teachers rarely have.

A few of the families were wealthy, but most were very poor. In one home, I smacked and killed a rat in the kitchen with a broom while my student and her mother scrambled up on the chairs and table. In another, my student shared information that forced me to call social service to report sexual abuse. I would have preferred to mind my own business and not get involved, but I had no choice. The situation for my student was grim. Worse yet, there were younger kids in the family. Even though convictions followed my reporting, it was not a very rewarding experience.

The toughest homebound job I had was in the burn-unit of the hospital. This particular student had been badly burned by an alcohol burner accident in a junior high science class. He had burns over most of his chest, arms, and face. I worked with this student for several months. What stayed with me long after that experience was his horrible pain and how it changed him. I watched a young, immature boy become an old man with his resigned, almost stoic acceptance of the painful, daily burn treatments.

By 1972, I had a wide range of teaching experiences. The first two years in North St. Paul were almost idyllic, fulfilling the romance of all that teaching could be. I had great students, great professional peers, great subjects to teach, all positives. The two years of substitute and homebound teaching removed the rose-colored glasses. Subbing in many classrooms throughout a school taught me that all teachers are not alike. Some are masters, but some should have chosen a different career. Homebound instruction took me beyond the classroom into the lives of students and their families.

Like most teachers, I came from a very positive, pro-education, middle class neighborhood and family. High school teachers rarely glimpse life on the other side of the classroom door or on the other side of the tracks. Those experiences, though not always positive, expanded my understanding of the educational experience. They added a great deal to who I was becoming as an educator. They gave me a broader understanding of the complex mix of factors that motivate student behavior. It was an invaluable perspective for both teaching and administration.

After two years of subbing and homebound instruction, I finally

secured a full-time job teaching social studies at West Junior High
School in Duluth in the fall on 1972. I finally had my own classroom
again and I loved it. Now I could plan and develop units of instruction,
not just single-day, sub survival kits. At the end of the 1972–1973
school year, I was invited to join a new faculty, teaching social studies
in Duluth's first alternative school. I accepted the new position and
taught in the Duluth Open School for four years, until it closed in
1977.

The open school was a unique professional experience. We had
the opportunity to experiment with many aspects of the education
business in ways that most educators just dream or theorize about.
For example, we had the scheduling flexibility to give a group of
teachers common preparation time. That planning time allowed us
to team-teach and provide inter-disciplinary instruction. Traditionally
students studied the French Revolution or WW I in a history class one
year and read the literature of that same period a year or two later.
Now we could examine a historical period from many disciplines at
one time.

When it was relevant, science, art, and/or music teachers would
join the team. Whether is was the renaissance or the reformation,
students and teachers alike gained a much richer understanding
of the milieu of a period, instead of the simple dates and facts, all
packaged in separate little boxes of curriculum.

The discussions that followed explored the mind set or worldview
of a historical period. A study of the industrial revolution prompted
important and still relevant questions about how technology can
influence so many aspects of the human experience. How did those
technological changes influence socioeconomic conditions and/
or the thinking of contemporaries like Dickens, Marx, Darwin, and
Freud? None of us believed we were breaking new ground. But we
were certainly thinking about the old ground in exciting new ways.

Our students rarely, if ever, had the same required assignment.
After a unit of instruction coordinated with several teachers, students
were encouraged to pursue the topic in ways that interested them
individually and demonstrate what they had learned. One student

presented a project demonstrating how the development of weapons leading up to WW I led to the stalemate of the trenches while another student discussed the influence of the trench warfare experience on the war poets and existential literature.

In traditional schools, student progress is measured in letter grades that are too often just indicators of how well a student plays the school game and pleases the teachers. Those letter grades are based primarily on multiple choice, pencil-and-paper tests that are easy for teachers to grade and measure little more than memorization skills. The rest of the letter grade calculation typically comes from those mind-numbing worksheets and homework assignments that are mostly repetitious busy work.

In all fairness, these kinds of assignments have their place, because students learn and achieve in different ways. It's when these methods are used exclusively and not balanced with more open and individualized assignments that the brightest and most creative students are turned off and the least motivated students drop out. When these tests and grades are calculated on a curve, only a certain percentage of the students can get A's and a certain percentage must fail. Students have to compete against one another, creating an atmosphere ripe for cheating.

We required students to demonstrate other skills such as analysis, synthesis, comparison, and evaluation in their project work. We allowed and encouraged students to help each other and collaborate on their projects and in their presentations. Occasionally the synergy from several students and/or several disciplines was truly remarkable.

One group of students wrestled with the concept of revolution. After comparing the American, French, and Bolshevik revolutions, they explored a definition of the term that had broader application. Then they examined its use describing the industrial revolution of the 19th Century. They compared those fast, violent, political changes to slower, technological, economic change. What other rapid or fundamental changes fit their evolving definition of revolution? The automobile and its impact on the demographics of cities? Sputnik and its impact on science curriculum? How about the "sexual revolution" of the sixties?

One can only hope that today, those students have a conceptual framework from which to evaluate the impacts of the personal computer, the internet, and the other recent information technologies on our lives. Most of these technologies did not exist in 1978.

This kind of instruction often required more than the traditional, 50-minute class period. Because the Open School was designed to be a faculty-run school, teachers could participate in determining the length of the class periods. Now we could structure the length of the class periods to fit the instruction rather than cram the instruction into a standard class period. Art classes, science experiments, or inter-disciplinary studies could now be scheduled for two hours or more as determined by the instructional need rather than by administrative dictate.

Sometimes the entire K–12 faculty planned for a week of instruction on a single theme. On one occasion we focused on environmental education for a week in all subjects at all grade levels. It was a great way to demonstrate the variety of ways our lives impact the environment and the variety of ways the environment impacts our lives. By its very nature, environmental learning should not be limited to a six-week unit in an eighth grade science class. Foreign language and culture, tolerance, and conflict resolution were other concepts that benefited from a similar, immersion approach.

However, those regular, consensus-driven faculty meetings were a mixed blessing! On the one hand, teachers were thrilled to have more control over their teaching environment—selection of courses, schedule of courses, methods of instruction. On the other hand, a lot of time was wasted reaching consensus concerning such routine administrative details as what time to break for lunch.

I was pregnant with my second son Max when I began my third year of teaching at the Open School. Planning ahead, I worked with the substitute teacher to cover my assignments when the baby was born. I taught the full day on Wednesday, September 10, 1975. Early on Thursday, September 11, 1975, I called the sub and the principal from the labor room at the hospital. Max was born just before noon.

My doctor gave me approval to return to work on Monday, September 29, 1975.

I already had a wonderful baby-sitter for my three-year-old son Erik. She and her husband had two young children of their own and they lived across the street from the Open School. They were all looking forward to the baby coming, so I planned to return to work as soon as possible.

What a relief to have a good sitter for the kids! More than degrees, credentials, and luck, it made working possible! Childcare, especially for an infant, was a constant stress. Even the best sitters in the world could not ease the guilt and worry when the kids were sick.

We used seven different sitters for one or both boys from 1972 to 1983, when Rick began working from his home office. During those 11 years, sitters changed because situations changed, theirs or ours. Each change was traumatic for us and for the boys. Finding and keeping a good sitter created an underlying anxiety that I never anticipated as an integral part of my working.

Three times we moved the kids abruptly when things didn't seem right. It was recurring diaper rash, unused diapers, illogical rules, or lack of supervision that got our attention. It was never anything horrific, just nagging concerns. A lot depended on how the kids behaved when we picked them up. In one instance, it seemed that almost overnight, the boys (ages 3 & 6) had become little monsters, fighting constantly. They were with a sitter who ran a licensed day-care. Her license allowed up to ten children and she had the full ten.

She had plenty of room and lots of toys, puzzles and hands on activities. I stayed to watch and visit several times after work. I realized that the kids were left alone most of the time and had to fend for themselves. It was survival of the fittest. She did not intervene in squabbles or referee in any way. We changed sitters within two months and the boys returned to the relatively civilized kids they had been.

In another instance, an older, socialist couple had agreed to watch Erik after school on days when Rick had to travel. When their German shepherd scared him as he walked up their long driveway from the school bus, they quickly agreed to keep the dog confined until Erik got in. She even gave him his first piano lessons. But when Erik announced to Max that there was no Santa Claus after the sitter had told him Santa was just a commercial scheme for making money, it was more change, more trauma for everyone.

When Max was born in 1975, Rick and I decided that two children were enough for us. We were thirty-one years old and did not want to fret about birth control for another decade. The day after Max was born, I had a tubal ligation performed. I returned to work on Monday, September 29, 1975, with my doctor's approval. I had missed just twelve days of school.

I was shocked to find that my September 26th paycheck was not waiting for me when I returned to work. I called the central office and the business manager told me that my sick leave claim had been denied. Those twelve days had to be taken as maternity leave without pay, as provided in the contract.

This can't be right, I said to myself. I had not applied for maternity leave because I had not intended to be out of work more than a few days. The maternity leave in the contract was specifically for extended leaves of many months following childbirth. Besides, I had thirty-six days of sick leave accumulated. That was more than enough to cover the few days I expected to be out of work.

Paid sick leave was approved for other medical procedures like appendectomy, tonsillectomy or vasectomy. Only pregnancy was excluded. *Not fair.* Fair was the operative term, motivating my anger and my actions. The concept of discrimination never entered my mind.

I called the union office and explained the situation. They were more than willing to help. In fact, they said, they had actually been looking for a case to challenge the maternity leave provision of the contract. I couldn't believe it had never been challenged before. It was obviously unfair.

On September 30, 1975, I filed a formal grievance under the contract provisions.

Initially, the challenge was no big deal for me. It didn't cost me anything and for the most part, the union's attorneys handled everything. This large organization fought my battle and the community was large enough that I didn't stand out like a sign-toting feminist. Naively, I felt shielded by the anonymity.

On October 23, 1975, the Superintendent denied the grievance. In his written denial, Superintendent Pearson concluded, "Disability due to uncomplicated pregnancy has consistently been deemed to be outside of the sick leave provisions based on illness or other disability. In other words, maternity disability has not been paid because it is not a disability which the school district has recognized in the past."

In other words, that's the way it is because that's the way it's always been. It had never been challenged. As Mr. Waters, attorney for the Duluth Federation of Teachers wrote, "This is a matter that continually arises and most individual teachers, as well as other female public employees in Duluth, as well as other school districts in the area, have simply acceded to the position of the various public employers."

Why did so many others simply accede to the status quo? Why didn't I? I'd always had a pretty hard line between what's fair and what's not. I can't recall a specific message about fairness at home, church or school. I was never treated unfairly as a kid. However, when others were treated unfairly, it upset me. The bullies in grade school really bothered me. They never picked on me, but I hated what they did to other kids.

Later in school, the little we learned about Indians in the westward expansion, slaves in the Civil War, and the concentration camps during WWII motivated me to read more on my own. What I read profoundly disturbed me. I was haunted by the Anne Frank story. I couldn't believe that these things had happened and nobody had stopped it. Books like *Black Boy*, *Black Like Me*, and *Bury My Heart At Wounded Knee* taught me that man's inhumanity to man had no boundaries in time or geography.

In junior college, I was selected to travel with a Methodist youth group through the southern states to visit the missions of the church. I was planning to enter the ministry and this would be a good experience. When we were in Mississippi, we stayed on the campus of a black college in Holly Springs. We had white and black students in our group and made black friends on the campus.

On Sunday morning, however, we either had to worship at separate Methodist churches or go to the black church, because our black friends could not attend the white Methodist church. This wasn't right and I was extremely frustrated that such unfairness was the policy of my church. The pastors all had the same, lame explanations related to different regions and different conferences. No one else was as angry as I was. I spent less and less time in church after that trip.

A more likely explanation for my obsession with fairness, equity, and equality may stem from what I learned while teaching. In North St. Paul and again in Duluth, I was assigned to teach Senior Social Problems. The government portion of the curriculum included civil rights and civil liberties. I read widely outside the classroom to prepare. We studied Miranda and Gideon, *Brown v. Board of Education*, Tinker, and countless others.

I relished the teasing from students when they invoked due process, equal protection, probable cause, cruel and unusual punishment in response to one of my deliberately arbitrary or unfair decisions. I'd play devil's advocate that way occasionally, just to test their grasp of the lesson.

Someone once said—or should have—that you don't really know what you know until you teach it. Teaching is a powerful learning process. It locks in the knowledge and makes it yours. The best way to motivate and excite students is to convey your own enthusiasm for the subject and I loved the subjects I was teaching. The basic lesson of civil rights is that you have to know your rights and be willing to take a stand for them. I internalized the same lessons I was teaching my students.

Although my experiences and reading hardened my sense of fairness, I believe teaching tipped the scale. The lessons I learned while teaching left me no choice but to fight back. However, this maternity leave challenge in Duluth would not be my last wrestling match with the question of "why me?"

In his denial of my grievance on the maternity leave issue, Superintendent Pearson stated that my daily rate of pay was $54.21

and that I was seeking sick leave in the total amount of $650.52. He added that, "While the monetary implications are not particularly significant in this particular case, an award in favor of the employee would certainly obligate the school district to pay similar claims in the future, at least to the extent of twelve days if based on official medical determination of disability."

However, those "monetary implications" were "particularly significant" to our growing family. As it was, we were just making it from paycheck to paycheck. That's why I challenged in the first place. I wasn't carrying any banners. I had a full-time job and two young children. I wasn't looking for a cause. In short, I just needed the money.

The Duluth School Board discussed my grievance at a meeting following Superintendent Pearson's denial. "Mrs. Richard Pearson sues Superintendent Richard Pearson for Maternity Leave" was the coverage the next day in the *Duluth Herald* newspaper. Rick and I chuckled about the coincidental names in the article, but not the rest of the story.

The Board also discussed "elective surgery of an unspecified nature" following delivery, according to the newspaper.

Now I was mad.

Our very personal decision to have the tubal ligation was broadcast to the world. It didn't take a medical degree for colleagues, friends, family, and all the rest of the people in Duluth to figure out what "elective surgery of an unspecified nature" following pregnancy meant. Now I wanted a banner to carry; any banner would do. Everything seemed so unfair; the missing paycheck, the public notoriety, and the blown privacy.

I agreed with the union to appeal the grievance to binding arbitration. However, the arbitrator could only rule on the interpretation of existing contract language. He did not have the authority to determine whether the contract language itself was unlawful. Therefore, at the union's urging, I reluctantly agreed to file a discrimination charge simultaneously with the Minnesota Department of Human Rights. This was the authority that could make a determination on the legality of the contract language.

Why the reluctance? This was my first encounter with the thought that I had actually been discriminated against, that I was a victim of discrimination. There was a subtle shift in perception from "them" being unfair to "me" being a victim. Victim was not a concept I identified with easily.

This was getting a lot bigger than I anticipated.

The arbitration hearing was held in December 1975. In early 1976 the arbitrator ruled in favor of the school district, deciding the issue strictly on past practice. All the arbitrator really determined was that the district had been consistent in its application of the existing contract language.

But the Minnesota Department of Human Rights, as it turned out, had plenty to say about the very legality of that same existing contract language. The MDHR investigation ran almost concurrently with the arbitrator's. In January 1976 they found probable cause that discrimination had occurred and ordered the district to settle. The school district stalled on settling, considering an appeal of that decision.

On February 25, 1976, the Minnesota Department of Human Rights wrote to the Duluth School district, "Nearly 60 days have elapsed since you received notification that a finding of probable cause has been made in the Pearson discrimination charge. If conciliation efforts have not begun in 10 days the charge against the Independent School District #709 (Duluth) will be sent to the Attorney General's Office and scheduled for a public hearing."

Shortly after that, the district settled. I received the sick leave pay for the 12 days I had missed after Max was born.

This was a very positive outcome for many reasons. As a result of the finding from the Minnesota Department of Human Rights, the contract language for the Duluth School District was changed to include pregnancy as a medical disability. Subsequently, contracts soon changed in all the area school districts. City and county contracts changed as well, and women in public employment could finally use accumulated sick leave for the usual and customary absence for pregnancy. Long term, maternity leaves of absence without pay remained as an option, not a mandate.

I had been treated unfairly and I challenged that treatment. Admittedly, I was only looking out for myself and my own rights. I won and received my $650. The fact that other women gained maternity leave options was a collateral benefit and, in retrospect, was probably my biggest victory. It is also the essence of civil rights.

As a credit to the District, I must note, there was never any animosity shown to me or to the union folks who represented me. Everyone behaved professionally. It proved that reasonable people could disagree and continue to work together.

I taught in Duluth for three more years. Every spring, the district placed me on unrequested leave of absence, due to declining enrollments and budget reductions. The district always laid me off properly, according to seniority and licensure. There was never any question of retaliation. Contrasting this experience, there was nothing to prepare me for the deliberate, mean-spirited retaliation I would encounter twenty years later.

The Duluth district called me back to teach every fall. But the retirements in my license area of secondary social studies could not stay ahead of the declining enrollments. The numbers fell fast. I knew that sooner or later, my seniority would be too low to get called back to teach in Duluth.

While teaching at the Duluth Open School in secondary social studies, I was asked by both principals to cover for them whenever they were out of the building for the day. I found I liked the problem-solving demands of administration. They and other Duluth administrators mentioned to me several times that I should consider getting my administrative degree. I could not hold a social studies position much longer, so I decided to go back to school for administrative licensure.

I needed to complete my master's degree before I could apply for the administrative program. First I had to convince my advisor to accept my thesis topic. I wanted to examine the impacts of television on individuals, families, and social institutions, from an interdisciplinary approach including communications, economics, sociology, and psychology. He resisted my choice because both the interdisciplinary approach and the breadth of scope were outside the traditional parameters. After several discussions, however, he finally accepted my thesis topic, "The Role of Television in American Society."

I had first become intrigued the idea in the mid-sixties while watching my youngest brother watch television. He was between two and four years old at the time. He'd play with his toys in front of the TV, paying no attention to it, until the commercials came on. Then he was mesmerized. He turned immediately back to his toys when the regular programming resumed. That behavior happened consistently as I watched him and other youngsters. Something other than simple content had to be coming out of that innocent box in the corner of the living room.

For years, I read everything I could find about television. I watched television and I watched people watching television. I never thought television was bad or evil, but I knew its impacts were deeper and broader than most of us understood.

Rick and I decided not to have a TV in our home. When Erik and Max were young, it was hard to resist the pressure. Of course they could watch it at the babysitter's or whenever visiting family or friends, so they knew what they were missing. We just didn't want it dominating our family life.

Friends and family often suggested, subtly, that we were abusing our kids, or at least denying them, keeping them isolated from the real world. After all, what else could a family of four possibly do on a cold Minnesota night in January? I assure you, we were never bored. We listened to Mystery Theater on the radio, played games, worked on craft projects together, built model airplanes—the list was endless. Either Rick or I read to the kids every night at bedtime. Sometimes it was both of us because the stories were so interesting. The *Chronicles of Narnia*, Alfred Hitchcock's *The Three Investigator* series, the *Encyclopedia Brown* series, again the list seems endless.

We certainly weren't opposed to technology, just one that could so pervasively supplant other valuable activities. In fact, we bought an Apple computer in 1981. That was three years before we plugged in our first television set. Rick's folks gave us their old set when they upgraded to a bigger set. We rigged it up with rabbit-ear antennae, extended with a couple of coat hangers. The reception left lots to be desired.

While Rick and I struggled with the computer instructions, Erik took to it intuitively. He beat Rick's score on the Depth Charge game every time. By fifth grade, the school's computer instructor was calling Erik regularly for help.

My television thesis fascinated the professors in my master's oral exam. The exam lasted beyond the scheduled time because the subject so intrigued the professors. Most interesting was the personal and defensive tone to many of their questions. Apparently the topic forced them to examine something in their personal lives and they didn't want to go there.

I completed the masters in 1977 and began the coursework for the Specialist Degree in school administration. I loved the classroom almost as much as a student as I did as a teacher. It was a treat to be reading and discussing books and topics so relevant to my daily work. But the full-time job, two kids, and shuffling sitters made school difficult. I could never have done it without Rick's support. For several years, I attended classes in the evenings, on Saturdays, and during the summers to get my administrative degree.

Several of the instructors in the administrative courses were current superintendents doing adjunct teaching for the university. Their real-life and up-to-date experience was a refreshing and practical break from the ivory-tower idealism of so many university professors. However, much of their advice to us clearly indicated that it was a man's world ahead.

One instructor urged us to practice our golf game because a lot of administrative networking took place on the golf course. "That's why," he said, "most of the state and national workshops are held at golf courses." I hoped that golf wasn't a prerequisite for school administration, because I had never swung a club. With family, job, and coursework, I had neither the time nor the money to worry about my "handicap."

Another adjunct told us that we needed to be involved in community organizations, like the local Legion, Rotary, and Kiwanis. At that time, those organizations admitted men only. Women or spouses were consigned to the auxiliaries. He didn't miss a beat as he said this, never registering the fact there was a woman in the class.

In spite of those slightly off-putting messages, I kept at it. Rick continued his supportive role as Mr. Mom. After I completed my Specialist Degree, my academic advisor wrote in a letter of recommendation for my placement file:

"I have known Ms. Pearson in her capacity as a graduate student and as a teacher working with my own children. Further, I've had the opportunity to observe her work with administration problems in the Duluth Open School. In every case I have observed a thoroughly dedicated, competent and intelligent person, dealing effectively with the multitude of tasks demanded of her. She has an incisive mind with excellent powers of analysis, while at the same time respecting the suggestions, ideas, and persuasions of other persons. She seems to be well organized and efficient. Above all, however, she has an understanding and compassion for young people that is at once realistic and caring. In my judgment she definitely has a career in school administration and will do a superlative job wherever she works."

When the Open School closed at the end of the 1977 school year, I transferred to Central High School. This was a big school, with a graduating class of several hundred. I was assigned to teach Senior Social Problems, Comparative Government, and American History, including the advanced or honors sections. It was such a different experience from the Open School. Bells rang when there had been none; rigid rules and regulations applied where there had been few; authority replaced consensus. Just using the copy machine required two authorizations and three numerical codes.

In many ways it was a welcome change. It was often frustrating at the Open School to spend hours in meetings coming to consensus on something so simple as when to schedule the parents' open house. A quick administrative decision was much more efficient and allowed teachers to attend to teaching.

I had often thought during our exciting, concept-driven, interdisciplinary Period Units at the Open School—how much more meaningful that learning would have been if students had previously completed basic survey courses in history. Now I was back teaching those traditional courses and I made it my mission to put life back into history, to make it more than the deadly, boring subject that kids hate.

I spent two terrific years at Central High School. I loved teaching high school students. The challenge in high school was to wake them up, motivate and involve them in their learning. At West Junior High, the challenge had been almost the opposite. The junior high students were awake all the time, involved in and motivated by too many things, little of which related to academics. The adolescent and social stuff was challenging and fun in junior high, but I preferred the greater emphasis on the academic material and intellectual development in the high school.

Although back in a traditional high school, I resisted the typical grading methods and systems. If I gave a test and 30% of the students failed, who had really failed? Either the test covered material that I had not taught or I had not taught it very well. The prepared tests from the text publishers were the worst. One simple word or phrase changed the correct answer in a true or false question. Multiple choice questions had options included to deliberately mislead students. Test questions were too often about obscure little facts that had nothing to do with the big picture. These kinds of tests were designed to trick students into the wrong answers, a proverbial game of "gotcha." These kinds of tests measure how well students take these kinds of tests and very little else.

I wrote my own tests to give students the chance to show what they knew rather than sneak up on what they didn't know. In my tests and assignments, I worked for a balance that would allow both the gifted and the slower students to achieve some measure of success.

Each test or assignment would have some emphasis on definitions of major terms and short answers that we covered in class and were easily found in the text. That might include identifying terms like isolationism, fascism, Hitler and kamikaze. A short answer question might be, "Which countries opposed each other in WW II?" These kinds of questions and assignments allowed the less accomplished students to be successful.

That same unit test would also include essay questions to challenge the brighter students. For example, "Compare the German government under the Weimar Republic to the American government under the Articles of Confederation" or "Explain why you think Truman was right or wrong to drop the A bomb on Hiroshima and Nagasaki." The essay questions were written to allow the students to demonstrate their reasoning and their understanding of the bigger questions. I usually gave the students a choice of questions and I usually allowed them to use their notebooks. That reinforced taking good notes during the classroom lectures and discussions.

None of this eliminated the quarterly grading dilemmas. I rarely failed students and only did so after I was certain that I had done everything I could to motivate them. That's the job isn't it? They actually had to work hard to get an F from me.

But the top grades were also tough to decide. Who should get the better grade—the gifted student who whips out an assignment at the last minute, or the student of more average ability that obviously put in tons of time and effort? I developed a dual grading system on project work, one grade for quality and one for effort. I even experimented with a self-grading system, allowing students to evaluate how much they learned and how much effort they had put into the project. That bombed quickly because, surprisingly, the grades dropped dramatically and parents complained. However, we had some great discussions trying to understand why they dropped their own grades.

The recognition that students come to school with vastly different levels of innate ability and vastly different levels of socioeconomic advantage is what's missing in all the political rhetoric and statutory reform like No Child Left Behind. Many students start school so far behind that even super-human teaching efforts cannot make up for the deficits. Every classroom teacher deals with these differences every day. No amount of standardized testing, legislated accountability, or extraordinary teaching can level these differences in student aptitude that originate outside the classroom.

The school reformers and their high-stakes tests that require schools to "close the gap," simply ignore the underlying problems. High-stakes refers to tests that have a lot riding on the outcome, such as student graduation, teacher pay, or school revenue. The structural problems of poverty in our society will doom these reform efforts. These kinds of reforms are oversimplified attempts to solve complex problems, band-aids on the symptoms that leave the underlying causes untouched.

In the spring of 1979, I was selected by the senior class at Central High School to give the commencement address in the city auditorium. I shared the public rostrums that evening with Vice-President Walter Mondale who gave the commencement address at East High School in Duluth. It was an honor to have been selected. Looking back, the theme of my remarks that evening may have been predictive of things to come. The title of my remarks was "Take A Stand."

During the years I taught in Duluth, we lived on an old farmstead twenty-five miles north of Duluth and Proctor. Rick and I liked the rural lifestyle and we wanted our kids to attend smaller schools. We had both taught in larger schools and watched kids get lost in the huge numbers. We wanted the more personal atmosphere of smaller schools for our kids. We bought the farm in 1975 and built a new home there in 1976.

We raised cows, pigs, chickens, horses, too many bales of hay, and tons of vegetables. I taught in Duluth and Rick taught in Proctor until 1974, when he left teaching to work for himself as a media consultant. Although he did his production work out of a home office, he was often on the road. I drove 35 miles to work and hauled the kids to the sitter's everyday. The commute and sitter stops added an hour on each end of the day, not counting groceries and other errands.

Our oldest son Erik started kindergarten in the fall of 1977 and Max began in the fall of 1981. They attended the Alborn Elementary School, a small feeder elementary program in the Albrook High School attendance area.

Albrook was the southern of six high school attendance sites in the large, sparsely populated St. Louis County School District (ISD 710) that stretched from just north of Duluth to just south of the Canadian border. It was geographically the largest school district in the state. The degree of sparcity was less that one-half student per squarc mile. The other five high school attendance areas were Toivola-Meadowlands, Cotton, Cherry, Cook, and Orr.

The district also had five feeder elementary schools including Alborn, Brookston, Makinen, Forbes and Alango. The district was over 100 miles between the most southern and northern schools, with attendance areas reaching 30-50 miles beyond the school sites. The central office was located in Virginia, halfway between north and south, but outside the actual district. The school board met once a month, rotating the meeting sites to the schools in the district.

During the 1977–1978 school year, many parents discussed concerns about a district proposal for combination grades in the smaller elementary schools. Teachers and neighbors urged me to run for the school board. I filed and was elected to represent the Albrook attendance area on the St. Louis County School Board from 1978–1981.

Along with the roles of parent, teacher, and graduate student in school administration, the school board experience was a fascinating addition to the education mix. I had to check frequently to make sure I had the right educational hat on. On the board, I learned the critical differentiation between policy and administration. The board made the policy decisions on curriculum and programs, the administration implemented those decisions. I served on the board negotiating committee for a teachers' contract that ended in binding arbitration. I received calls from angry teachers who felt I was a sell-out and comments from other board members who felt I was too pro-teacher. I learned the price of making tough decisions. The board chair or the superintendent often asked me to make the toughest motions involving the termination of employees or the closing of schools.

I participated in successfully lobbying the Minnesota state legislature for sparcity aid to large, rural school districts in 1980. This targeted aid brought over $1 million in additional revenue to the district every year. My understanding of the education business broadened again.

By 1978, Rick had returned to education on a limited basis. Albrook, our local high school, was rural enough that it had trouble getting substitute teachers. The principal had repeatedly urged Rick to sign on and help out. He agreed and even took a long-term substitute position for six weeks. However, his business as a media consultant was expanding rapidly and by 1980, he turned down most subbing calls.

Then in 1980, Albrook still had an open math position late in the fall. After a summer of posting with no luck, the principal called Rick and asked him to take the position as a long-term sub for one year. Rick was reluctant because he had a major media contract pending and this would mean lots of late nights doing two jobs. But the principal was persistent and Rick finally agreed.

Because I served on the school board, state law required that I abstain from voting to hire Rick and required that the remaining vote be unanimous. Superintendent Nachitalo and the board chair called to inform other board members of the legal requirements for this vote. No one raised any objections. The issue was on the regular school board meeting agenda in late September at the Albrook School. School had started weeks earlier and Rick was already in the classroom as is often the case with late summer teacher hires.

The motion to hire Rick was made and seconded. There was no discussion following the motion. The clerk called the roll. I abstained and Chester Larson, board member from Cotton, voted "no." His vote caught us all by surprise. He had given no indication to the superintendent, the Board chairman, or to me that he had any concerns. We were all upset. Had he or anyone else raised questions or objections, the district would have reposted the job and kept looking, using a short-call substitute in the interim.

I was furious.

Chester had blindsided the board in public and me in my home district. The in-service training all school board members received from the Minnesota School Boards Association stressed "no surprises." He had, apparently, never learned that lesson.

After the meeting, he explained to board members that he didn't like hiring relatives of board members. That hardly explained his perverse tactics.

No one could understand why he had not expressed his concerns when called before the public meeting. He and I had a brief, private exchange following his explanation. I used a few intemperate words. My frustration had nothing to do with what he had done; it was how he did it.

That evening and the next day, the superintendent, the chairman, other board members, and the Albrook principal called Rick to apologize for Chet's surprising behavior and to urge him to stay on until they could find another long-term sub. Again Rick agreed for the good of the kids.

As it turned out, those five classes of math students had six more substitute teachers before the school year was over and the district had to transfer an experienced math teacher from Cotton the next year in response to all the parent complaints.

After the angry words between Chet and I that evening, the subject was dropped and forgotten—at least by us. Rick could now devote full time to his media business. Chester Larson and I continued to work together on the board for another year, until I decided not to run again at the end of my term. By then, I was serving as a high school principal and was too busy to run for a second three-year term. Little did we know that this incident would become part of a "whodunit" mystery ten years later.

Change came as fast in my career as it did in Rick's. With the layoff in the spring of 1979, after several years of the annual spring layoffs and fall recalls, it was clear I would not be called back to teach in

Duluth that fall. The rate of enrollment decline and subsequent staff cuts had finally overtaken my seniority. Even though I knew it was coming, it was a shock to face being out of work when school started. I began applying for work within a 50-mile driving distance.

I accepted a coordinator position in August with NE ECSU (Northeast Educational Cooperative Service Unit), a regional, educational service organization with offices 45 miles north of us in Eveleth, Minnesota. I was not teaching, but I was still in education and back home on the Iron Range, at least for my job. When I left the Duluth School District after seven years, I received the following recommendation from the Director of Secondary Education:

"I have known Ms. Pearson for the past seven years during which time she has served as 1) a crucial faculty member for the life of one of this district's secondary alternative programs - "The Open School" and 2) a member of the Social Studies department of Duluth Central High School. These two kinds of experiences were at almost opposite poles in terms of structure, organization, and relations between and among staff and students, but Judy both accommodated herself to both situations and impacted favorably upon them to her great credit.

"Ms. Pearson is a dynamic, highly energetic individual who both leads or cooperates with others who lead toward finding solutions to problems or enterprises and goes about implementing them. She is impatient with persons satisfied with the *status quo* simply because 'that is the way it has been done'. She is equally dissatisfied with procrastinators and folks in 'neutral'. She is a mover and a doer.

"Judy, in summary, is a complex, flexible, realistic person who is humane and tolerant of others. She values variety of experience, has an active imagination which aids her to contribute creative solutions to problems and instills enthusiasm in others involved with her in activities. She is very intelligent and has a mature well-developed interest in aesthetics without losing her sense of practicality and her interest in more mundane things if such happens to be the topic of the moment. In my opinion she is an outstanding teacher and would be an excellent administrator should she select that role in education."

As I looked ahead to my new job north in Eveleth, I dreaded another search for a babysitter and another adjustment for the kids. Our sitter in Duluth had spoiled us for years. However, grandmothers would be closer in Virginia and Gilbert and could help with the kids in a pinch. After all, Grandmas are the next best things to Mom when kids are sick.

I worried about the distance as well. This new commute would double my time, double the miles, and double the costs. I had cause to worry.

Gas prices skyrocketed after the Iran hostage crisis in 1979.

My days got longer.

Chapter 2

1979–1986

PROMOTION AND DEMOTION

*"The Cook Chamber of Commerce asked to visit potential
candidates for the principal in Cook."*
Cook News Herald, 7/3/86

I MISSED TEACHING AND I missed Duluth, but I liked
my work as planner for the NE ECSU (Northeast Educational
Cooperative Service Unit).

I assisted the 26 school districts in the region in their planning
for staff training, curriculum development, student assessment, and
general inservice programs. With my school board service on the
geographically large county school board and my work for a regional
planning agency, I covered a lot of territory. I worked with many
schools and got to know many school administrators. I had served
just two months in the NE ECSU position when once again, my career
shifted.

In late September 1979, I received a call from the Superintendent
in Buhl, Minnesota. He asked if I was interested in the high school
principal position. That summer, the Buhl School District had hired
a principal for grades 7–12. In early September, he had simply walked

off the job. I was told that the new principal had not appreciated
the kind of parent involvement that was almost instinctive on the
Iron Range. When parents directed criticism at his decisions, he was
particularly offended.

In most of the small towns on the Iron Range, parents don't need
to be prodded to get involved. It's their right. Most of them had deep
roots in the area and had graduated from the same school their kids
now attended.

I went to Buhl for an interview the next day and was offered the
high school principal position at the conclusion of the interview. The
superintendent wanted me to start as soon as possible. School board
action followed a few days after the interview. The Superintendent
had been covering both superintendent and principal positions and
the board wanted full-time administrators in both positions.

I didn't realize it until later, but I was the first woman to serve as
high school principal in northeastern Minnesota. Women had served
as assistant principals, but none had held the top job.

It's a good thing I had headed north to find work in administration.
Although I had won the 1975 discrimination challenge in Duluth on
maternity leave, other equal opportunity issues in Duluth remained
the way they had always been. As I prepared to leave Duluth in July
1979, a Duluth School Board member wrote a letter to Superintendent
Richard Pearson about the district's failure to hire any women for the
secondary principal positions. A few women held vice-principalships,
but none had been able to move up. She wrote:

"If women ask me to give an honest assessment of their
opportunities in the Duluth School System, I must say that in my
opinion it is intolerable. What are the symptoms of an intolerable
system? If you investigate woman by woman the successful ones, you
would find it takes something beyond competency – even instead of
competency. There are three routes to take:

1. Put up with having your head patted.
2. Put up with having your fanny patted.
3. Strengthen your credentials, then threaten, fight, sue.

If you wish to check out the success stories of women in

administration in the last ten years, you will find they fit one of these patterns – head, fanny, or fight. If the few women are all applying in other districts, due to substandard treatment here, maybe you will lose them. Then what kind of education are you providing?"

I never applied for an administrative position in Duluth because I had not completed my Specialist Degree when my teaching layoff was final in the fall of 1979. I often wonder what would have happened if the final layoff had taken place a year later. At any rate, I was headed for a principal position 60 miles north of Duluth. I came to a fork in the road and I took it.

Like all first time principals, anxiety reigned those first weeks on the job. It was a huge jump in responsibility. There's a lot to learn quickly. In addition to the names of the 38 teachers and other staff people I now supervised, I had to learn the ins and outs of the school building, the master schedule, the discipline policies and procedures. You just know that there's no way the coursework, administrative degree, and license can prepare you for every contingency and surprise that lies ahead. School was already in session when I came on board; so much of my anxiety related to playing catch-up. It had nothing to do with being a woman doing what had always been a man's job.

Although that thought never entered my mind, apparently it grabbed the attention of others.

In the teachers' lounge at Buhl, they had a board with bets on how long I'd last. Big bets had been placed. After all, my predecessor had not lasted long. He was a big, burly guy who was there one day and gone the next. I was a rookie, a woman, and this was the Iron Range. It didn't bode well; the odds were good on a short tenure.

I hadn't been on the job two weeks when I heard loud voices in the outer office. As I hurried out there, I saw a little old lady, slight and bent, with a babushka tied under her chin. "I demand to see the principal!" she screamed. By now, several teachers had joined the secretary behind the counter, trying to calm her down.

"Can I help you?" I asked as I stepped up to the counter.

"I want the principal, not another damn secretary!" The air reeked with the smell of booze as she spewed this out.

"I'm the principal, how can I help you?"

"You can't be the principal, you're a woman. I want the son of a bitch that runs this place!"

I led her into my office and sat her down. Once I offered her coffee and a cigarette, she calmed down. (This was 1979, before all the smoking bans). I had suspended her grandson the day before for swearing at a teacher and she didn't want him at home another day. She questioned me several times, trying to get her mind around the fact that a woman was principal. Of course, she was so loaded she couldn't get her mind around much of anything. I listened to her rambling complaints about kids these days who had no respect for their elders and then I walked her out of the building.

Where did I get the idea that I could do a "man's" job? That I could and should compete with the guys? That's how I was raised. Whatever the fix-it project or family activity, my dad expected me to carry my share. I received no pampering or exception as the only girl. In fact, as the oldest, more was expected of me. It made no difference whether we were finishing the cement slab under our boathouse at the lake, wallowing in the sludge to unplug the septic tank, paddling the canoe, or picking berries. And make no mistake; I compared blisters with the rest of them and bragged the loudest when mine were bigger.

In school, I'd bring home a pretty good report card, like five A's and two B's. My mom would give the reinforcing "Five A's, very nice job!" My dad would look over his glasses and say, "How come you got two B's?" Maybe the balance of those combined messages was a recipe for the self-confidence I seemed to have from the beginning. Mom affirmed what we did; dad pushed us to do better.

Tomboy probably played a role as well. Instead of passively playing with paper dolls, I liked to compete with the boys. The boys' activities were more competitive than the girls'—maybe too competitive. I broke my collarbone playing football in grade school, broke it again playing softball in junior high, dislocated my jaw playing ice hockey, and broke my leg racing down the ski hill.

While others may have been skeptical about a woman doing the high school principal's job, I had no doubts. I just assumed that if I worked hard, used common sense—which isn't all that common—and gave it my best, I'd do a good job.

As a teacher, I appreciated a school environment that valued and facilitated teaching. After all, that's what schools are for! As principal, I worked to create a streamlined system, minimizing as much of the red tape for teachers as possible. This ultimately freed teachers to focus more time on their classroom responsibilities, curriculum, and students. Lesson plans had long been a sore spot for the Buhl teachers. They had to turn in the weekly plans in duplicate on forms provided by the district. The Superintendent told them it was to ensure there were current lesson plans to give to substitute teachers.

I knew from my own experience teaching and subbing that weekly lesson plans were inaccurate after the first day or two. In addition, most substitute teachers lacked the training to provide any new instruction scheduled on the lesson plans, whether it was on Macbeth, French grammar, or solid geometry. When I discussed this with the superintendent, he made it clear that the issue was more about authority and control than accurate planning.

Working with my high school faculty, we developed a process that did a much better job of providing substitute teachers with up-to-date lesson plans for the day. I simply had the substitute teacher call the absent teacher before the start of classes to get current or workable instructions. This pleased the substitutes because their days were much more successful. The teachers were happy because they seldom came back to find their classroom in chaos.

Elimination of the duplicate lesson plan requirement took a little finessing with my boss, but he eventually agreed to let me determine how to supervise and evaluate my high school teachers on their instructional planning. Teachers lost the onerous, duplicate lesson plans and I gained a measure of their confidence. I had listened to their concerns, thoroughly understood them, and facilitated a resolution. I think the fact that I remained a teacher at heart resonated with them and made a difference.

One by one, the teachers eventually came around and I received all the acceptance and support I could have asked for.

It was surprising, however, that the very last teachers to accept a woman boss were the other women on staff.

Why?

It wasn't jealousy. None of the women seemed to have any aspirations for administration, even though they were strong, competent, and extremely skilled at their profession. Perhaps there was some resentment, in the sense that my presence as principal reminded them of aspirations they could have had.

I think it was also fear. Fear of losing control is a pervasive undercurrent in most classrooms and schools. Lurking in the back of most teachers' minds is the nightmare of a confrontation with a rowdy teenager, a classroom out of control, the loss of authority. A big, tough principal has to be there to physically handle this predicament, right? How could a woman deal with these things? None of the staff had worked for a woman before, which was true across most of the Iron Range. It was a change. Change can be threatening in and of itself.

These attitudes and concerns created a pressure for me to be extra tough, extra strict, extra hard-nosed, just to prove I could handle the job. I learned the hard way about giving in to that pressure and imposing hastily conceived rules or solutions. Once, when high school boys were smoking in an unsupervised basement washroom, I had it locked up. Surprise! They moved one floor up, to the elementary boys washroom. Now I had a more serious problem to solve, requiring more resources.

School board members complained that kids were smoking downtown at noon, so I closed the campus at noon. I got cheers from all the authoritarians. Students couldn't leave the school grounds at noon, which ended the growing complaints from downtown. But, in doing so, I had created an angry hornets' nest. Many parents wanted their kids to come home for lunch. So then, I had to require that parent permission slips be brought in, which we then had to keep track of. With each solution we contrived, another problem was created.

Could one parent give permission for several students to come to their home for lunch? Of course, some of the notes turned out to be bogus, so now there was another set of behaviors to investigate and punish. I was learning fast to think twice before acting.

The following year, I resisted the pressures to be tough for tough's sake and relied more on common sense. Why close the campus for all students when only a few were causing the problem? Punish the offenders, not the innocent. I learned a couple lessons that guided my decisions for years. First, passing a rule that does only what you want it to do and nothing more is not as easy as it sounds. *Isn't there some law of unintended consequences?* Second, use as little authority as necessary to get the job done. Imposing a rule that is unenforceable or no one is willing to enforce is just plain dumb. Rules for the sake of rules are even dumber and the kids all know it.

Those pressures to be quick and tough were constant and I learned most of those lessons the hard way. All principals experienced the same pressures, but too often women felt them more keenly. At regional and state meeting, we discussed it often. Tough or "strict" were never intrinsically admirable administrative traits to me. Fair is more complicated, but more effective.

Buhl was like a lot of the smaller Iron Range communities. Most of the men worked in the mines or other blue-color jobs in the service industries that supported the mines. For generations, this mining-based economy and culture had kept most women at home. The all too familiar refrain was that women belonged at home, barefoot and pregnant.

Stereotypic Rangers bragged about surviving the long, cold winters and their reputation for being hard drinking, opinionated, and tough. Outsiders or newcomers to the Range were derisively called "pack-sackers," which could apply to someone who had moved in as recently as 30 or 40 years ago. Strong ethnic ties bound neighborhoods, communities, and churches. Finnish, Norwegian, Slovenian, Serbian, and Italian traditions and foods dominated the holidays.

Most parents wanted their kids to go to college so they wouldn't have to work in the mines. A hockey scholarship was a common dream. Many parents were more intensely involved and committed to their peewee hockey organizations and blue-line clubs than to their churches. Hockey coaches could schedule ice-time at any time day or night, weekends or holidays and parents drove kids to practice and games. Parent behavior at hockey games could get as rowdy and profane as a barroom brawl.

I understood the culture and values because Buhl was back home on the Range for me. While I missed the classroom, which was my first love, I discovered I also loved school administration. The principal can make a big difference in school atmosphere and in the morale of staff and students. School administration was never boring. Something unpredictable happened every day, sometimes every hour. Problem solving on the run could be fun, but sometimes situations came at me like 90 mile an hour fastballs whipped out of a pitching machine. I quickly developed tactics to buy time to think and evaluate my options before responding. Whenever possible, it was, "I'll check it out and get back to you."

Conflicts occurred constantly, between students, staff and students, parents and teachers, parents and students, administration and parents, and bus drivers and students. As any school principal will agree, the possible combinations for conflict in any school environment are infinite. The hands-on person for resolving conflicts of all varieties is the building principal. My primary job was to diffuse and mediate. I frequently found myself teaching students–and sometimes teachers--how to apologize for their part in the conflict, even scripting the actual words.

Many students never experienced successful conflict resolution at home. They had never given, received, accepted, or even heard an apology. Teachers too often felt that any apology or compromise on their part diminished their authority. Occasionally, when I screwed up, I'd use the opportunity to model as well as teach the art of apology. A teacher once told me that I was the first principal he ever heard apologize to the faculty. *How sad is that?*

Every conflict was unique and tested my creative ability to facilitate a resolution. What worked in one situation would bomb in another.

Conflict resolution is critical. Conflicts threaten the individual student or teacher's ability to function as well as the stability and productivity of the institution itself. Unresolved conflicts can fester and poison a system. When the resolution left both sides equally unhappy, I knew I had done a good job. Apparently the superintendent concurred. He wrote in a 1/9/80 performance evaluation:

"I would like to take this opportunity to commend you on your job performance to date as high school principal. I am *VERY* satisfied with your ability and the way you have handled the many different situations that have arisen since you came. You have handled them as well, if not better, than a principal who has had many years of experience. I appreciate your ability to see the problem and take appropriate action. You keep me well informed as to what is happening and are not afraid to ask for help or to come to me to discuss a situation you are unsure of. I also believe one of your strong points is your ability to get along with and work with the students and staff."

Things were going well and the response to my developing administrative style was generally positive.

A Buhl School Board member wrote in a May 1981 letter of recommendation:

"Her professional skills and her personal charm have made Mrs. Pearson a respected and well-liked administrator at our school. Her intelligent and direct manner is refreshing to those working with her; and her firm, but friendly mien with the students has resulted in a noticeable rise in student morale and school spirit. In fact our truancy lists have dropped considerably in the last two years. She has been innovative with our curricula, and she has been quite helpful to the school board in revising and expanding policies relating to our students. I would say Mrs. Pearson has contributed greatly to the renewed vitality and good will in our school."

Soon after I started in Buhl, I began attending professional meetings of the Range Principals' branch of the Northeast Division of the Minnesota Association of Secondary School Principals. Twenty-two years later at my NE MASSP retirement party, I learned that I had been the first woman to attend the Range meetings. One of the retired principals, who was already an old hand when I joined in 1979, came to our 2001 retirement party. He talked about the good old days. In the roast and toast tradition, he remarked that he and others were so outraged when I first came to the meetings they tried to circulate a petition to keep women out of the Range Principals' meetings.

I must have been naive back then because I never sensed any hard feelings from the group. On the contrary I found the guys to be friendly, helpful, and supportive. I called several that first year to get help with scheduling and procedures for student suspensions and expulsions. I always received great cooperation. Apparently the hard-liners mellowed some, because in January 1980, they selected (railroaded) me to be the regional NE Division representative to the MASSP State Board of Directors for a two-year term.

I was also the first woman to serve on that statewide Board. At that time, there were only about 40 women serving in secondary school administration in the state, which had about 1,500 secondary administrative positions. Several women from around the state greeted me when I arrived for my first state board meeting. They expected me to be their representative on the board. I gently reminded them that I represented a group of pretty hard-line guys up north who expected me to represent their issues. I did what I could when there was no conflict of interest between the two groups.

I received interesting advice from some of the women. After board meetings and formal sessions at the conventions, it was common to stop in small groups for coffee or a social drink. I enjoyed this informal time. It was a great place to trade war stories in a more informal and relaxed setting. I learned more about the administrative business in these informal sessions than in all the formal workshops put together. However, the women warned me not to let the guys buy my drinks because they would expect something in return. I never experienced anything like that and never heard of anyone who had.

However, I was occasionally frustrated in these informal gatherings when the guys would not allow me to buy a round. They insisted that they pick up the tab out of old-fashioned chivalry, I suppose. Women's business clothes didn't have easy-to-reach multiple pockets to hold wallets and money. By the time I got my wallet out of my purse, one of the guys had already paid the tab. This bugged me because I wasn't being treated as a peer, wasn't paying my fair share.

I was not and never have been an ardent feminist. The closest I came to those concepts growing up on the Iron Range was through my grandmother Nana, who belonged to the local BPW (Business & Professional Women's) club in Virginia, Minnesota. Most of the women my grandmother introduced me to at their meetings in the early 1960s were secretaries, teachers, or retail saleswomen. The women socialized and discussed equal work for equal pay, but they were anything but radical. I never heard any strident messages against men or business as usual.

Therefore it surprised me when a little thing like men complimenting my appearance at work or at professional meetings rubbed me the wrong way. I had never been super-sensitive to gender issues. However, I came prepared to work and participate, not make a fashion statement. I dressed for work, not for a date. I resented comments on my appearance. I felt demeaned, objectified, and put in my place, instead of respected for my competence and intelligence. Comparable compliments and fashion comments were never made man to man, why to a woman?

I trusted that no put down was intended and that those compliments stemmed from well-intentioned, traditional patterns of behavior. After all, in the good old days, women expected compliments on their appearance. So why did it set me off? Was it my own insecurity in an unfamiliar setting? Were the men just clumsy at exploring ways to relate to women stepping into traditionally male domains? I stewed over this petty irritation many times.

My mom chided me gently about these sensitivities when we'd visit over lunch or coffee. "Don't make a mountain out of a molehill," she'd say. "Don't worry, be happy!" was her anthem long before the tune became popular. She just had a knack for putting things in perspective. Her steady, calming, and reassuring influence was suddenly gone in July 1981. She died unexpectedly at age 61 from a massive cerebral hemorrhage following surgery to remove a brain tumor.

I missed her so much, so often. I missed her when I was sick, I missed her when my kids were sick. Holidays were hell without her. I missed her so many times in the following years when I needed a gut-check on perspective.

My dad was just as lost without Mom and after a couple of months, I encouraged him to start getting out and seeing other people. He's one of the lucky ones because he found a wonderful, second partner to share the rest of his life. In December 1981, he married Ruth Hill, a widow who had lost her husband recently. A couple of my brothers were initially upset but soon realized that nothing about Dad's getting married again compromised their memories of Mom in any way. This was about Dad's future, not theirs. In December 2006, the family gathered to celebrate Dad and Ruth's 25th Anniversary. We all acknowledged that Ruth was great addition to the family and to Dad's life.

When I started in Buhl in 1979, the district had about 650 students in grades K–12. But by the early 1980s, the iron mining industry had slumped and the surrounding mines had made significant layoffs. Buhl and neighboring communities and schools were hit hard with declining enrollments and shrinking revenues. By 1982, the Buhl School District had lost 150 students and the Board was talking to other school districts about consolidation. I was the least senior administrator in the area and if consolidation came, I would probably be laid off again. I needed to update my credentials and document my resume.

The executive director of MASSP wrote a letter of recommendation based on my service on the state Board of Directors:

"I have the utmost respect for Judy Pearson. She is a very outgoing person, is a sound thinker, and expresses herself very well. She is not afraid to take a stand on issues confronting her. Whenever our organization needed representation at a meeting, Judy was one of the first people to be considered as that representative. She is the type of person who 'works with you' and evidenced this support whenever I called on her on behalf of the association. Her cooperation and support helped make the Minnesota Association of Secondary School Principals a more effective organization."

One of those representative appointments I received from the MASSP was to serve on the Program Board for the Principals Fellowship Program, sponsored by the Blandin Foundation. I served on this Board for five years. In 1982, the Program Coordinator for the fellowship program concluded a letter of recommendation:

"Based on my experience with and knowledge of Judy Pearson, I believe that she is a professional, very competent, and caring school administrator who can handle either the principalship or superintendency even in trying circumstances. I believe she has the potential to be an exceptional leader in education in our state. Her service to the Principals Fellowship Program has been marked by thoughtful, active participation. She does her 'homework', and her insights and ideas are always helpful. Judy is bright, competent, constructively decisive, and she sincerely cares about education and youth."

If he had known what I would face in a few years, he might have qualified his potential state leadership prediction with a caveat against staying in Northern Minnesota.

One of the NE Division principals I represented on the state MASSP Board of Directors was later elected as the MASSP State President. He wrote in his October 1982 letter of recommendation:

"Judy Pearson provided executive leadership on a state level by serving on the Minnesota Association of Secondary School Principals state board of directors. It was in this position that Ms. Pearson received a reputation of total reliability and the highest of professional standards. It was at once obvious that she continuously met pledges and responsibilities promptly. While demonstrating quality standards of honesty, morality, and ethics, Ms. Pearson provided the necessary direction and leadership which assisted MASSP through a very difficult year. Finally, I feel Ms. Pearson is the finest high school administrator I have seen in twenty-one (21) years in this profession."

However, all the statewide service and kudos did little for job security, which was again tenuous at best. My administrative degree and license were for secondary school administration. I decided to add the coursework necessary for a superintendent's license, so that I would be qualified for more administrative positions. I completed the courses in the spring of 1982 and received my superintendent's license.

It was just in time. In the fall of 1983, the Buhl Superintendent left the district abruptly and I was asked to take over. I served as Superintendent for the Buhl School District from 1983 to 1985.

In January 1984, I attended the winter workshop of the Minnesota School Boards Association with several of the Buhl School Board members. After one of the breakout sessions, I ran into Chester Larson, who was still serving on the St. Louis County School Board as the representative from the Cotton attendance area. It had been three years since I left the board in 1981, the last time I saw Chester.

Surprisingly, Chester seemed compelled to tell me that he had made a mistake when he voted against my husband's long-term sub position at the Albrook School. He continued to explain that he had received nothing but complaints afterwards. I assured him that it had worked out for the best for Rick and we parted company. I had forgotten the incident and was surprised he mentioned it after all that time. Besides, admitting a mistake was totally out of character for the Chester I knew.

By the fall of 1984, the Buhl school board had entered into a formal, consolidation agreement with the neighboring Mt. Iron School District. As Superintendent, one of my most challenging tasks was to pass a referendum on the consolidation. Petitions had been signed in both school districts requiring the issue be put to the voters. After countless public forums, discussion groups, and media interviews, the referendums passed.

The consolidation agreement provided that there would be a joint school board for planning one year prior to formal consolidation. As a result, during the 1984–1985 school year, there were three school boards meeting regularly once, sometimes twice a month. The Mt. Iron Superintendent and I served as superintendents to our respective school boards and districts to plan the district shut downs. We also served as co-superintendents to the newly elected Mt. Iron-Buhl school board as it staged up for the start of the 1985–1986 school year. It was a very busy year.

We worked hard at it and the consolidation proceeded smoothly for three years. That was amazing due to the number of contentious issues that had to be resolved. Previous consolidations on the Range had left bitter feelings between the communities. Consolidation meant two separate school districts would cease to exist. Traditional community identities were involved, as were community politics. How many board members would be on the consolidated board? Which community would dominate? How many schools would be kept open in each community?

Most critical in the minds of many, was athletics. What colors would the new athletic teams wear and what would they be called? Where would the varsity games be held? These issues may seem petty compared with issues of governance, finance, and facilities, but they form an integral part of the historical identity of any community. They were settled by compromises. We used one color from each of the former varsity programs. The new teams were called the MIB Rangers and they played in alternating home field or court locations.

In preparation for the formal start of the new Mt. Iron-Buhl School District (MIB) on July 1, 1985, the consolidated school board had to select a new superintendent. Robert Duncan, the Mt. Iron Superintendent and I both applied. Duncan was awarded the position, which I felt was fair and proper. He had a doctorate, more experience, and more seniority.

I was back in the business of updating my credentials and resume. In April 1985, Superintendent Duncan explained the situation in a letter of recommendation:

"It is my opinion that if any school consolidation takes place, it is imperative that the Superintendents of the districts involved be able to rise to the occasion, by putting the future of the district as a first priority and cooperatively provide the type of leadership which allows a consolidation to take place. I have the greatest respect for Ms. Pearson's ability to do this. It is unfortunate that because of the consolidation process, there was only one Superintendency position available in the new district. That position was filled by myself, the more senior of Ms. Pearson and myself. I am confident that Ms. Pearson will be a great asset to any school system which employs her as an administrator."

The Chairperson of the new Mt. Iron-Buhl School Board explained my "demotion" in an April 1985 letter of recommendation:

"Consolidation has presented many difficult and unique challenges to Superintendent Pearson, who has devoted herself unselfishly to accomplishing a smooth and educationally progressive transition. Ms. Pearson served as co-superintendent during the transition year of the consolidation. In the consolidation process one superintendent needed to be cut. She was the junior administrator in the two districts and was regretfully cut from her position as Superintendent for the new district. Fortunately for I.S.D. #712 she will continue to serve our children as Junior High Principal. I can honestly state that her knowledge, enthusiasm, and willingness to work for our children as been one of the most rewarding benefits I've received as a Board Member."

At this point, the inclusion of these flattering evaluations of my teaching and administrative performance seems gratuitous, so I'll try to explain. In the immediate situation, they help explain my demotion from superintendent to principal. But it's more that that. I admit a definite need to establish my competence and credibility before the tide turns in my career. By 1985, I had a strong and enviable professional reputation. Simply asserting that would be suspect, so I've used other's words. During the bruising battles just ahead, my competence and integrity would be publicly questioned repeatedly. How else do you counter those biting innuendos about "people who sue?"

In addition to the new, consolidated MIB superintendent position, I applied for several other superintendent and administrative positions in the area. In all cases the positions went to men, but also to candidates with stronger credentials (more years of administrative experience or doctorates). I had no complaints about these selections.

I always felt that the most qualified person should get the job. My definition of affirmative action stops at open, fair, and encouraging procedures for recruiting, screening, interviewing, and selection. I wanted the job on merit, not because I was a woman.

I've often joked that my definition of affirmative action is simple. "Please don't give me a job just because I'm a woman, but heaven help you if deny me a job just because I'm a woman!"

In the meantime, in the newly consolidated Mt-Iron-Buhl district, I was assigned the position of principal for a new junior high program that was housed in the Buhl school building, beginning July 1, 1985. This appeared to be a demotion, stepping from superintendent back to being principal. But I was committed to making the consolidation work. Besides, demotion is a state of mind.

This new position turned out to be a terrific and exciting challenge. Over half of the students in grades 6–9 were from Mt. Iron and resented being bused to the Buhl School. As any school person knows, that is a relatively rambunctious age group of students under normal circumstances. Most of them started the fall of 1985 angry and suspicious of their new classmates and teachers.

Students of that age group typically challenge teachers more often than at other grade levels. As a result, junior high teachers require more administrative support and can be more challenging to work with. Add to that, over half of the teachers assigned to the new junior high program were from the former Mt. Iron school district. They also resented being assigned to the Buhl building, particularly to work for a woman! I suspect there is a critical mass of conflicts that one person can resolve in any given day and I was close to meltdown many days of that first year at the junior high school. My adrenalin pump seemed stuck at full-throttle.

These were tensions unique to this new junior high school, in addition to the usual issues with that age population. I needed every trick I knew and then some. I rediscovered lessons learned the hard way those first years in Buhl and learned new ones. Some things never change.

Gum chewing and boys wearing hats were minor but perennial

complaints of classroom teachers. How much authority and how many resources did I want to commit to tackle those issues? The teachers wanted after school detention, but between those two behaviors, several detentions could be filled daily. Did I want to spend my valuable and very limited resources on those issues? What about the no-shows for detention? Did I want to back detention up with suspension from school? How much authority "capital" would I have to spend to make detention effective?

Whether supervising students or teachers, I tried to use as little authority as necessary to accomplish the task at hand. It was a new school, but the same principal principles applied. Authority should be a means to an end, not an end in itself. I resisted the internal and external pressures to be tough for toughness' sake. I avoided imposing general, broad rules or consequences on an entire group for the misbehavior of a few. If a teacher is coming late most mornings, why install time clocks for everyone? If a few students break the rules and drive at noon, why ban all student cars? Why make the whole class stay after school if one student took a pen off the teacher's desk?

Correcting or humiliating adolescents in front of their peers is bad practice. It can also have unpredictable and explosive consequences. Such a response by a teacher could escalate a minor issue, result in the "F" word, and mandate major consequences. Kids will do most anything to avoid being embarrassed in front of their friends. When correcting someone, student or staff, I did it privately and addressed the behavior that had to change, not the worth of the individual. "How" is much more important than "what" in effective discipline.

I'd also try to "catch them," students or staff, doing something right and make sure they heard about it. That can shape or modify behavior as powerfully as punishment.

Parents were always on my mind. I called parents regularly, about attendance, discipline—or just for advice what we could agree might motivate a change of behavior. Often when disciplining a student, I would hear about others involved in the incident, either from the student or his parents. The information was usually preceded by a demand for confidentiality. This is not surprising in a small town.

Without revealing my sources and therefore without imposing punishment, I'd call the other parents just to alert them with an early warning.

Some of those parents chastised me for not having proof. Most of them appreciated the warning and the chance to parent and make an early intervention. I was thinking as a parent, which is a solid, common sense guide for educators. Wouldn't I want to know as soon as possible if my kids were making bad decisions? Wouldn't I appreciate the warning? How would I want to be treated as a parent?

When's the last time anyone's heard a parent complain because they were given too much information from the school? As a general rule, the more information parents had, the more they were involved in their child's education. The more parents were involved, the more successful the students were.

Two factors helped make that first year in the consolidated junior high successful. The first was humor, my constant companion. It guaranteed that I never took the job or myself too seriously. The second was the support and partnership of a terrific secretary, Marilyn Dimberio. This was her first school position, but she had all the skills of a seasoned pro. She demonstrated the first principle of a master secretary. A good secretary gets the job done accurately and efficiently. A great secretary does all of that and makes the boss look good in the process! Plus she had a great sense of humor!

The proof of just how good she was at making the boss look good came at the end of that first year. One morning in April I found a letter on my desk, signed by the entire faculty.

"We would like to take this opportunity to thank you for making this first year of consolidation a good year at Martin Hughes Junior High. Your positive approach and concern for the education and well being of the students has been apparent all year. We have four hundred students placed together for the first time. All of them are experiencing the pains and joys of early adolescence. We especially appreciate the enormous time, effort, and skill needed to maintain a positive learning environment. Congratulations on a great job!!!"

The last week of that first school year at the junior high, the student editors handed out the first yearbook, entitled "Ranger Reflections." I was surprised when it was dedicated to me at the graduation ceremony. We had lots of tensions and fights between students that year. I suspended and disciplined more students that year than I had any other year.

However, I have always believed that there are no bad kids, just kids making bad decisions. My curriculum as a principal was decision-making. Every bad decision or misbehavior presented a potential teaching opportunity. Make no mistake, the lessons taught had to include consequences to ensure real learning. It was more often about how the consequences were delivered than what they were. I suspect that process is the determining factor in most successful human interactions. Apparently my approach and actions were perceived as even-handed. The yearbook dedication read:

"This first annual Martin Hughes Junior High "RANGER RELFECTIONS" is proudly dedicated to our devoted and caring principal - Mrs. Judy Pearson. Throughout the year, Mrs. Pearson energetically and cheerfully guided us with a firm, but fair hand. Her dedication, time and understanding far surpassed what we expected from her. Thank you, Mrs. Pearson, for being a prince of a pal. Enjoy the first "RANGER REFLECTIONS" - it's especially for you!!!"

Those unsolicited approvals meant a lot to me, especially the phrase, "…firm, but fair hand."

I served two more exciting years as principal of the junior high before layoffs threatened again in Mt. Iron-Buhl due to continuing financial trouble. In March 1986, the Mt. Iron-Buhl School Board voted to eliminate several positions for the 1986–1987 school year, including one administrative position. That would be me, the least senior administrator in the district. Fortunately, three months later in May, they voted to reinstate the administrative position. My position was secure, if only for one more year. But I knew I had to start job-hunting again. *Will I ever be senior enough to have longer than one year's job security?*

Two events dramatically altered what the future held for me, both personally and professionally.

The first event was our purchase of a new home.

After 14 years on the farm north of Duluth, we realized our jobs kept us too busy to enjoy the work and chores on the farm. Rick and I had both wanted to raise our sons in the rural, farming lifestyle. They could grow up with baby chicks, lambs, and calves, while shucking peas. However, the boys did not see cleaning the barn, raking hay, or weeding the garden through the same rose-colored glasses we did. Erik was in ninth grade, Max in fifth, and both were chafing at the rural isolation from their friends and social activities. A move seemed right for them.

Working from his basement office in our small farmhouse, Rick had outgrown the available space. He was producing, duplicating, and distributing nationally syndicated radio shows for clients from North Carolina to the Twin Cities. His business was booming, increasing ten-fold in four years. My work in the Buhl and then Mt. Iron-Buhl districts was more than 50 miles north and included lots of evening supervision. With my long drives and night duties, I had too little time with the family and almost none for the farm.

We decided if we weren't going to work the farm we should move. Rick needed more office space, my career had moved north, and all of us loved to catch and eat fresh fish. We put a protractor on the map and drew a circle 50 miles from my Mt. Iron-Buhl job to see what lakes would be included. We had fished Lake Vermilion previously and loved the beauty of the lake. The Cook end of the lake was within our selected radius.

On June 13, 1986, we looked at several homes for sale on Lake Vermilion. Rick fell in love with one and called the agent that same evening when we returned home. We drove to Cook and made an earnest money offer two days later. By June 25, 1986, we had a signed contract. We agreed with the owners to take possession the following summer, giving them time to finish the new home they were building and giving us time to close out the farm.

We all had mixed feelings about the move. The boys were sad about leaving their friends and anxious about starting in a new school. We would all miss the farm, the animals, the gardens, and the great, homegrown food. Nobody would miss the smell of manure and the blisters from shoveling the barn every spring. At the same time, we were all excited about the swimming, saunas, boating, and fishing. The thought of catching and eating fresh walleye balanced much of the melancholy about leaving the farm.

Erik and Max would be attending the Cook School in the fall of 1987, Erik in grade 10 and Max in grade 6. The Cook School was part of the same large St. Louis County School District as the Albrook School and had the same smaller school benefits we had looked for when we bought the farm. It was a good decision for both boys. In these smaller schools, they could participate in a wide range of activities. For most kids in the larger schools, participation meant focusing and practicing on one sport or activity in order to make the cut.

Erik and Max took part in speech, drama, band and choir, football, basketball, golf, and did well in regional and state competitions. Erik made first chair in the trumpet section of the band, Max in the saxophone section. Max sang solos in the choir. They both played lead roles in the school plays. In competitive speech, Max was state champion in the category of Creative Expression his senior year. Ironically, the title of his performance was "Family Values." He wrote a satirical flip on the current political rhetoric, describing his family where Mr. Mom was home baking the bread while mom was out earning the bread. Erik was a Merit Scholarship semi-finalist and Max was accepted to all three service academies, selecting the Air Force Academy after graduation. "Smaller is better" worked for our kids.

While both boys were successful academically, they played the school game from different perspectives. We were called to school by one of Erik's primary grade teachers. She said he wasn't achieving up to his potential. He had the highest standardized test scores, but his daily work and in-house tests never qualified him for the top reading group. When asked about it later, Erik said he didn't want to be in the group with all the girls, so he deliberately missed just enough points to stay in the reading group with his buddies. We chuckled and decided to leave it alone.

Max made the top group every time.

In junior high, Erik was barely receiving passing grades in his English class. At conferences, the teacher explained that he was losing a lot of points because he refused to do his spelling assignments. He said that if he made perfect scores on the spelling pretests, he shouldn't have to write each word 10 times and turn it in. From Max's teachers we received compliments; from Erik's it was concerns.

Erik's high school principal called us into school because there were complaints about devil worship in the school. Erik was mentioned as one of the students that knew all about it. After a few questions, we realized that it was just his Dungeons and Dragons hobby, which he worked on whenever he got the chance. D & D was a fairly complex, role-playing, adventure game that had challenged Erik for years with plenty of reading, writing, calculating, and sketching. We chuckled and left that alone too.

Max always met all the school requirements, often beyond the call of duty. Erik did just enough of the required work to get what he wanted—the right reading group, study hall time for D & D, or the bottom of the 'A' honor roll—which we required to maintain access to the car keys. They both mastered the school game, but Max maxed it, graduating first in his class.

In early July, shortly after signing the contract on the new home, Rick and I attended an Alborn Little League game for our sons' team. Neither of the boys was a star player, but one of us always attended for support. This happened to be one of the few times we could all go together. It was a hot, dusty, dry day. While grabbing a cool drink, we visited with Bob Larson, the Alborn elementary principal. We knew him from school events and from my three years on the school board representing that attendance area.

"Did you hear about the Cook job?" Bob asked me.

"Sure, I heard Roy was retiring last winter," I responded.

"No, that's not what I mean," he said. "They already had a bunch of interviews and didn't like the candidates. So they're reposting it."

"Really, that's interesting."

"Why don't you apply, we need someone good up there?" he

suggested. *Rick glanced at me with a look that said "Aha!"*

"Very interesting," I said. "Last week we signed a contract for a new home on the Cook end of Lake Vermilion and we'll be moving to Cook next year."

I had not applied for Cook originally because I had hopes of securing a superintendent's position again and staying on that career track. Now that our new home was going to be further north in the Cook attendance area, the range of superintendent possibilities had narrowed significantly.

Rick and I discussed the position and whether I should apply. If I got the position, for one year, our last on the farm, I'd have a much longer drive. But the possibility of my eventually living and working in the same community was an exciting prospect for the entire family.

My low seniority and the continuing financial trouble of the newly consolidated Mt. Iron-Buhl district were already dark clouds on the horizon of job security. While Rick facetiously said he would miss being the only father at the mother's day programs in school, we made the fateful decision to apply for the Cook School principal position.

It was not a simple decision. In addition to the financial and lifestyle commitment with the new home on Lake Vermilion, we were essentially deciding that I would end my search for another superintendent position and step off the traditional career path. Once having served as superintendent for a Range school district, most would not be content to drop back to building principal in a rural school.

However, we liked the smaller schools for our kids and we really loved rural living. The lake was the cream of that lifestyle. We especially loved the saunas. There is nothing so invigorating as pouring water on the hot rocks until you're all steamed up and sweaty in the sauna and then jumping in the cold lake, to "close your pores." It's year-round magic to watch the ice come and go with the seasons, to hear the loons every summer evening and the mystical wailing sounds of the winter ice. Standing on the dock on a cold night in December, watching a spectacular display of the northern lights while listening to the harmonics of the shifting ice is a truly surreal experience.

The boys were already worried about changing schools, leaving old friends, and making new ones. We did not want to subject them to more moves for my job. There's more to life than career. Rick's business operated from home—wherever home was—as long as Fed Ex delivered to the door. So I applied for Cook and held off searching for other statewide postings. We hoped to settle down for the long haul.

Chapter 3

1986–1987
JOB DISCRIMINATION

"Hell will freeze over before we hire a woman
principal at the Cook High School."
Pascuzzi Deposition, October 1987

JULY 8, 1986. THAT'S the day everything in my professional
and personal life shifted dramatically.
I applied for the Cook Principal position.

I was thrilled about the prospects of living and working in the
same school the boys attended. I would be close when they were
sick or injured and I could attend their games and events. By now,
over two hours of drive time from the farm to Mt.Iron-Buhl took its
toll everyday. The Cook position had been reposted with a deadline
for applications on July 18, 1986. The July 3, 1986, *Cook News Herald*
(official newspaper for the district) reported on the selection and
reposting process:

"(Superintendent) Dr. Nachitalo reported on the search for a
principal for Cook. He said the Cook Chamber of Commerce had
asked to visit potential candidates. The three members from the
Chamber were joined by three parents and five teachers to talk to
prospective candidates. Nachitalo said he wasn't prepared to make a
final recommendation. He said they would readvertise for additional
candidates and that the ones who had already applied would still be

considered."

On July 22, 1986, Dr. William Nachitalo, Superintendent of the St. Louis County School District, called me to set up an interview for the Cook position. We knew each other well, from my service as the Albrook representative on the school board from 1978–1981. We had also worked together as peers from 1983–1985 when I served as Superintendent for the Buhl School District. After setting the time for the interview, he continued,

"You know, of course, that you're the most qualified applicant," he said.

"That's good to hear," I responded.

"There's a rumor out there that I set up the position for you," he added.

"That's just ridiculous," I replied. "I never even applied when it first opened. We just bought a new home on Lake Vermilion and that's why Cook is now an option for us."

This was the first of what would be many references to rumors about my application for the Cook position.

Nachitalo set the time for my interview on Tuesday, July 29, 1986, at 8:30 a.m. in the central office in Virginia. He indicated that the district interview would last until about 10:30 and then the process involved a drive up to Cook to meet with a citizens' committee at 11:00 a.m. He said the Cook meeting might include a tour of the community and that I should plan for most of the afternoon.

The interview on July 29, 1986, was an interesting experience, to say the least.

The interview committee included Superintendent Nachitalo, Assistant Superintendent Willard Niemi, School Board Chairman Chet Larson (from the Cotton attendance area and the "no" vote on Rick's substitute teaching position in 1980), and the newly elected school board member from the Cook attendance area, Don Anderson.

The formal interview in the central office in Virginia went well. Prepared questions were asked of all candidates. The interesting part came in the more casual time at the end of the formal questioning. The Superintendent again mentioned rumors that I purchased our new home because I knew in advance he was going to give me the job based on our previous relationship.

I assured the interview committee that our decision to buy a new home was made before the reposting of the position, well before I knew anything about the Cook position being reposted. I told them, as I had in my letter of application, that my motivation for applying was fragile job security caused by the deteriorating financial health of the Mt. Iron-Buhl district. After having purchased a new lake home in the area, it was also motivated by a desire to live and work in the same community.

What's with all the rumors? I asked myself as I left the meeting.

As I left the building, Chester Larson stopped me on my way to the car.

"You know," he said, "the Baptists in Cook, Don Simonson in particular, are against a woman for the job. Simonson is anti-woman's liberation."

"Thanks for the heads-up," I responded.

"Don't use Ms. for your title, be sure to use Mrs." he added.

"Thanks again," I added quickly, anxious to get on the road to make the meeting on time. *What's going on?* I wondered. Although Chet and I had that minor falling out when we served on the school board together, that was years ago. *Is this just friendly advice or an ominous warning of strange stuff ahead?*

I arrived at Smitty's diner in Cook on time and met with the people present. The group included Gary Albertson, editor of the *Cook News Herald*, and chamber members Don Simonson, Russ Pascuzzi, and Keith Aho, who arrived about 11:15. The small size of the group surprised me, having read in the *Cook News Herald* that it numbered 10 or more, including parents and teachers. While the first interview in the central office was interesting, this one at Smitty's was astounding.

I was asked about my father, my husband, and my sons' athletic interests. I was asked three times about my relationship with Superintendent Nachitalo.

"How well do you know the superintendent?" Pascuzzi asked the second time.

"As I started to explain before, we…"

"Help me out, Don. Remember what we were talking about last night?" Pascuzzi interrupted, turning to Simonson.

The group had several conversations like this among themselves, as if I wasn't there. I was often interrupted in responding to their questions, but I finally had the chance to answer. I explained that I had known the Superintendent professionally during the three years I served on the School Board and as a peer at regional and state meetings during the two years I served as Superintendent in Buhl.

"Our relationship would best be described as one of professional acquaintance and respect for each other. We never met socially."

The men spent some time discussing the superintendent and their perceptions of his troubles in the district, the fact that the board had rejected his recommendation for his personal secretary. Pascuzzi asked the group if this was the first time that the superintendent had been asked by the board to leave. Albertson assured them that the board had never asked Nachitalo to leave. *What does this have to do with me or with the job in Cook?* I wondered.

"Don't you think it will be difficult to be the principal when your own kids will be attending the school?" Simonson asked me.

"It is a common issue because most principals…" I began.

"Do you think it's fair to require a principal to live in the community?" Simonson interrupted.

"I don't think it's fair or even legal, but it is understandable," I said, answering his second question first. As I returned to his original question, Simonson interrupted again.

"It might be better to hire someone from outside, who lives in Virginia, say, than someone who lives in town," he announced to the group in general.

This really threw me because selling the community and encouraging the new principal to live in Cook was supposedly the impetus for the citizens' committee. In a letter to the School Board in March 1986, the Cook Chamber had written to encourage, "the ISD 710 School Board hire a replacement who would reside in the Cook area and become an active member of the community."

What is this all about? I wondered, recalling Chester Larson's comments as I left the Central Office.

Thirty minutes after we started, Simonson abruptly stood up and concluded the interview. I was surprised when the session was cut short and there was no tour of the community. Nachitalo had told me to plan for the afternoon. Gary Albertson walked with me to the parking lot.

"These men don't think a woman can do the job," he said. "I'm not sure of that either, but if any woman could, it'd be you."

Then he said, "If I tell you something, you won't get mad?"

I shook my head. *This can't get any worse.*

"The rumor is that you are sleeping with Bill," he proceeded.

"You've got to be kidding me," I quipped, feigning light-heartedness and struggling to keep my composure until I reached my car.

The confidence I had going into the interview process vaporized. I did a mental checklist of the positives several times. I had years of experience as teacher, 7–12 principal, superintendent and board member in the district. I had great recommendations from supervisors and Board members. I had the Specialist Degree in School Administration from the University of Minnesota Graduate School, not the less rigorous and more common six-year certificate most administrators had. Nachitalo had told me when he called to set the interview date that I was the most qualified candidate. *My credentials should be enough to outweigh any prejudice, right?*

Relax, wait and see, I told myself as Albertson's comments forced me to replay the chamber meeting.

The uneasiness remained. Puzzle pieces were fitting together and it wasn't a pretty picture. *Am I on candid camera?* I asked myself. Had the rumor about my sleeping with the superintendent prompted the repeated questions about my relationship with him? Where did the rumor come from? Was this just the prevailing attitude that any woman who got ahead did it on her back?

If not, who started the rumor and why? Why would somebody do that? Is this for real? They interrupted me so often I couldn't answer their questions. Did they have their minds made up already? What was this business about hiring someone who did not live in the community when they had been so public about wanting to encourage the new principal to live in the community? The questions hammered incessantly.

Calm down, I argued to myself. The credentials speak for themselves. I certainly knew, as did Nachitalo, that there was absolutely nothing to the rumors. I reminded myself several times that this citizens' committee had no authority to make the final decision. Only the school board can hire. But I lost the argument to calm down.

I pulled over to the side of the road. I took out a pen and paper and wrote down the names of the people present at Smitty's and their questions and comments. The writing helped. I didn't want to forget a single comment. The pounding in my head dropped a few decibels, temporarily.

"How did it go?" Rick asked when I got home.

"Grab us a cup of coffee and sit down. You're not going to believe this," I said.

When we were settled with our coffee, I began to describe my interview experiences.

"Forget about Chet," Rick said when I repeated Chet's comments about the Baptists in Cook being against a woman for the job. "He's a loose canon anyway."

"Maybe not," I said as I continued.

"Just where the hell is this going?" Rick reacted to the repeated questions about my relationship with the superintendent.

By now, Rick was on his feet, pacing. I finished my account with Albertson's parking lot performance.

"I can't believe this crap!" he exploded, slamming his fist on the table. "Who do those SOB neanderthals think they are?"

I had hated to tell Rick because I knew how angry he'd be, but there was no holding this stuff in. He was absolutely furious.

There was never any question about the substance of the rumor. Rick just raged about the way I had been treated and at the insult to both of us. Although his anger was in my defense, it would become another factor to deal with. The struggle to cope and to contain the anger, for both of us, for the family, was just beginning.

I knew principals would be at work in the schools in two weeks or less, so I expected to hear soon from Superintendent Nachitalo. I heard nothing by Friday, so I called his office. He was not in, so I left a message. On Monday, August 4, he returned my call at home. He told me that he had met for lunch with the committee from Cook the previous Thursday, July 31, at the Four Seasons restaurant north of Virginia. He said that by consensus they had decided on a young fellow named Bill Putnam.

Nachitalo went on to explain, however, that the administrative committee had some concerns about Putnam. He was only 34 years old, had held positions of assistant principal in California last year and positions of superintendent/principal and principal in Minnesota before that. Nachitalo expressed concerns to me that this fellow moved around a lot, from job to job. He said Putnam had been reluctant to accept the position at first, but that he had just done so. He indicated that the School Board would hire him at their next meeting on August 12, 1986. He concluded the conversation by telling me that if it was any consolation, the teacher leadership had recommended me.

I said little during the telephone conversation. I was too busy taking notes. I couldn't believe it. I had better credentials and he admitted they had concerns about the guy. Baseless rumors were floating around and a few chamber members had forced the hiring decision over lunch.

Anger spiraled to rage. Rick and the boys were home and I had to get away from them. I hid out in the gardens and yanked weeds furiously until my hands, legs, and back ached in exhaustion. It took enormous effort to keep it all from boiling over and burning everyone around me. The emotional muscle it took to keep control sapped my energy for weeks to come.

Albertson's and Nachitalo's comments echoed and ricocheted in my head like gunshots in the Grand Canyon. I couldn't turn them off. I didn't sleep. I paced. I couldn't eat. Food tasted like cardboard. *How could this happen in this day and age?*

On Tuesday, August 5, I called Gary Albertson. I needed answers. Where had the rumor come from, whom had he heard it from. I wanted to know if all the Cook interviews were as short as mine. I wanted to know who exactly was at the luncheon meeting and how the decision was made. I had pen and paper ready as I made the call.

I was determined to maintain a matter-of-fact, "just curious" tone in the conversation. In no way did I want to reveal my emotional state or the fact that I was taking fast and furious notes. *Madame DeFarge knits again!* Albertson said he couldn't remember where he heard the rumor. He said that in the second round of interviews that I participated in, all meetings in Cook were 30 minutes.

He confirmed that the rumor was behind all the questions about my relationship with Superintendent Nachitalo. He told me he thought I had done a good job.

"It was fun watching you change their minds about a woman doing the job."

"But those guys are a real bunch of chauvinists," he said. "If you had been a man, you've have had the job."

That might have been a naive shot at consolation, but it just fired my jets.

I kept my cool as I listened, wrote, and occasionally interjected an innocent question. However, it took very little encouragement to keep him talking. He rambled on with far more information than I had expected to get.

"I won a steak dinner from Pascuzzi because you didn't get the job," he jokingly volunteered. "Russell bet that the job was 'greased' for you."

He confirmed that the decision was made over lunch at the Four Seasons restaurant the prior week. I remember grabbing for more notepaper, scratching out notes as he volunteered more and more information. I asked him who had attended the luncheon meeting and he said Superintendent Nachitalo, himself, the board member from Cook, Simonson, Pascuzzi and a Musech (whom I had never met).

Albertson had confirmed my worst scenario. This was blatant

discrimination, pure and simple. I was in an absolute fury; a rage that lasted for days. I shut down, closed up. I didn't trust myself to keep it together. I felt like I was going to explode.

Rick knew enough to give me lots of space. Besides, he had his own anger to deal with. Between the affair rumor and the steak dinner "joke," he was just barely holding his temper. It's as if we instinctively understood that if either of us brought it up before we cooled down, the combined anger levels would hit critical mass.

The boys were old enough, ages 11 and 14, and bright enough to read the pressure gages and stay below the red lines. The physical exertion of bringing in the hay crop over the next several days helped relieve the tension, even though we were all sort of hunkered down and rigged for silent running.

In the following days, even before the school board took action, I heard from family, friends, co-workers. It's small town country and they had all heard what happened, even though I had not spoken to anyone. I couldn't. I was too angry and humiliated.

I received the letter on August 12, 1986, officially informing me that William Putnam had been hired for the Cook position. The six School Board members voting on that decision were Chairman Chester Larson, Don Anderson, newly elected from Cook, Jim Raridon from Orr, Dave Clement from Cherry, Larry Anderson, who had succeeded me on the board from Albrook, and Diane Goodnai from Toivola-Meadowlands.

I had to fight back somehow. What Nachitalo and Albertson had told me left no choice. They had hired a less qualified man. Although I had not seen Putnam's credentials, Nachitalo had told me about their concerns. I started searching for an attorney. I had no idea how to proceed or what my options were, but I needed someone representing my rights who could get the district's attention. Maybe they would reconsider if confronted with the laws they had broken?

None of the local attorneys I called would take the case. Too small-town, too many conflicts of interest, too contrary to the popular milieu, too little experience with these laws, who knows? I called my association attorney looking for referrals. Each rejection fueled the rage.

I spent two weeks non-stop on the phone, trying to find someone to represent me. It seemed impossible to convince them that I was credible, that I wasn't just another whining malcontent. Frustration and anger dominated our lives, an invisible presence like the proverbial elephant in the living room.

More fuel was added to the fire on Monday, August 18, 1986. I was interviewing teacher candidates for the Mt. Iron-Buhl junior high school in the central office in Mt. Iron. It was after 4:00 p.m. I was finishing a review of credentials for additional interviews. John Roszak, a Twin Cities attorney for the Mt. Iron-Buhl School District came into the office for a meeting with Superintendent Duncan. I had worked with him when I was the Buhl Superintendent. He was also the attorney for the St. Louis County School District at that time.

Roszak volunteered that he had a conversation with Nachitalo at a workshop the previous week. According to Roszak, Nachitalo told him that the people in Cook refused his recommendation to hire me for the principal position in Cook.

"They had the two of us in bed," Nachitalo had complained to Roszak.

Nachitalo told Roszak that he was personally upset about the rumors. I took notes on the conversation as soon as I left the office. I called him later that evening to see if he could confirm the dates or names of the people in Cook. He was not as forthcoming on the phone, as if he knew he had already said too much.

Rick exploded again after a phone call on August 22, 1986, from the real estate agent who had sold us the house on Lake Vermilion. The agent called with information on our closing documents.

"They were talking about Judy after church on Sunday," he told Rick.

"Hell will freeze over before we hire a woman principal for the Cook School!" Pascuzzi had asserted, following questions about women candidates.

"What the hell's going on?" I heard Rick shout as I came downstairs to see who had called. "Who do those bozos think they are?"

What were we hearing? Wasn't this crap against the law?

Throughout my administrative training I learned repeatedly about how to interview and hire in non-discriminatory ways, the dos and don'ts of posting, screening, questions that could and could not be asked in interviews, about factors that could and could not be considered in hiring decisions. *How could they get away with this?* I kept asking myself.

For two weeks, I followed every lead and referral to find an attorney to represent me, made countless telephone calls, told the story over and over. That process of finding an attorney is one of the worst I've ever had. The rejections left me feeling like there was something wrong with me, not them. I felt like the rape victim whose behavior or dress is questioned. Frustration was mixed with a growing helplessness.

Finally, on August 25, 1986, the dynamics shifted in my favor. Sharon Fullmer, an attorney with Popham, Haik, Snobrich, Kaufman, and Doty, Ltd., a large Minneapolis law firm, expressed an interest in my case. As Buhl Superintendent, I had worked with one of the firm's senior partners on a school bond sale and he vouched for my competence.

However, the firm wanted 30 days to research the case and the relevant law. Those 30 days seemed like 30 years. I wanted to get going, to hold someone accountable for the unfairness, hurt, and humiliation. I could handle not getting a job because I wouldn't move to town or lack of experience or a doctorate degree, even a poor interview. Those were all factors that I could change. But like race, gender can't be changed. You are helpless and hopeless, there's nothing you can do. This is the fuel of rage.

As if the gender wall wasn't enough, there was always the rumored "affair" to kick the rage up another notch!

On September 16, 1986, I received a letter from Sharon Fullmer outlining the research she had been doing. The factors she explored included possible monetary damages, tort (a wrong caused by a breach of legal duty) liability of the district, and defamation charges. She indicated she would recommend to her firm that they accept the case, but the decision would not be hers to make. She thanked me for my patience. *If she only knew.* The waiting was torture.

On an emotional pain scale of 1-10, waiting is a 10. I paced because I couldn't stay still. Still no sleep. The interviews, phone conversations, and doubts recycled constantly. I kept reminding myself that I had a strong professional record and reputation. *Then why do I feel like a failure?*

Lots of other conversations and rumors came to my attention. They came from my parents and brothers who lived and worked in the area, my in-laws who lived and worked in the area, from teachers I had worked with, people I met while on the school board, and area administrators I worked with. By September, Erik and Max were hearing the stuff at school. That really made Rick mad. We were trying to keep the trouble from the kids.

One rumor was that I had bought the house on Lake Vermilion because I was promised the job. Another rumor was that the job had actually been reopened for me and then I bought the house. Other rumors were that I had been offered the Assistant Superintendent position in St. Louis County and that three of the building principals were upset that the job was being held for me. The calls and comments were supportive, but the rumors were untrue and ridiculous. I explained everything again and again. Each time added salt to the wounds. I felt like I was under fire from all sides.

Finally in late October 1986, Sharon Fullmer called and said her firm had decided to take my case. It had taken three months, but now I could begin to fight back.

Rick and I drove to Minneapolis and met with Sharon Fullmer and several senior partners in the firm. They spelled out our options. She had already prepared charges to file with the Minnesota Department of Human Rights (MDHR) and with the U.S. Equal Employment Opportunity Commission (EEOC).

I was amazed to learn that you couldn't simply sue a government institution, such as a public school district. You have to request permission to sue from the Justice Department. The attorneys said we would have to file the charges first and then request the right to sue. The state or federal agency would take a year or more to investigate the charges. The attorneys suggested we not wait for the agency investigation, but request the right to sue immediately. The "no waiting" option got my attention immediately.

The attorneys also had a grave warning for me.

"You understand that once you file this lawsuit, your career in school administration is over," said one of the partners.

"You mean I'll be blacklisted?" I asked. "Isn't that kind of thing illegal?"

"Oh, it doesn't have to be that formal to be effective," he explained.

"The 'old boys network' will take you out," Fullmer said.

I didn't think much of their comments at the time. I was too angry and impatient for someone to be held accountable. Besides, I had challenged in Duluth and had still been treated fairly. I still had the romantic notion that if you worked hard and did your best, you could always get ahead.

At the end of our meetings with the attorneys on October 24, 1986, I signed a complaint to be filed with the state and federal agencies. I also signed a retainer agreement with the law firm. The agreement required us to write a $5,000 check to the law firm which they would keep until the case was completed. I would have to pay out of pocket expenses such as filing fees, deposition costs, travel expenses, and copying charges as they were billed. The law firm would receive one third of any award or settlement I received.

The $5,000 was almost three months of take-home pay for me and was difficult to come up with. Rick and I agreed that we had no choice. What the district had done was wrong and illegal. Worse yet, it was done on my home turf, where I had grown up and established my career and professional reputation.

The November 6, 1986, issue of the *Cook News Herald* headlined "Sex Discrimination Suit Filed Against ISD 710." It read, "ISD 710 is being sued for sex discrimination, apparently because a male was hired for the position of Cook principal and not a female. Supt. Nachitalo dropped this bombshell at the end of the regular board meeting held

Monday, Nov. 4, at Cherry. There are no female administrators in ISD 710, which is probably one of the reasons for the suit."

The article was technically incorrect because we had not yet received the right to sue, but the MDHR and the EEOC notify defendants within 10 days anytime a complaint is filed. That was the bombshell that the superintendent had reported. Later in November, another bombshell fell. Nachitalo informed the Board that he was resigning to take another position and would only serve through the end of 1986.

Apparently, higher powers concluded that I had a legitimate complaint, because on December 8, 1986, we received the right to sue notice from the U. S. Department of Justice. We were given 90 days to file our lawsuit.

On February 17, 1987, we filed the lawsuit at the Federal Court House in Duluth, Minnesota. The suit named the St. Louis County School District, the six school board members, Superintendent Nachitalo, and the five chamber members who were either at the interview at Smitty's or at the luncheon meeting when the decision was made. Those five were Gary Albertson, Don Simonson, Russell Pascuzzi, Keith Aho, and John Musech.

I was reluctant to name individuals in the suit but the attorneys insisted it was best until we found out more about how things actually happened. The Cook Chamber of Commerce was not named in my original suit. That became a big issue later on.

Fullmer warned me that once the suit was filed in Federal Court, the news media might pick it up. I thought I was prepared. When I got to work at the Mt. Iron-Buhl junior high on February 19, teachers were gathered in the office waiting for me. It was in that morning's addition of the *Duluth News Tribune*. I wasn't prepared at all.

When they brought it up, it was as if all the air had been sucked out of the room. I kept a good poker face, but inside I was falling apart. I had worked hard for six months to wall off the anger and humiliation, keep it buried and compartmentalized. Here it was, right in my face. Not only was I personally ashamed about not getting the job I was qualified for, now I was publicly branded as "the kind of person that sues."

Minutes later, the other Mt. Iron-Buhl principals arrived at my office for an administrative meeting. John Gornick, the elementary principal, jokingly put his arm around my shoulders.

"Was it good sex with Nachitalo?" he asked.

"What in the world are you talking about?" I demanded.

"Did you guys find any good parking spots on the back roads?" teased Rocci Lucarelli, the high school principal.

"What's this stuff all about?" I asked again.

"Haven't you read the morning paper?" Lucarelli asked.

What the hell were they talking about? What had the newspaper reported? I hustled to get a copy and read it for myself.

The article referred twice to the rumor that I had an affair with Superintendent Nachitalo. The "affair" rumor made the headlines, but it only took up 10 words in the entire twenty-page complaint filed in Federal Court. The article reported that I was suing for $2 million dollars. It was exasperating that the paper took the two most sensational aspects of the filing to make the headlines.

The reporter never called my attorney or me before printing the story. He wrote it from the complaint and from comments by the school district's attorney, John Roszak. This was the same John Roszak that had reported Nachitalo's concerns about the hiring decision to me in the Mt.Iron-Buhl office.

"The school district's position is that if people acting on their own in Cook said things offensive to Pearson, that conduct should not be our responsibility," Roszak was quoted in the February 19, 1987, *Duluth News Tribune.* That was certainly a creative spin on what he had told me back in August.

Two weeks later, a letter to the editor by the Chairman of the Advisory Committee for the Hiring of the Principal appeared in every area newspaper from Cook to Duluth. The letter was signed by ten members of the original committee appointed at the end of the 1986 school year to help in the selection of a principal for the Cook School. This committee, which was disbanded after the first round of five interviews, had included teachers, parents, and

Chamber of Commerce members. The letter stated that the original committee had, in fact, recommended a woman as their first choice. After making their recommendation to the board, the original, first-round committee disbanded.

"Dr. Nachitalo and the board then extended the date for applications for the job," read the letter. "The committee which interviewed Mrs. Pearson was not the original appointed committee. It did contain three of the original members who represented the Chamber of Commerce of Cook, plus other Chamber members."

Some of those original committee members told me later that the Chamber members were against the recommendation for a woman in the first round but were out-voted by the majority. The chamber members walked out of the meeting in a huff, right after they lost the vote.

While it was not surprising that many guys in northern Minnesota did not think a woman could be effective as a high school principal, it was dismaying to realize that they could have such undue influence over the superintendent and the school board. It was obvious to me that those Chamber members had prevailed in getting the first-round recommendation for a woman set aside, in forcing a reposting of the position, and in manipulating the second-round selection to insure a man was hired.

I called Corrine Spector, the women recommended by the first-round committee, introduced myself, and explained my concerns. She had no interest in joining me in a challenge. In fact, she did not believe it was discrimination but my "relationship" with Nachitalo that caused her recommendation to be set aside. Her cool and curt responses surprised me.

The publicity also affected me in ways I never anticipated. I knew that headlines fade in the public mind and the story would be old news after a couple of days. It never faded in my mind. I had heard too many negative comments and jokes about people who sue throughout my professional training and association. All the administrative training included major emphasis on liability issues and how not to get sued. Anecdotal stories and jokes referred with derision and ridicule to the kind of people who sue. I identified with every one of them. I felt like a traitor. I wanted to crawl into a hole.

I had always been an outgoing, sociable extrovert. I became less comfortable around people. I dropped out of a fellowship program I had been accepted to, resigned from the Blandin Fellowship Board of Directors, refused another appointment to the St. Louis County Variance Board of Adjustment, and stopped attending political caucuses. I shut down. I avoided any social gatherings that weren't required in my job. Guilt and shame at being a litigant—"litigious bitch" was the term used—kept me home. Besides, I was no fun to be around.

The suit was on my mind constantly and I found it almost impossible to engage in the small talk that is part of social gatherings. First thing in the morning and last thing at night, my stomach knotted up as the suit boiled up to the surface. *How does what I'm thinking about manage to churn my stomach, anyway?* I couldn't block any of it. Talk about a conflicted, split mind. It was a righteous suit, but I was ashamed of suing. This split mind was a discordant little lick in the plaintiff blues.

There were lots of reminders, in case it ever slipped my mind. In June 1987, we moved from the farm north of Duluth into our new home on the Cook end of Lake Vermilion. A couple of weeks later, eleven-year-old Max and I canoed down to a store around the point from us to get an ice-cream cone. The clerk asked us where we were from. I described the location of our new home.

"Oh, you're that woman," she said.

I ducked any more conversation, paid for the cones, and we left.

"How come we just got here and everyone knows who you are already?" Max asked on the paddle home. I knew he was worried about starting in a new school and this wasn't helping.

That first Christmas after we moved to the lake, the December 17, 1987, *Cook News Herald* had an editorial about the Christmas spirit. Albertson complained he couldn't get into the spirit this year due to, "the lack of Christmas decorations on the main street of Cook. I never noticed them much when they were there, but I sure miss them. The

Cook Chamber of Commerce has put them up in the past, but they have some financial problems and weren't able to do it this year. The cost for putting the lights up was around $450."

My lawsuit was not mentioned specifically and I had not filed against the Chamber, but everyone knew what he was referring to. Rick and I heard it from friends and neighbors, the kids heard it in school.

Three weeks later, Albertson's editorial in the January 21, 1988, *Cook News Herald* read, "Ridiculous lawsuits are raising insurance rates. I think they should force a person who brings a lawsuit to pay all expenses if the person loses. The USA is one of the few countries in the world that doesn't have laws like that." No doubt what that was really about and it wasn't the last editorial on the subject. Many more would follow.

We were six months in our new home and community and didn't feel particularly welcome. You know you're the topic of discussion when you walk into a room full of people and it suddenly gets quiet. While it's possible some of those quiet conversations were supportive, it didn't feel that way to us.

Meanwhile, everyday after August 1987, I drove the 50 miles to and from work in Mt. Iron-Buhl. I passed the Cook School every morning, long before my kids arrived and every afternoon, long after they left.

Daily reminders.

Chapter 4

1987–1990

LAWSUIT DISCOVERY

"A person bringing a frivolous lawsuit
should have to pay all the defendant's costs."
Cook News Herald, 6/9/88

AFTER LOSING THE POSITION in Cook in 1986, I continued to work in the Mt. Iron-Buhl School District. Due to the predicted budget woes, I lost my administrative position to more senior principals and was bumped back into the classroom in 1988.

When we filed the lawsuit in February 1987, I had more questions than answers about who did what when. I knew what I had heard from Nachitalo, Albertson, Chester Larson, and Roszak. I knew what I had experienced at the interview and Cook meeting on July 29. I knew the dates for the job posting, the date I had applied, the date I received the "Dear Judy" letter, and the date the school board hired Putnam. The rest was unanswered questions.

Was I really the most qualified, as Nachitalo told me?

When did Putnam apply, before or after the posting deadline?

What were the specifics of Putnam's credentials?

Who vetted Putnam and when?

Who attended the luncheon meeting when the hiring decision was made, according to both Nachitalo and Albertson?

Did the chamber committee have that much influence or was something else going on?

Who started the rumors?

Who was behind the decision to hire Putnam?

Why would they hire a less qualified man?

Our attorney Sharon Fullmer said that such unanswered questions were not uncommon and the discovery process would help get some answers. Discovery, she explained, is a pretrial procedure by which each party asks to see information held by the other side concerning the case. Common types of "discoverable" materials are official documents, interrogatories, requests for admissions and depositions. The judge hearing the case receives notice of all of these requests, from both sides.

My legal vocabulary expanded on a daily basis. I needed at least a layman's understanding to figure out what was going on. Interrogatories are a list of written questions that one side presents to the other. Interrogatories are intended to expand the basic knowledge of the case through the written answers provided. Admissions are written requests in which one side asks the other for an admission of fact. In this case one side might ask the other for an admission that, "Putnam's interview followed Pearson's on July 29, 1986." The other side would likely admit this and it then becomes an uncontested fact upon which both sides rely.

A deposition is a formal interview, under oath, in which an attorney questions a witness to learn more about the events in question. The attorney from the opposing side is typically present and may also ask questions of the witness or object to questions from the other side. When the interview is complete, it is "certified" by the witness and the court reporter as a true and complete record. At this point, it becomes a part of the court record and may be used during the trial.

We served our first request for the production of documents and interrogatories at the same time we filed the lawsuit in February 1987. The list of documents we requested is too long to cover here, but it included relevant School Board minutes, credentials from all candidates, reimbursement receipts, relevant billing records, communication between the School District and the citizen's committee, relevant personal and official calendars, and notes taken by the parties in the interview and selection process.

We were entitled to see any documents they might use or refer to in their defense. It was a challenge to list everything that we thought we needed but not so much that it would be impossible to read and sort through. The calendars and billing records we requested from the beginning would play a significant part in the trial later on.

Although the process, procedures, and legal jargon were beginning to make some sense, I was confused and worried about the people. Nachitalo had resigned as Superintendent to take a position in southern Minnesota. Assistant Superintendent Niemi had left the district months before Nachitalo. Two school board members decided not to run for re-election. I'd never get answers if more and more participants and witnesses changed positions or left the area.

There was some good news from the administrative resignations. When Niemi left, the district assigned AlBrook School Principal Bob Melander to fill the Assistant Superintendent position. In December 1986, the district appointed English teacher Corrine Spector interim principal in Melander's place. The first-round citizens' committee had selected her as their first choice for the Cook position in June 1986. She was fully licensed for the position, as she had been when passed over the previous summer when the board caved into chamber pressure. Even though she had not accepted my interpretation of those events, I was glad to see a woman administrator in the district.

She was the first woman to work as High School Principal in the St. Louis County School District. The following year, she was assigned as Principal for the Orr School. Perhaps just filing the lawsuit had made a difference as the district scrambled to offset the perception of sexism in the public eye.

April 1987 brought terrible news. For every step forward, it seemed like there were two steps backward.

Sharon Fullmer called to inform us that her Minneapolis firm would have to drop my case because they found a conflict of interest. She was upset and apologetic, but indicated that the firm would send back my $5,000 retainer and would find me substitute counsel. Rick and I drove to the cities shortly after her call to interview two firms who had agreed to take the case. We chose Richard Williams of the Hvas, Weisman & King firm in Minneapolis.

We had paid Fullmer's firm the retainer with the understanding that they would bill for ongoing expenses and would receive 1/3 of any settlement or award I received. The financial arrangements were quite different with Williams. His firm did not require a retainer and would not bill us for anything until the case concluded. Then we would be billed for everything. There was no contingency arrangement related to a settlement or award. All bills would come due at the end of the case. We had no idea how long that would be or how high the bills would be.

Driving home, we talked about the potential financial risk for the family. We had committed to the new home and the financial responsibility for that investment. If we proceeded with the lawsuit, it would likely wipe out any savings we could manage for the boys' college expenses.

"This is really risky business," I said to Rick. "Maybe we should just drop it?"

"Yah, but could you live with that?" he asked.

The silence that followed was deafening as we each contemplated the risks of going ahead. There would be a price to pay either way.

"Forget that question," Rick finally broke the silence. "I'm not sure that I want to live with just dropping it. Then those sons of bitches get away with this crap."

"Agreed. I can't just do nothing. There's really is no choice, is there?"

We would owe a tremendous amount of money, win or lose. It was hard to anticipate all the implications of the new financial arrangements. It was also difficult to change attorneys. We had developed a supportive and trusting relationship with Fullmer. It was discouraging to start back at the beginning, explaining everything and everyone again. Defendants were leaving and changing positions constantly. The geography of the case covered over 5,000 square miles. The uniqueness of the St. Louis County School District, the number of defendants, and the number of attorneys further complicated this case.

Williams had little time to get up to speed on the case.

On April 27, 1987, we received an Order from the Federal Court. None of the defendants' attorneys, the school district, or the individuals named had answered the complaint (lawsuit). The Order stated that they should have responded within 30 days of the filing. The Order directed us to notify them that they had to respond. *Why is this our responsibility?* I wondered. If they failed to respond, we had to file an application for default within 10 days or the case would be dismissed. Somehow, we were responsible for their failure to do their job. Furthermore we were still in the process of substituting attorneys, which alone takes more time than the 10 days provided in the Federal Order.

Dick Williams had to hustle.

By April 29, 1987, he notified the six law firms of the court's order.

By May 6 all defendant attorneys had responded or requested extensions. Extensions would become a familiar procedure before the case was over. Motions filed and dates set routinely received extensions. Is that because time was on the side of the attorneys? Their billable hours just kept climbing. Time also seemed to be on the side of the defendants.

If enough time went by, more witnesses would have moved, changed jobs, or lost their memory, which had happened to a few immediately. How were we ever going to prove what we believed to be true? When would I get answers? Patience was not one of my long suits and time became my greatest adversary in this process. It was already a year since the Cook interviews. Passing time was another riff in the plaintiff blues.

On July 14, 1987, we received the court's Pretrial Order setting the dates for the end of discovery and pretrial motions. All discovery and depositions were to be completed by April 1, 1988. Any "substantive" motions (relating to the rights and duties of the parties, as compared to procedural motions referring the steps or process used to enforce or define those rights and duties) to dismiss the case on behalf of the defendants had to be filed by May 1, 1988. While I was glad to see some deadlines set, it was almost another year to wait. How could this process take so long?

The stalling tactics of the defendants chewed up the calendar. Everyone received the court's deadlines in July. We had filed our original discovery request for district documents back in February. The first round of depositions was scheduled for August 10. We had not received any of the documents requested. On July 24, Williams wrote to the defendant attorneys, "I am not going to produce my client for her deposition prior to getting my discovery from school board unless compelled to do so by an Order of the Court."

Depositions finally began on Monday, October 5, 1987, after Williams received the first set of district documents on Friday, October 2. We had no time to pour through the boxes of documents on the hiring process, the credentials of candidates to compare, the calendars with dates and times of interviews and meetings, and the phone records of arranging contacts, etc. Every document we requested throughout the discovery process came late. We began depositions with a significant disadvantage. *Was that deliberate or coincidental?* I wondered.

In spite of having little time to review the discovery documents, we began depositions in October 1987. Attorneys scheduled three days, October 5–7, 1987, for the first five of what would eventually be 11 depositions. This first set of depositions was held at the St. Louis County Court House in Virginia, Minnesota. We deposed Superintendent Nachitalo and three of the Cook Chamber members--Albertson, Simonson, and Pascuzzi. The defendants, including the school district and the five chamber members involved, took my deposition during these three days as well. Six attorneys questioned me.

It was cold, grey, and drizzling when I arrived at the courthouse that morning. *An ominous sign,* I thought.

Inside the courthouse, it was also cold and grey. Ten men in suits turned toward me as I walked up the stairs to the courtroom. I nodded slightly and went to sit on the bench on the other side of the huge, grey marble hallway until Williams could break free to join me. My footsteps echoed in synch with the beating of my heart. I'd never felt so alone and intimidated in my life. *What have I gotten myself into?* I thought to myself.

The suits included six attorneys: Williams for me, Bartel (from Roszak's law firm) for the school district, Prebich for Albertson, Peterson for Simonson, Roche for Pascuzzi, and Colosimo for Aho. The superintendent, some of the chamber members, and some of the school board members were also there.

Not only was the setting scary, the costs were staggering. With the addition of the court reporter, I estimated that the costs of these meetings were well over a thousand dollars per hour, most of which I would be responsible for if I lost. The only consolation was now maybe I'd find out the who, when, and why of hiring a less qualified man. This first round of depositions took the entire three days scheduled. Nachitalo's deposition took the first day; mine the second day; and Albertson, Simonson, and Pascuzzi the third day. The transcripts of the depositions totaled 561 pages.

It was very discouraging. My first face-to-face encounter with the other side produced few answers. Instead, we got more questions and confusion. The lies I heard astounded me. I was so naive. I believed when you are under oath you have to tell the truth. For certain, Nachitalo and Albertson lied, either in their conversations with me or in their depositions. Which was it? All four denied making any decision over lunch at the Four Seasons. Their depositions clearly contradicted what they told me at the time. Simonson denied everything.

Simonson tossed out a clue, however. He stated that Chet Larson had called him just before Putnam arrived at his meeting in Cook.

"We like him here at the Central Office," Chet told Simonson. "You're going to like this man." Simonson further indicated in his deposition that the only person he ever talked to from the district office was the board chairman, Chet Larson.

The only relatively bright spot in the three days was Russell Pascuzzi, who mostly told the truth, as I knew it then. He admitted hearing all the rumors, about the job being held for me by Nachitalo and about the affair. Of course, he couldn't or wouldn't remember who told him about the affair. He admitted the steak dinner bet with Albertson, over the job being wired for me. Yes, he had told folks outside church one Sunday that he did not believe a woman could handle the principal's job. He admitted the statement,

"Hell will freeze over before we hire a woman principal for the Cook High School."

Some of the testimony that seemed relatively mundane at the time surfaced later as critical for us. Superintendent Nachitalo's testimony about the routine vetting or checking credentials of the candidates became a key to my case, close to a smoking gun.

"Who did you contact with respect to Mr. Putnam's background check?" asked Williams.

"I called officials—board members and superintendents—from districts where he had worked—in Minnesota and California. I talked to them *prior* to calling him in for an interview."

"Did you share that information with the members of the board who were doing the interviewing process?"

"Yes. We talked about what I had heard."

According to Nachitalo, all the vetting calls on Putnam were made *before* interviewing and recommending him for the job. He stated several times that the central office interview team made the decision to recommend Putnam immediately following the interviews. He denied that the Cook committee made the decision two days later at the luncheon. Nachitalo said he merely informed folks at the luncheon he was going to recommend Putnam. Very interesting, because Simonson, Albertson, and Pascuzzi all stated they heard no conversation about the Cook job at the luncheon. *Unbelievable. Were they at the same luncheon?*

The name mentioned most often in the depositions was Chester Larson, Chairman of the School Board. According to the depositions,

Chet had made several calls to folks in Cook about the candidates, particularly in support of Putnam. Nachitalo referred to him many times as having a major role in this decision-making process.

I had served with Chester for three years on the school board, from 1978–1981. Aside from the few angry words following his no vote on Rick's long-term sub position, we had the same professional relationship as did all members of the board. I assumed that when he had made his suggestions to me following the central office interview, he meant to be helpful.

Now I began to wonder about Chet. His name had popped up too many times. Nachitalo testified that Chet Larson told him about discussions with one or more folks from Cook regarding their concerns about hiring a woman for the job. *Why was he so involved?*

Shortly after the first round of depositions in October, Williams requested an extension of time from the Court on the cutoff date for amendments to the pleadings or original complaint. The district had responded late with the original discovery documents and still had not provided the signed answers to our interrogatories, also requested eight months earlier in February.

During the depositions I began to realize that Dick Williams was not going to be a very supportive attorney to work with. He warned me right up front that he didn't do much "client handholding." That was fine with me, but a little support would have been helpful during those first three days of depositions. Instead, he chewed me out for talking too much in my deposition (my first opportunity in 14 months to explain how wronged I had been).

"This is a deposition, not show and tell," he hollered at me. "Just answer the questions!"

Following the depositions, I had only one telephone conversation with Williams in November. When I asked about what he had found in the boxes of district documents he received just before the depositions, he indicated that he had not had much time to look through them. I asked him to get me the documents so I could go through them. I'd find whatever time it took. In particular, I hoped the calendars and telephone records would explain what really happened when.

He was abrupt and impatient with me whenever I asked questions or made suggestions.

After reading through the deposition, it was clear to me we should drop the charges against some of the individuals. I never wanted to include them in the first place. After some discussion, Williams agreed to drop Aho, Musech, and Pascuzzi from the lawsuit. When asked about Aho in his deposition, Nachitalo had stated, "I didn't recall he was even there (luncheon at Four Seasons restaurant). He was not a major actor in all of this."

In relation to Pascuzzi, Nachitalo said, "I can't even recall whether he was there, to be honest with you. Again, I think the relationship with Mr. Pascuzzi is similar to what I described as the relationship with Mr. Keith Aho."

Throughout the depositions, there were only two individuals in Cook who had contacts with the Superintendent and Chairman of the Board. Albertson and Simonson. Nachitalo referred to them at least five different times as the people from Cook he talked to. Musech never appeared in the depositions as having any comments or involvement other than attending the luncheon. He was not at the interview at Smitty's. We decided to drop the three less mentioned and keep Albertson and Simonson.

The entire "drop" process was delayed and complicated by motions from the defendants to bring the Chamber of Commerce into the suit as a third party.

Albertson and Pascuzzi filed Third Party Complaints against the Cook Chamber of Commerce in November 1987. Apparently they or their attorneys thought they could hide behind the chamber shield. So another party joined the lawsuit. It would take additional time for another attorney to get up to speed. The Chamber issue was frustrating because throughout the process, the local newspaper referred to the lawsuit as the reason for the Chamber's financial troubles, always implying that I sued the Chamber.

Nine months after I filed suit, Albertson, the same editor who implied that I caused the Chamber's financial woes, dragged the Chamber into the lawsuit.

Albertson filed first against the Chamber in November 1987. His editorial about Christmas spirit a month later never mentioned that fact. The fact that I had not sued the Cook Chamber never appeared in the *Cook News Herald.* Two negatives make a positive, so by inference I had. Our first Christmas in Cook was less than merry as well.

Six more months passed before the remaining depositions began. I had little contact with Williams or direct involvement in the case during this time. However, in March, Williams had to petition the Court again to extend the cutoff dates for discovery from April to June 1, 1988. We had not yet received the chamber's response to the actions bringing it in as a third party.

By April 1988, Aho, Pascuzzi, and Musech had been dropped from the suit and the Chamber of Commerce was officially included in the suit through the third party complaint by Albertson. Although I was not directly involved during these six months, the legal letterheads kept flying. I received copies of the correspondence and motions. Stacks piled higher and higher. My life, my case was the impetus for this flurry of paper, but I remained an outside observer. This litigation game was an economic bonanza for attorneys, while the clients were benched on the sidelines.

The *Cook News Herald* kept the issue in my face and in the community minds. The steady pounding in the paper drove me further into a shell. The March 31, 1988, editorial included a quote on civil rights and white males. "The only time a white male has equal or civil rights is when he is dealing with another white male."

In an April editorial, Albertson wrote, "A year and two months ago, five Cook businessmen, the ISD 710 school board, Superintendent William Nachitalo, and ISD 710 were sued because a person didn't get a job they applied for. Well, three of the Cook people have been released, to date. We sure have an interesting legal system. When this is all over I think it would be interesting to figure out how much it cost the people from Cook."

On May 19, 1988, referring to an article titled "A Chilling Flurry of Lawsuits," his editorial stated, "We have more lawyers per capita than any nation in the world and they have to keep working. I believe there have been a lot of crazy lawsuits because of this." I was never mentioned by name, but in a small town like Cook, everyone knew who he was referring to. In fact, on several of these "editorial" occasions, I received phone calls from friends warning, "He's after you again."

The best (or worst) was Albertson's June 9, 1988, editorial. He wrote, "It is only fair that a person bringing a frivolous lawsuit should have to pay all the defendant's costs. Right now, anyone can bring a lawsuit against anyone else and they don't have to have anything to base it on." *He must have forgotten when he told me on the telephone, "If you'd been a man, you'd have had the job."* I cursed to myself.

The lawsuit involved me more directly in April 1988.

The defendants, specifically the new chamber attorney, wanted another deposition from me.

The defendants' attorneys deposed me the second time on April 4, 1988, in the St. Louis County Court House in Virginia, Minnesota. It lasted two hours and was relatively uneventful. Don Bye now represented the Cook Chamber of Commerce. Old ground was covered again, except for one subject.

Bartel, the attorney for the district, asked several questions about the incident when Chester Larson voted against hiring Rick for the long-term sub position at Albrook High School. *Where did this come from and what does it have to do with anything?* This exchange bothered me because it seemed to suggest that I had done something wrong.

After my deposition, I bugged Williams to get statements from the 1981 Albrook Principal and the Board Chairman to set the record straight, to prove how unreasonable and unprofessional Chet's vote had been. I wanted to prove that Rick had only agreed to the job for the one year to help the school and the kids, that his business was growing fast and it would have been a sacrifice for him to take the teaching position. I kept at it until Williams finally slammed his hand on the table.

"Drop it, Judy, just drop it!" he shouted. "Don't you get it? If you prove Chester Larson's behind this because of bad feelings from that incident, you lose the lawsuit."

"I don't understand," I said.

"If Chet took you out of the position because he was angry with you personally, that's not discrimination," he explained impatiently, as if I was being deliberately dense.

"It's unethical, unfair, and petty," he concluded, "but it's not illegal."

This exchange weighed heavily, producing a sort of cognitive dissonance that troubled me throughout the rest of the process. I wanted the truth, didn't I? Who did this to me and why? But was the truth contrary to my interests in the lawsuit? *How could this be?*

In April 1988, Bartel petitioned the court to compel me to submit to an adverse psychiatric exam. This was a shock. I had never claimed any psychological damage as a result of the discrimination and I had never seen a psychologist or psychiatrist. We simply asserted that the discrimination and resulting rage and frustration had caused a lot of emotional distress. Rick and I joked about what the outcome of a psychiatric exam might mean. It seemed like a lose-lose proposition to us. If I passed the exam, there would be no damages awarded. If I failed the exam, the lawsuit would benefit—but I'd still be nuts.

This final round of depositions began with mine on April 4 and took until June 6, 1988, to complete. Most of these depositions were held in Virginia. After my deposition, we deposed board chairman Chet Larson and William Putnam on April 28, 1988, and Cook board member Don Anderson on May 20. On June 6, 1988, Williams deposed former Assistant Superintendent Willard Niemi and school attorney John Roszak in Minneapolis.

In his deposition, Chet Larson denied that he talked to me right after the central office interview. I knew that was a blatant lie. He denied any contact with Simonson from Cook, although the other depositions contradicted this. Williams asked Chet about my July 1986 interview.

"Now, at the time that this interview had been held, had you ever hear of any rumors that were going around that Judith Pearson was having some type of sexual liaison or affair with Dr. Nachitalo?" he asked.

"I believe, yes, I had," Chet answered.

"And from whom had you heard that?" followed Williams.

"Just a community rumor," said Chet. "I don't know who I heard it from."

"What community was that rumor being spread in?" asked Williams.

"Albrook, Cotton, I guess the whole school district," Chet replied.

"You must have heard it from a variety of different sources?" Williams persisted.

"Yes," said Chet.

"Surely you remember at least one source?" Williams repeated.

"No I don't," insisted Chet.

In his deposition, Roszak denied talking to me about his conversation with Nachitalo regarding the citizens' committee in Cook. I knew that was yet another lie. Again it was demoralizing that these folks, especially an attorney, would lie under oath and commit perjury. Perjury is a criminal offense for giving false statements under oath. I suppose I expected the invisible hand of justice to reach out and smack them on the spot. On the contrary, they never paid any consequences for their lies. Regarding my conversations with Nachitalo, Roszak, Chet Larson, and Albertson, it was my word against theirs. Except I knew they lied and there was nothing I could do about it. The frustration was enormous. Their "inventive" testimony became the improvisation in my plaintiff blues.

Most of the other side's defense was now established from the depositions. Their unanimous testimony was that the candidates had been vetted before interviewing. The central office interviewing team selected Putnam immediately following our interviews on Tuesday, July 29, two days before Nachitalo's luncheon with the chamber members on Thursday, July 31, 1986. Not only did no one challenge my qualifications, several praised my career and credentials.

"I've already indicated in my testimony that Judy was a very strong candidate, a very capable person. It came down to 'splitting hairs,'" Nachitalo replied when Williams asked him to compare our credentials.

"But Mr. Putnam in my estimation, based on the interviews, had "charisma.'"

Superintendent Nachitalo stressed that Putnam was charismatic in his interview several times. Assistant Superintendent Niemi said Putnam's interview made the difference. From the frequent references in their testimony, it was clear that "splitting hairs" and "charismatic" would be a major thrust of their defense. It would be almost impossible to refute.

All of the testimony stated that no decisions were made at the chamber luncheon. The chamber members were merely informed of the decision that had already been made. They were not involved in making it.

There were contradictions throughout the depositions, but Williams assured me we could use those contradictions as evidence. He was not surprised by the lies, as if perjury was a standard operating procedure. *I wonder if he even believes me.* It was beginning to dawn on me that very little of this lawsuit process was about the truth. Strategy mattered, truth was coincidental at best.

At my second deposition on April 4, 1988, Williams brought me the unopened boxes of district documents he had finally received back in October. I took them home after the deposition and started pouring through the stacks, looking for clues about what really happened, who decided what when.

The night before Chet Larson's deposition on April 28, Rick and I found what would eventually turn out to be the missing piece, the closest thing we had to a smoking gun. Buried in one of the boxes of documents were over one hundred pages of the district's phone records. Checking Bill Putnam's resume against the phone records, we found three pages with long distance phone calls to communities where Putnam had been employed.

The defendants testified that Nachitalo had vetted Putnam before the interviews and before the chamber luncheon on July 31.

The phone records proved otherwise.

I compared the telephone bills with Nachitalo's notes on those vetting calls. The records revealed a frenzy of phone calls beginning at 1:57 p.m. on Thursday, July 31, immediately following the luncheon—at which no decisions were made? There were 10 long distance calls to six different school districts that afternoon. Nachitalo was still calling Putnam's former districts at 8:42 p.m. that evening from his home. The calls continued from his home at 6:45 a.m. the next morning, Friday August 1. *Damn, he never checked the guy out until after the luncheon. The decision really was made at that luncheon.*

Many of Nachitalo's background notes were negative, similar to the concerns Nachitalo had shared with me on the phone.

"Very green," read a note from the call to one of Putnam's former superintendents.

"Never finished any job, got along with kids, but over his head," more notes taken during the same phone call.

"He did lose his patience a few times and might talk too much at times," were notes from another former school district.

"Needs more experience," read another.

I marked up the telephone bills and the vetting notes and gave them to Williams first thing the next day at Chet Larson's deposition.

For the first time, Williams seemed excited about the case.

Williams asked Chet Larson about those vetting calls.

"I take it that you had this information before a decision was made to hire Mr. Putnam; you didn't decide to hire him first and then find out how he did on his other jobs afterwards?" asked Williams.

"Correct."

"Did you have this information before you interviewed Mr. Putnam?"

"Yes."

"You were aware of the fact that there were some reservations about his performance, is that right?"

"Correct."

"You were aware about that at the time that you interviewed him?"

"Yes."

Finally we had some proof of lies about the vetting process. The only frustrating part of this for me was that this critical evidence had gathered dust in unexamined boxes in Williams' office for more than six months!

Putnam's deposition followed Chet Larson's that day. Williams asked Putnam about his finally deciding to take the Cook position, after testifying he had initially turning it down.

"And you were advised by Chet Larson on the phone that you were head and shoulders above the other candidates and that the rest of them were sort of in a pack behind you, and you said based upon those representations, you'd take the position, is that correct?" Williams asked.

"That's absolutely correct," Putnam responded.

Chet Larson is mentioned again, along with more contradictions. If the decision between Putnam and me was about "splitting hairs," where did the "head and shoulders" come from?

Just three days before Roszak's deposition on June 6, David Bartel (from Roszak's firm) informed us that his law firm would be dropping their representation and a new law firm would take over for the school district. Although no explanation was given, I assumed it was due to Roszak's direct involvement and pending deposition. The new law firm's representative appeared at his deposition.

Extensions were granted again to allow motions for substitution of attorneys. Another new lawyer had to get up to speed for the major defendants. More time was lost.

However, we got a break on June 14.

After two months of legal letterheads on the issue, Mary Rice, the new lawyer for the district defendants, dropped the motion compelling me to participate in the adverse psychiatric exam. The trade-off was that we had to agree not to assert a claim for psychological or psychiatric damage.

"No problem!" I told Dick Williams.

And then, suddenly, there was startling news.

On the front page of the July 28, 1988, *Cook News Herald*, Albertson reported that Putnam had resigned. Of course, he found a way to work me into his article about Putnam's abrupt departure, one more example of the yellow tinge to his reporting.

"Putnam's tour as principal is remembered by the fact that one of the other applicants for the job filed a lawsuit against the district, the school board, and five Cook business people who met with the applicants for the purpose of selling the town. The person filing the lawsuit felt she should have received the position."

Cook School staff told me that Putnam left because he was in over his head and essentially, could not handle the stress of the job. That seemed to confirm that he was less qualified to begin with. However, another key witness was gone. Later on, I wondered if the deposition process three months earlier had scared him off. No one wants to be involved in a lawsuit.

There was more good news in August 1988.

The District hired Bonita Gurno as the K–12 Principal for an open position at the Cotton School. With Corrine Spector continuing to serve as principal, now at the Orr School and soon to be transferred to fill Putnam's vacancy at Cook, there were two women principals in the school district. *Would this be true if I had not filed the lawsuit?*

The discovery part of the process was finally complete by mid-June 1988, three months later than the original pre-trial court order. Now came substantive and dismissal motions. We dismissed Simonson in July 1988. Three defendants remained (the School District, the Cook Chamber of Commerce, and Albertson).

These three parties immediately filed motions for summary judgment. Motions for summary judgment are standard procedure and essentially ask the judge to decide, after discovery, whether there are issues that should be resolved by a trial. If the judge decides "no" and grants summary judgment, we lose. If he decides "yes" and denies the motion, we go to trial.

In other words, the defendants were asking the judge to throw the case out for lack of evidence or legal grounds. We were entitled to file a response to their motion for summary judgment, which we did, defending our legal position. The summary judgment hearing was scheduled for November 16, 1988. However, it was postponed because the defendant's new attorney, Mary Rice, petitioned the Court indicating she needed more time to review and respond to our brief. It was rescheduled finally for March 3, 1989. Another four months lost. Just another little lick of the plaintiff blues.

At the summary judgment hearing at the Federal Court House in Duluth, Minnesota, Williams arrived late and seemed unprepared. He was on the defensive constantly with the judge, apologizing for the length and complexity of the original complaint. He argued that it was Fullmer, not he, that had prepared the original complaint. I was disappointed with his performance. His blame shifting seemed unprofessional. He had two years to amend the complaint if he felt it was necessary.

When we left the hearing, Williams did not even know if we had any charges left to take to trial. The judge appeared to grant the defendants' motions for summary judgment on almost everything, throwing most of our complaint out the window. Williams said we would have to wait for the written judgment to figure it out. My confidence hit a new low.

In the meantime, Williams had asked me about possible expert witnesses. I suggested Dr. Clifford Hooker, who had taught a seminar I took in 1980 on school law, with a major emphasis on hiring and firing. Williams interviewed and hired Dr. Hooker to examine the applicants' credentials for the Cook principal position and the process used to select candidates, interview, and hire. The cost was $60 an hour. This included Hooker's reading time as well as travel expenses for a deposition and then the trial, if we survived summary judgment. The school district also hired an expert witness, Dr. Harry Vakos. The costs continued to skyrocket.

Three weeks later, on March 21, 1989, we received the written summary judgment order from the court. The bad news was that the judge granted summary judgment on 15 counts in the complaint. Those issues were thrown out. The good news was that he denied summary judgment on several counts, so I still had a chance at a jury trial. But the judge ordered new briefs and filings on the remaining claims, to be filed with the court by June 2, 1989. So did I have a chance at a trial or not?

Three months later, in August, Judge Donald Alsop granted

summary judgment on all the remaining claims except discrimination and conspiracy to discriminate. Conspiracy is a combination or two or more persons committing an illegal act or committing a legal act by unlawful means. We had lost ground again, but after months of summary judgment proceedings, I would get my day in court! We had finally established a *prima facie* case. That means our case was sufficient on its face and statement of facts to entitle us to go to a jury.

However, going forward was getting tougher all the time. There were several U.S. Supreme Court decisions in June 1989 that made it more difficult for plaintiffs to prevail in employment discrimination cases. In the *Wards Cove Packing Co. v. Antonio* case, the court shifted the burden of proof in job discrimination cases to the plaintiff. In the *Price Waterhouse v. Hopkins* case, the court said that the plaintiff must prove by direct, not circumstantial, evidence that discrimination had been the motivating factor in the employer's decision.

Circumstantial evidence is indirect or secondary evidence, by which a fact may be reasonably inferred. Direct evidence is evidence that proves a fact without any inference or presumption. Price Waterhouse meant that the plaintiff had to have the equivalent of a smoking gun. I couldn't imagine how that would be possible, particularly after hearing the lies in the depositions.

Williams was worried and began pushing me toward a settlement out of court.

On October 5, 1989, the court issued an order for a pre-trial conference on October 24, 1989. The order emphasized, "Trial counsel and a representative of each party with authority to enter into a compromise settlement agreement *must* attend." In preparation for this conference, on October 20, 1989, we sent the defendants a written proposal to settle. Our monetary request was for one and a half times actual damages (salary differential and driving costs), a minimum amount of punitive damages, and attorneys' fees. We also requested that the district hire me for the Cook Principal position when the next district opening occurred, with Putnam's seniority date in 1986.

The Cook Principal position was of paramount importance to me.

I wanted to get away from all the driving and I wanted to be closer to my home and my kids. I wasn't asking to displace the present Cook Principal, but to be given the position when the next district opening occurred.

Our proposal was not constructed without tension. It seemed Williams had lost enthusiasm and just wanted it over. He low-balled all my requests, but I had already risked too much to just give up. He was abrupt and short with me now most of the time. I was miserable and would have been glad to have it over. I was disillusioned with the whole process. It was depressing to lose confidence in your attorney at this late stage of the game.

After all our tension and conflict to construct a settlement proposal, there was no response from the district to our settlement offer at the pre-trial conference in October 1989. There was no counter-proposal. In fact, there was absolutely no response from the other side, in spite of the court order.

In February 1990, we received notice from the Court that my case would be on the trial calendar beginning April 9, 1990. Williams continued to press me to reduce settlement terms, whittling away at the money for damages and my insistence on the job in Cook. His discussions with me were full of impatience and frustration.

Five months later, on March 5, 1990, we got a combined settlement proposal from the district and Albertson.

They proposed $35,000 total.

No attorney's fees.

No job.

No deal!

"I would rather go to trial and take my chances than settle for nothing. My entire career, years of education, two graduate degrees, training, experience, professional reputation, family sacrifice, and support throughout this process are at stake," I wrote in response to Williams on March 21, 1990. We had struggled to put together a compromise proposal in October as required by the court. We heard nothing for five months and then their proposal amounted to nothing. Williams' fees and the out-of-pocket costs already exceeded their meager proposal.

In early April 1990, Williams called to tell us that we were off the April calendar and rescheduled for the October 1990 calendar. No explanations, just another six months lost. It was an emotional roller coaster. Tighten up; steel yourself to get ready, then crash when delays and extensions brought more months of waiting. This was agony. My whole life was on hold until this was over. I wondered if I'd ever sleep well again, appreciate good food, or read a novel for enjoyment. Life moved in black and white, all the colors were gone.

I struggled to maintain at work and at home. I talked to no one at work about what was going on. I had been bumped back to teaching for my day job in 1988. Fortunately, teaching makes its own demands. It gave me focus and kept the lawsuit from dominating everyday.

I said little at home in front of the kids. Their school lives were busy and full; they didn't need to worry about this stuff. Rick and I would try to hash it over in the evening after the kids went to bed. But suppressing our anger for over four years was costing us. Talking about it always held the risk of unleashing a beast, or igniting a flash fire that could consume everything in its path. If one of us exploded, what could the other one say? Our anger would just feed off each other's. There's no response, no discussion possible.

Instead, the pent up anger and frustration would burst out at totally insignificant and unrelated, petty irritations. Rick put a hammer through the garage door when he banged his leg on a trailer hitch. I totally shattered a Tupperware container I had taken out of the refrigerator, slamming it on the kitchen counter, after the turkey legs inside fell out and rolled across the floor. *Keep a lid on it, just contain and maintain,* I had to keep telling myself.

To this day, Max loves to regale audiences (at my expense) with his tall tales and embellishments about how that shattered Tupperware incident terrorized him as a child and shaped his destiny! He hasn't lost his "creative" expression skills.

Finally, the formal Trial notice arrived. The trial date was set for November 5, 1990. Another month had passed. Maybe time only mattered to me. But this time the schedule stuck. We were on for

November 5 with an estimated trial duration of two weeks.

I heard nothing more from Williams until he called at me home on Sunday, November 4, the day before the trial was to start. He was sick and could not make it up to Duluth the next day. He said the judge insisted that we proceed with jury selection, so one of his associates would come up to Duluth for it.

I felt abandoned. He had been flat and cold for a long time and now a no-show on the first day of trial? I didn't know what to think. It had been four years of anticipating truth, justice, vindication, relief- –my day in court.

All I felt was dread.

Chapter 5

1990–1991
MY DAY IN COURT

*"The burden of proof is on the plaintiff
to prove every essential element by the
greater weight of the evidence."*
Judge Alsop, Jury Instructions 11/26/90

RICK AND I MET with Williams' young associate John
Daley for the jury selection on Monday, November 5, 1990.
Walking into the courtroom was like walking into a cathedral. You
instantly lowered your voice and whispered. Everything was huge, dark
and daunting. The judge's bench seemed enormous. The courtroom
smelled of old wood and leather, very official and intimidating.

Both sides went through their questions for the prospective jury
members. This process is called a *voir dire* examination, to determine
if there are reasons to challenge (excuse) potential jurors. Questions
involved jurors' work experience, including any involvement in
discrimination. They were also asked about any experience they may
have had with the judicial system.

Both sides were allowed three preemptory challenges of jurors and
both sides exercised them. Preemptory means that no reason had to
be given for the challenge. Gut or instinct was all it took. Rick and I
were concerned because Daley did not seem to take the whole process
seriously. *Was it due to lack of vested interest or lack of experience?*

Daley kept asking us for our opinion on which juror to keep and which to challenge. Sometimes it's flattering to be asked your opinion. This was not one of those times. He's the lawyer, the expert. Years of watching "Perry Mason" and "Matlock" hardly left us feeling qualified. But by 4:30 p.m. we had a jury composed of seven women and one man. Defendant's attorney Mary Rice struck two men that we wanted, so the predominantly female make-up of the jury was, surprisingly, their doing.

Dick Williams was sick all that first week, so we did not have our first day of trial until Tuesday, November 13, 1990. That Monday was a holiday because Veteran's Day fell on Sunday, so court was not in session. I drove 90 miles down to Duluth that Monday evening to meet with Williams at 6:00 p.m. to prepare for trial the next day. He was late getting in and lost his temper when there was no reservation for him. His secretary had screwed up. He managed to get a room anyway, but he remained very uptight. He hadn't eaten anything, so by the time we hauled his files up to his room and got him something to eat, it was after 7:00 p.m.

Because Williams had been so short and impatient with me in the past year or so, I had written out a list of questions to remember to ask him. I knew nothing about what the trial would be like, about what would happen when, who goes first, or when would I testify. He had never initiated any conversation about the trial process or given me any supportive direction or information. If he had any idea of what I was going through, he never gave me a clue.

I had no chance to ask my questions. Williams blew up several more times when he couldn't find documents in his files and couldn't find the notes from his partner on jury selection. When I tried to ask a question, he cut me off.

"Stop it, Judith! Just stop it! You're not going to try this case!" he hollered. I didn't know what I had done wrong, if anything. I toughed it out, providing a lot more support to him than he was providing to me. Williams had no time to go over my potential testimony on emotional distress, which he had told me to prepare months ago. It had been bothering me ever since. I had no idea of what he thought should be included. I was anxious about keeping my composure on the stand while describing the hurt and humiliation of the discrimination. What about the turbulent, emotional roller coaster ride of the past four years? Could, should I include that in the testimony?

When I finally got a chance to ask about the emotional distress testimony, he told me to keep working on it and we'd get to it later.

The last thing he told me, as I left that evening, was that we would probably have a settlement offer first thing in the morning, before the trial started. He told me to think about what I'd accept to settle. We finished after 11:00 p.m. and I drove the two hours home.

I still had no idea of what would happen the next day.

It was a dark, miserable drive home. It matched my mood perfectly. Williams' attitude bothered me. *Does he dislike me that much or is he just nervous about the trial? This is his job, doesn't he do this all the time? Why is he so uptight?* I wondered. *Doesn't he realize that this is an intimidating first time for me?*

I did not sleep at all that night, stewing again over the emotional distress testimony, the potential settlement offer, and Williams. *How much would I give up to get out of this nightmare?* Rick and I had to leave home about 6:30 a.m. to be certain to be on time for 9:00 a.m. court in Duluth.

I was a wreck that first day of trial. I had no sleep the night before. My stomach flipped from nauseous to acidic and back again. I felt rushy, as if my heart was beating triple speed. I was upset with Dick Williams, his temper and lack of preparation. He seemed arrogant and impatient all the time. Rick drove as I kept trying to organize scattered thoughts and late-night notes on emotional distress.

Maybe I would be called to testify that first day, maybe not. My brain had turned to mush. I was in a panic. I couldn't seem to remember anything. I had spent countless nights (I was teaching a full high school load at the Mt. Iron-Buhl High School during the day) going over the depositions and documents. Now the dates, names, and sequences just blurred in my mind. I kept returning to Williams' behavior the night before and how unsettling that meeting was. I had very little confidence left.

A settlement offer from Gary Albertson delayed the start of the trial. His attorney Prebich made an offer of $10,000 to settle out of court and Williams wanted me to accept it. I had argued to drop the other four defendants, but Albertson had played such a key role. His comments had prompted me to file the suit in the first place. Besides, he had lied throughout his deposition. Most important, we were still struggling to figure out who did what, when, and why. I believed he had many of the answers.

But I gave in.

In truth, I was relieved. I had hated suing individuals right from the beginning. In my mind, people can believe whatever they want, hold whatever bigoted, biased opinions they want. They just can't act on those beliefs to take away someone else's rights. The only defendant in this suit with the legal authority to deny my rights was the school district. The district may have been pressured by the chamber members involved, but only the district had the legal responsibility to know and observe the laws in this case.

The attorneys went before the judge to settle Albertson out. Williams, of course, kept the money. That was fine by me. It was the first money he had received against his costs and bills. That was our agreement, but I felt guilty about his not having received any compensation to date. I also wondered if that was why the case did not seem to get his full attention or preparation.

Before we went into the courtroom, Williams said he had to talk to Mary Rice about the trial schedule. He wanted them both to talk to the judge about agreeing to work late that first day of trial. He wanted to leave early the second day to get back to the cities for his son's cross-country banquet that evening. The judge agreed.

Rick and I were totally ignored in this discussion. Nobody asked us. It was my trial, but my time, my schedule didn't matter to them. We were furious because getting out early that first day mattered to great deal to us.

Max, now in ninth grade, had been selected for a regional high school honor band performance that evening across the bridge in Superior, Wisconsin. We hoped to finish early enough to attend.

However, our desire to attend our kids' events was never factored in. How ironic! This whole lawsuit mess had started in large part because I applied for the job in Cook so I could finally work and live in the same community my kids went to school in, so I could attend their events.

By the time the trial started, at 10:30 a.m. Tuesday, November 13, 1990, there was no settlement offer from the district as Williams expected. I lost sleep on that score for nothing. The trial started with opening arguments, which are brief statements by both sides summarizing the facts and theory of the case that they intend to develop during the trial. Williams went first, took 30 minutes and was absolutely horrible.

He got the geography wrong, the dates wrong, and referred to me as a teacher, not a principal. He reminded me of a teacher unprepared for class. I was shocked by his poor performance. Mary Rice's opening statement was much better, smoother, and hard-hitting. She hammered away at our burden of proof. "The entire burden of proof falls on the plaintiff in this case," she repeated to the jury several times.

After the opening arguments, we had to present our case. The district would then present their defense and both sides would have time for rebuttal. A total of 16 witnesses would be called, six by us and 10 by the district. Both sides entered many documents and exhibits into the record. The court was in session only seven days from November 5 through November 26, counting jury selection. Williams' illness, Veteran's Day, Thanksgiving, and no sessions on Fridays took up the rest of the month. A blow-by-blow description of those seven days would require a book by itself. But there were distinct highs and lows worth describing as the trial moved toward a verdict.

Williams called me as the first witness after the opening arguments. He took me through my professional background and my experiences in the Cook principal selection process in July and August of 1986. Whenever I referred to the rumors, either Albertson's comments about the affair, or the job being saved for me, or our having purchased the lake home on the promise of the job, Mary Rice objected. The judge sustained or ruled in favor of her objections on the grounds the rumors were hearsay and not admissible.

Hearsay refers to oral statements of someone other than the witness testifying. Those statements are admissible only to show that the other person spoke certain words and not to show the truth of what the other person said. It was a confusing and frustrating concept. None of that critical information got into the record. The same thing happened when I recalled hearing about Pascuzzi's statement, "Hell would freeze over before there would be a woman principal at the Cook High School." It was also thrown out as hearsay.

I was devastated by the rulings and struggled not to show it on the stand. *Was our whole case out the window?*

Williams lead me through my testimony for about two hours without asking me about the emotional distress he told me to prepare for. When he finished asking me questions, Mary Rice would begin her cross-examination, defined as questioning of a witness by a lawyer other than the one who called the witness. The cross is limited to issues raised in the direct testimony. The objective of the cross-examination is to clarify or discredit testimony already given. It can neutralize damaging testimony or present facts in a light more favorable to the party against whom the direct testimony was offered.

I was already upset after Williams' behavior the night before, his poor opening performance, and the judge's rulings on hearsay. That all added to my anxiety about Rice's adversarial cross-examination.

However, at 3:45 p.m., Williams and Rice agreed to postpone the rest of my testimony and cross-examination until the next day. *Good,* I thought, *we'll still have a chance to go over the emotional distress testimony.* Rice requested the postponement because Williams needed to call our second witness, Dr. William Nachitalo. We had subpoenaed him to be there, but he could only stay one more day. A subpoena is an order of the court compelling the appearance of a witness.

Williams took Nachitalo through the sequence of events in the Cook principal selection process. When Williams got to the vetting calls on Putnam and the critical telephone records, he had to ask the court's indulgence and have Rick go out to his car to find the copies

I had marked up. I was appalled. They were our best evidence and he forgot them?

I had given them to him two years before. Williams did not have his questions for Nachitalo prepared or his notes and exhibits organized. He had done nothing to coordinate Nachitalo's vetting notes on Putnam, which were so contradictory to Putnam's letters of recommendation. It was our best evidence and he blew it. Either he hadn't expected to call Nachitalo until the next day or he just wasn't prepared.

At 4:45 p.m., partway through Nachitalo's testimony, the judge adjourned the first day of the trial. There had been plenty of low points in the past four years getting to this point, but this was rock bottom. The judge had ruled out everything I thought was critical testimony and evidence. *And what's with Williams? Is he entirely unprepared, nervous, or just plain terrible?*

As Rick and I drove home late that evening following Max's performance, we contemplated the worst. We were glad no one else had come to the trial with us. The two of us were in this together, alone. We would probably lose the case and have to find a way to pay Williams' costs and fees, which were way over $50,000 by this time. We would have to file for bankruptcy, sell our home, and lose everything.

Because we had left the courthouse right away to get to Max's performance in Superior, Williams had the entire evening in his hotel room to prepare for the next day.

It showed.

He was more organized and scored some direct hits with Nachitalo, who was on the stand the entire second day. Williams began the second day by finishing Nachitalo's testimony on the Chamber of Commerce committee in Cook, the luncheon, and the telephone records.

Nachitalo stated that when he called to offer the job on Friday, August 1, Putnam initially turned it down. When Putnam called back later that day, Chet Larson was in the office. Nachitalo said Chet Larson took the call and convinced Putnam to take the job. Nachitalo made several statements that contradicted his 1987 deposition. I had

gone over the depositions again and again in preparation for the trial.
I knew them by heart.

Over the noon recess, I found Nachitalo's contradictory deposition
statements and gave them to Williams. He used them effectively in the
afternoon to impeach (discredit or challenge) Nachitalo's testimony.
In his deposition, Nachitalo stated he had called to check Putnam's
references before the interviews. The telephone records proved that
was not true.

When Nachitalo defensively responded, "I don't recall," to one
of Williams' repetitious questions on the timing of the vetting calls,
the stoic judge who had thus far seemed bored and disinterested
jumped in.

"Just a minute, Dr. Nachitalo. You just testified to that. Now which
is it? You either recall something or you don't. You can't have it both
ways," admonished Judge Alsop.

Nachitalo's poise was crumbling and it was apparent to every
one. He stated that Putnam's paper credentials were very good and
that was why he selected him for interview. But in his deposition, he
admitted that he had passed Putnam over for interview. His stammered
response to this contradiction was that he had been mistaken and had
forgotten that someone else had placed Putnam in the interview pile.
Who was that someone else?

During the trial I was reminded of my grandmother's advice. If you
just tell the truth, you don't have to remember so much. Nachitalo
should have listened to his grandmother. During Nachitalo's cross-
examination on his schedule the week of the Cook interviews and the
chamber luncheon in 1986, he pulled a calendar out his pocket.

Williams shot out of his chair to object. We had requested copies of
all calendars covering the events in question three years earlier. This
was the first time we saw his. That calendar turned out to have little
significant information for us, but the fact that they had not provided
it during discovery was a big score for our side.

Williams and Rice finished with Nachitalo and the judge adjourned
early. The judge explained to the court that Williams had to leave to
get home to the cities to attend his son's cross-country banquet. The

judge went on to say that he had three kids himself and knew how important this could be. *Irony of all ironies,* I cursed to myself. *Trying to join up with my kids' lives was what got me into this mess.*

That second day ended better than the first. We had a glimmer of hope. However, Williams left immediately for the cities to attend his son's banquet. I had no chance to ask him about the next day and what it would hold for me when my postponed testimony and cross-examination resumed.

I had tons of questions for Williams but no chance to ask. He was on the road to the Twin Cities. I was cut adrift again. What about my testimony on emotional distress? Am I limited to describing the emotional response to not getting the job or can I describe the emotional distress over the past four years, the plaintiff blues? Did I have to worry about saying something that would screw up the agreement we made to get out of the adverse psych exam? Could I use my notes on the stand? When was that going to happen? How would that testimony be cross-examined?

I wasn't looking forward to it, but I knew it was important if we were ever going to have a shot at any compensatory or punitive damages. I needed to be emotionally steeled for it. With so little sleep and so much stress, I was afraid I would break down. There were no answers and no sleep that night.

Several kinds of damages would be considered if we won. Actual damages are those suffered by the injured party directly related to the defendant's action. Salary and benefit differences and expenses incurred that would not have been incurred but for the actions of the defendants would be included. Those expenses would include daily mileage for four years to and from work in Mt. Iron-Buhl. Compensatory and/or punitive damages are compensation in excess of actual damages awarded as a form of reparation to the injured and/or punishment to the wrongdoer, awarded only in rare cases of willful and malicious misconduct.

Williams got in Thursday morning just two minutes before the gavel sounded. He began with me again on direct testimony, but struggled with the actual damages related to the extra driving. He messed this up. He still didn't grasp the distances and the geography that were such an integral part of my daily existence. He couldn't remember where I had worked when and what distances were involved in my commutes.

This was particularly frustrating because it was a huge part of my motivation for applying for the Cook job in the first place. I had spent a minimum of two hours a day commuting, in good weather. Winter roads added to the time and stress on a frequent but unpredictable schedule. I had made so many white-knuckle drives that his failure to comprehend really grated. Williams was obviously having another bad, unprepared day.

Mary Rice completed her cross-examination of my testimony. It was much easier than I had anticipated. Her questions were brief and I had no problems responding. Williams rested our case and the judge ordered the morning recess.

As we walked out of the courtroom, I asked Williams about my emotional distress testimony. He pulled up in mid-stride. He had forgotten about it! He raced back into the court to catch the judge. Too late. The judge ruled our primary case closed. Mary Rice would begin the district's defense after the morning recess.

I almost exploded at that point!

I had worried about it day and night for weeks, worked and reworked my notes, all for nothing. Didn't he understand that? Was he totally oblivious to my concerns?

After the recess, Rice began her case. She called six witnesses during the rest of the day. In order, they were chamber member and *Cook News Herald* editor Gary Albertson, chamber member John Musech, former Cook School Board member Don Anderson, School Board Chairman Chester Larson, former Cook Principal Bill Putnam and former Assistant Superintendent Willard Niemi.

There were memorable moments in the court that day.

School Board Chairman Chester Larson was absolutely resolute in his testimony. He stated he did not know and had not talked to anyone in the Cook community about the principal position. He denied talking Putnam into taking the job after he initially turned it down. Larson said the district interview committee had selected Putnam immediately after the interviews concluded on Tuesday, July 29.

Chet stated emphatically that the affair rumor was all over the district, but he could not recall a single person he heard it from. I think everyone in the courtroom found this curious. His testimony contradicted both Nachitalo and Cook Board Member Don Anderson. Chester was quickly becoming the most interesting player in this process.

Rice never asked Larson about the 1981 incident, when he had voted not to hire Rick for the math position at Albrook. I had no idea if it was part of the puzzle, but I wondered about it. He had brought it up out of the blue at a state school board conference in 1984 and it was referred to in his deposition two years before in 1988.

What would have happened if she had asked him about it? What if he had answered that he held that incident against me and took me out of the Cook position as a result? I wondered if she even knew about the incident? Had she read the earlier depositions, taken before she took over the district's case?

The most memorable witness that day was Bill Putnam. He was currently teaching and no longer an administrator. He was noticeably nervous as he took the stand. I assumed that was because Federal Court is an intimidating place. Putnam stated definitely that Chet had talked him into taking the job. Putnam testified that Chet told him on the telephone he was, "head and shoulders above every other candidate." Chet had denied this conversation just a short time before.

But as Rice and then Williams on cross-examination took him over his credentials and professional background, it became clear that he had omitted jobs from his resume. He had actually held seven different jobs in six years. He became increasingly agitated and upset as Williams pushed him on his past jobs. His voice trembled with emotion. He appeared close to breaking down at several points. There was palpable tension in the court.

"You better back off him," I said to Williams during a recess. "He's going to crack up there."

"But I'm not even half-way through his resume," Williams responded.

"The point's been made. Besides, none of this is his fault," I argued, "and I don't want to see him come apart up there."

Williams drove home one final, but major point that day. The district had rested their defense primarily on the assertion that Putnam gave a much better, charismatic interview in the original selection process. Williams suggested to the jury that now they had had the opportunity to compare their own "interviews," since both Putnam and I had testified on the stand at length. That comparison was clearly in my favor.

I often wondered what would have happened if Williams had pressed on with Putnam. Was there more trouble buried in his confusing resume? He had resigned and left Cook a few months after his April 1988 deposition. Was this kind of exposure what he ran away from?

The court adjourned about 4:30 p.m. that third day, Thursday, November 15. Court was not in session on Fridays, so Monday, November 19, was the fourth day of trial. Rice called her last two witnesses. She called current Superintendent Dan Mobilia to discuss transfer policies and possible openings. She called former board member Raridon to testify that he was there when Putnam's credentials were selected for interview.

During Raridon's cross-examination, he stated that Chet Larson was also involved in selecting candidates to interview. Rice rested her case mid-morning and Williams called four witnesses in rebuttal. They were Bob Champpa (former Cook Board member and member of original citizens' committee involved in the first round process for the Cook job), and chamber members Don Simonson, Russell Pascuzzi, and Keith Aho.

Humor crackled through the courtroom after the third witness referred to Putnam's "krismic" interview. Nachitalo had used the word charismatic repeatedly in his 1987 deposition. All the practice and coaching of witnesses had neglected pronunciation. Was it coincidence that all mispronunciations were exactly the same? It was hard for anyone in that courtroom to imagine Putnam having been "krismic" after watching him testify the day before.

One of the best moments for us came when Simonson was asked whom he had talked to in the central office about the interviews and meetings in Cook.

"Chet called up to Cook and told us to wait for Putnam to come up, that we'd like this man," Simonson responded to a question by Williams.

"Chet called after our meeting and said, 'You liked him didn't you?" he admitted in a follow-up question.

His reference to Chet by his nickname twice electrified the courtroom. Chester Larson had just stated emphatically, several times, that he did not know or talk to anyone in Cook. The contradiction hung almost visibly in the air. It was one of those magic moments. Williams had warned us that a trial took on an almost organic quality, a life of its own that could produce unpredictable events. This was one of those and it landed squarely in our column. Discussing it later on the drive home, Rick and I wished the boys had been there to share the moment, because it was too hard to describe.

When Williams asked Russell Pascuzzi what he had said about having a woman principal in Cook, Mary Rice jumped up and objected.

The judge ordered the jury removed.

It was the only time the judge removed the jury. As the two lawyers spared back and forth about the rules of hearsay, the judge stopped them, turned to Russell, and asked him what he had said.

"Sure, I said hell would freeze over before we'd hire a woman in Cook," Russell answered the judge.

"I didn't believe it then and I still don't believe that a woman can handle the high school principal job. I'm just thinking back to when I was a kid in school."

Even though Russell was there in person admitting what he had said, the judge ruled his testimony inadmissible hearsay, apparently because I had heard about his statements from third person. The judge told Williams in chambers that this might be grounds for an appeal. Somehow I did not find that comforting. The jury never heard what I had thought was proof of the Cook Chamber members' prejudice against hiring a woman. If that gun wasn't "smoking," it was locked and loaded—and we lost it!

Pascuzzi was the last witness that day. The court adjourned at noon on Monday, November 19.

All along we had been working from the theory that the Chamber members were so against a woman for the job that Superintendent Nachitalo caved under their pressure, instead of doing what was right. Driving home that day, Rick and I came up with a new theory. Too many contradictions in deposition and testimony pointed to Chet Larson. He was the Chairman of the Board and not someone Nachitalo could ignore. It appeared that Chet had pulled Putnam's file for interview at the last minute, used the Cook Chamber to push Putnam through, and bullied Nachitalo into submission.

Chet was an unusually involved chairman. He was retired military and spent more time in the central office than all the rest of the school board members put together. Chet was there when Putnam called back and Chet had talked him into taking the job. *Why would Chet deny that?*

Chet's the one who said the affair rumor was all over the district. I was now certain he had started the rumors. We finally had it figured out and it was too late. The last two witnesses were the experts for each side. We had no way to focus on Chet's role. The only question bugging me was why would he do that? Was it bias against women or our past history?

On Tuesday, November 20, the trial resumed with the two expert witnesses, called by each side to examine the candidates' credentials and the hiring process. Naturally, I thought Dr. Hooker had the better credentials for the expert job and was the more credible of the two. Williams scored final points and some good chuckles when he cynically asked their expert, Dr. Vakos, why a sharp superintendent like Nachitalo would do something so stupid as announce to a citizen's group at a luncheon that he was recommending a candidate for a job before he had checked references? Rice objected and the judge sustained, but the question hung in the air as the last words of trial testimony.

Before the judge dismissed the jury and adjourned for the day, he read a humorous seven-page story, from authentic 1921 court transcripts, lampooning the value of expert witnesses. It was not very complimentary to expert witnesses. However, Rick and I had a hearty laugh, the first in a long time. I can't recall the story itself, but I remember the laughter to this day because it felt so good at the time. It provided a welcome release of all the pent up tension. Rereading the judge's story years later, it wasn't that funny.

The judge adjourned Tuesday at noon after he set up the final schedule.

There would be no court session the next day, but Williams and Rice were to meet with the judge in the Twin Cities, Wednesday, November 21, to wrestle over jury instructions. Thursday was Thanksgiving, so closing arguments were not scheduled for six more days, on Monday, November 26.

When Williams, Rick, and I left the courthouse, we walked to a restaurant for lunch, so we could plan for Monday's closing arguments. We needed some way to make the geography and the distances clear for everyone, particularly the jury. Rick agreed to put together a big map for a tripod display. Dick said he would come up to our home on Sunday afternoon and spend the night, so we could go over the final summary of the case. It was one of the more relaxed conversations we had with him. Williams asked about some of the witnesses Mary Rice called, including Dan Mobilia.

I explained that I knew the current ISD 710 Superintendent Dan Mobilia from 1983–1985 when I served as Buhl Superintendent and he was Babbitt Superintendent. We had been the only two range superintendents to risk investing in wood gasification boilers. These were alternative systems to heat our buildings. I chuckled, explaining how I had crawled inside the huge wood-chip drying chamber with the consultant engineer to understand the system and to see why our new boilers were accumulating carbon deposits and shutting down.

The green wood chips were piling up on the conveyer screen bed and not getting dry enough. Too much moisture was getting into the firebox. I asked the consultant why we couldn't install some simple device, like the float in the back of a toilet, to signal or stop the conveyor once the drying bed was full of green chips. He remarked, "A whisker switch, of course! Why didn't I think of that?" Mobilia still laughed at my role in solving one of the major mechanical problems we had in bringing the gasification systems on-line.

This little anecdote is not about the whisker-switch or Mobilia. It's about Williams. As I recalled this quick little story from the time Mobilia and I worked together, Williams physically turned his chair and faced Rick to ask about the boiler.

"Was it a hot-water or steam boiler?" he asked Rick. I knew it was a steam boiler so I answered, but Williams directed his attention, body language, questions, and comments on this subject to Rick. Try as I might, I could not establish eye contact with him. It was so blatant that Rick was embarrassed. He could hardly keep a straight face, even winked at me a couple of times. Otherwise I would have blown up. I fumed all the way home. What was this? A woman can't figure out a mechanical problem? Or any woman who does is threatening? This was my attorney in a sex discrimination case and he couldn't converse eye to eye with a woman about mechanics? No wonder I was a wreck.

The wait during the Thanksgiving recess from Tuesday, November 20 until the following Monday was hell. Sleep was the enemy and nighttime was a war-zone. How do you get something like this off your mind? The entire trial, word for word, raced through my mind on a continuous loop. It was especially difficult to be around our families that holiday. I couldn't talk about the trial because my emotions were too close to the surface. Yet it dominated my thoughts. *How do you not talk about the only thing on your mind?*

Williams indicated he would call and discuss the issues related to jury instructions, but of course he never did. Instead of Sunday afternoon as we had scheduled, he came in late on Sunday evening, about 7:00 p.m. He hadn't eaten so I re-heated dinner and cleaned up. We worked on geography and timelines for several hours before we turned in. Rick stayed up even later to complete the maps and charts we had designed.

Monday was snowing and stormy, so we left early for Duluth. I drove Williams so he could prepare for his closing and Rick followed behind. It was a terrible drive for both of us. The closings were relatively brief. Williams completed his closing without ever referring to the maps and timeline exhibits that Rick spent all night preparing. He forgot! Mary Rice said repeatedly that we had not offered any testimony on emotional distress! *Whose fault was that?* I screamed silently. Each time I heard it I wanted to wring Williams' neck.

After the closings, the judge read 22 pages of instructions to the jury. On the burden of proof, he read, "In a civil action such as this, the burden of proof is on the plaintiff to prove every essential element by the greater weight of the evidence. If you find that the evidence is evenly divided between the parties then you must rule against the party having this burden of proof."

The judge charged the jury and sent them out just before noon. Williams and Rice had to stay to straighten out the exhibits, which had to be available to the jury. Rick and I left because it was still storming heavily outside. It took us over six hours to drive home, triple the normal time. We were exhausted. Rick had driven me to each day's trial proceedings and had stayed with me throughout the trial. I could never have made it through without him.

We were relieved that it was finally over, but discouraged by the jury instructions. They set such a high standard of proof, we didn't think we could possibly win.

When we got home, I found that Williams had not even made his bed that morning. I know he was under a lot of stress, but what about me? He was a professional but so was I. Yet he expected me to cook, clean, make beds, drive, haul files, read mood swings, and be supportive of him–all traditional roles of women. The little sensitivity I had to that chauvinist attitude boiled to the surface. I don't know if he was a chauvinist or just the prima donna center of his own universe, but that was the last straw.

We never saw Williams again. All further communications were handled by phone or mail and that was just fine by me.

We waited at home for news from the court. The next day, Tuesday, Williams called about 9:30 a.m. to say that the judge had called him. One of the jurors had gotten trapped by the storm in Wrenshall and couldn't get into court. Did we want to dismiss her? We agreed to let her stay if she wanted to finish.

Williams called again at 2:30 p.m. to tell us that the judge had gone ahead and dismissed the trapped juror in the interest of time and for the convenience of the other jurors. Williams complained at length about how bad the roads were on his trip home to the cities after court the day before. Both he and the judge got trapped in Moose Lake for the night. That we had driven through the heaviest part of the storm was of no interest to him.

It was ironic that I never had the chance to give the emotional distress testimony, including the stormy 50-mile commutes I had made for the past four winters driving to work in Mt. Iron-Buhl. Lots of those were white-knuckle drives just like the one the judge, lawyers, and jurors had faced the day before. They never heard about the daily reminders on my drives past the Cook school my kids attended or about all their activities I missed. *Too bad Williams forgot that testimony.* The lawyers, judge, and jury had just experienced why I applied for the Cook job; to drive less, get off the winter roads, and work closer to home.

At 4:30 p.m. Williams called with the verdict.

"We won on all counts! The jury was unanimous on all counts!" he exclaimed, sounding almost surprised.

Erik was still home from college on his Thanksgiving break and the three of us were just sitting around the kitchen table visiting, waiting for Max to get home from basketball practice. We were just describing some of those magic moments in the courtroom to Erik when Williams called.

With his abrupt two-minute telephone call, Williams had the house in motion.

I have to tell you there was a bit of screaming, laughing, and lots of hugging. I spent more time swinging through the air than I did shouting, "I can't believe it! We did it!" Rick had to leave shortly to pick Max up at the Cook School, but when they returned, the hugging and celebrating started all over again.

Williams had been in a hurry and had no time for questions when he called. He took just enough time to tell us the jury found the school district, Nachitalo, Chet Larson, and the Cook Chamber of Commerce guilty of discrimination and conspiracy to discriminate. They had figured out Chet Larson without any help from us. The jury awarded $45,000 in actual damages and $90,000 for emotional distress. The emotional distress award amazed me because I never testified directly on that issue.

We were ecstatic. It had been a long, long haul. However, our elation was short-lived. Max came home from practice the next day with a little different spin on our victory and dampened our celebration. He was upset over comments he heard at school. Bill Conger, the current board member from Cook, had complained to him that the school district would have to cut teachers or programs to pay for the lawsuit. Max liked and admired the guy. He was really hurt by Conger's comments.

I was furious. I called Williams and told him what happened. He agreed to warn Rice that her clients were spreading misinformation.

Max didn't need the guilt trip that his mom was causing his teachers to be laid off. He was only in 9th grade. Besides, it wasn't true. Mary Rice worked for the insurance company that carried the district's errors and omissions liability insurance. The insurance company would do the paying. School districts were required by law to purchase those policies. All school board members knew this because they voted to authorize the purchase of that insurance every year. The guy's comments to Max were just sour grapes, those of a poor loser. How childish and insensitive can you get!

The trial was finished, the jury verdict was in. *C'est fini*, right? Wrong!

In December 1990, the defendants filed a motion asking the judge to override the verdict or order a new trial. On December 20, 1990, the *Cook News Herald* reported, "ISD 710's Attorney Files For New Judgment or New Trial." Of course, the article reminded readers that it was, "A jury of seven females and one male found against former Supt. William Nachitalo, board chairman Chet Larson, and the Cook Chamber of Commerce last November."

I couldn't believe it! How could this be? With a single motion, the defendants could get the whole thing overturned? What had the last four years of hell been all about? Could a jury verdict be so abruptly and casually discounted? Am I in some twilight zone in another dimension, where nothing's real, there's no order, no rules?

The court gave Williams until February to reply. Both attorneys prepared huge briefs again. Could this go on forever?

After five more months of numbing frustration and uncertainty, Judge Alsop issued his final Conclusions and Order on April 16, 1991.

He wrote in reference to the jury's decision, "The court (Judge Alsop) is fully satisfied, however, based upon its own independent assessment of the evidence that plaintiff has met her burden of proof. It is undisputed that plaintiff established a prima facie case of discrimination. Defendant ISD 710 did assert several non-discriminatory reasons for its decision not to hire her. Plaintiff, however, successfully refuted these reasons and demonstrated that they were a pretext (a motive alleged to hide the real intent) for sex discrimination."

Finally, a final victory. No celebration followed this anti-climatic decision. By this time I was too exhausted and disillusioned with the whole process. I refused to get excited again, only to be let down by more procedural baloney.

Judge Alsop reduced the amount of actual damages to $35,324 and upheld the emotional distress award at $90,000. But we would have to petition yet again to get my attorney fees paid. These fees were over $80,000 so it would be another round of briefs and hearings before I would know if there was any award left. It wasn't over yet.

Judge Alsop included injunctive relief, but it was less than what we had requested. Injunctive relief is a court order requiring a party to do or to refrain from doing something. We had requested that the school district be required to hire me for the Cook position when the next opening came in the district, with a retroactive 1986 seniority date. Instead the judge ordered the district to offer me every secondary school principal position that became available until I took one or December 31, 1993, whichever came first. He also ordered the district to give me the same 1986 seniority date that Putnam had.

His order only provided a two-year window of opportunity for a principal position and it did not specify the Cook School. If Albrook was the school that opened, or if the district used its transfer authority to move openings to Albrook or Toivola-Meadowlands or Cotton, I could be driving greater distances than ever before. It was certainly not the remedy I was hoping for.

Williams's petition for fees was dated May 16, 1991. Rice's response to his petition was dated June 17, 1991. It was not until August 1991 that Judge Alsop ruled on the issue of fees. Although he granted us attorneys' fees, he reduced them significantly. The difference in fees and costs came from our settlement. I was still frustrated with Williams and jokingly thought to myself that we deserved half of his fees anyway. He had been unprepared much of the time. We had found all the critical evidence, including the explosive phone records and the contradictory testimonies Williams missed in the depositions.

Nine months after I won a unanimous verdict, I still had nothing to show for it. No money, no principal position in 710, and only one year left of the two-year window. If this was winning, what was losing?

Those growing doubts and publicity on the home front combined to dampen any enthusiasm we had for the legal system. On December 17, 1990, the *Timberjay* had headlined, "Cook Chamber of Commerce Considers Bankruptcy."

The article read, "The Cook Chamber of Commerce, at a special meting Monday, December 10, discussed the possibility of declaring bankruptcy as a result of a legal judgment against the School District #710, in a sex discrimination charge." The implication throughout the years of coverage was that the chamber's problems were my fault, that I had sued the chamber.

However, credit goes to the *Timberjay* for digging beneath the surface and reporting the whole story. The *Timberjay* quoted the president of the chamber, "The chamber became involved in the case only when the attorney for one of the defendants used his client's affiliation with the organization in an attempt to shield his client from a possible judgment. It's an unfortunate situation, one that is attributable to just a few people."

Albertson pounded away on the stacked jury concept. On January 17, 1991, the *Cook News Herald* reported that the Minnesota School Boards Association had recognized Chet Larson for his tenure on a school board. Albertson's editorial congratulated Chet Larson and read, "It is too bad that the one blotch on his record is from a lawsuit on sex discrimination that was decided by seven women and one male. It would appear there was sex discrimination as far as the jury selection was concerned. That issue isn't over, either."

On that last threatening note, Albertson was right.

Nothing was over.

Chapter 6

1986–1992
Bogus Credentials

"MIB Official Falsified Past Reference"
Mesabi Daily News, 4/7/91

WHEN I LEFT THE chronology (1986) to follow the
ISD 710 lawsuit through to the trial, I had just completed
my first year as junior high principal for the newly consolidated Mt.
Iron-Buhl School District. I served two more years, from 1986–1988
in that position before the district's continuing financial troubles
caught up with my seniority again.

The last two years as junior high principal were just as challenging
and exciting as the first one had been. It was such a busy place. The
numerous combinations of potential conflicts remained in play on
a daily basis. Students and staff demanded my attention constantly.
That was, without doubt, a good thing because it kept my mind off
the lawsuit during the school day. My only real Mt. Iron-Buhl worry
was job security. The consolidation of the two school districts had not
resolved the financial woes the districts had experienced. Minnesota
State Department of Education officials eventually became involved,
because the district continued to slide further into statutory operating

debt.

The state officials recommended closing a building. One of the compromises that sold consolidation to the voters in the 1984 consolidation referendums was keeping high school buildings open in both communities. Now it was clear that one of the high schools would have to close.

In late spring 1988, the school board voted to close the Mt. Iron High School and cut two administrative positions. I was still the least senior administrator in the district and was placed on ULA (unrequested leave of absence) for the 1988–1989 school year. Our contracts provided that administrators who were laid off could bump into the classroom. Two of us, elementary principal John Gornick and I, were laid off and assigned to the classroom for the 1988–1989 school year. I taught high school seniors while he was assigned to an elementary classroom.

I applied for several other administrative openings in the area, but the positions all went to men, equally qualified as far as I knew. However, I had a growing suspicion that the publicity surrounding the lawsuit and the informal networks I had been warned about were at work, stacking the odds against me.

My teaching assignment that year was American and World History in the Buhl High School building. I was discouraged at first over losing the administration position, but teaching quickly demanded all my attention. Teaching is great brain food. I hadn't taught or read much history for nine years, so I was back on the learning curve. Teaching required studying and thinking in ways I hadn't practiced for years. Apparently parts or processes of the mind are not tapped often in administration. These reawakened brain cells were now re-firing on all cylinders, forcing me to focus on something besides the lawsuit.

Teaching was again exhilarating. I was fortunate to rediscover this. So often we move onward and upward and never have the chance to go back. Circumstances had given me the extraordinary opportunity to go from teacher to principal to superintendent to principal to teacher. What a rare set of insights into the education experience.

That atypical career progression also necessitated some candid introspection. Which educator did I want to be? Which of those jobs had I liked best? Which was I best at? I had enjoyed all of my education positions, but each had its pluses and minuses. Each position required subtly different skills, exercised different intellectual muscles, and made different demands on my time and energy. I never resolved those comparative questions about the positions I had held, but I believe wrestling with them made me a wiser educator.

The next few years were exciting times in a social studies classroom. I tried to teach history in ways that made students think. I wanted them to understand why things happened, not just when. I incorporated the perspectives of historiography, which is the study of the theories, methods, and biases of historians. Students should understand history not as the truth about the past, but as an interpretation of past events. History changes over time and place. Revisionism will always be a part of the historical landscape.

For example, in his 1942 college text, *Growth of the American Republic*, Pulitzer Prize winning historian Samuel Morison described the life of a slave. "As for Sambo, whose wrongs moved abolitionists to wrath and tears, there is some reason to believe that he suffered less than any other class in the South from its 'peculiar institution.' The majority of slaves were adequately fed, well cared for, and apparently happy." By 1982, the Harcourt, Brace, Jovanich text described, "Their owners had complete control over their lives. An owner could separate a husband and wife, or sell a child and keep the child's parents." In 1986, the Merrill text described, "Discipline was often severe. The most common punishment was whipping. A slave's crime might be oversleeping or using a less than humble tone of voice." Slavery hadn't changed, history changed.

I taught what I called Pearson's Principle. "We can learn as much about the times in which a history book is written as we can about the times it was written about." Older American history books focused solely on white male heroes. More recent editions included a politically correct smattering of blacks and women. Hispanics will be next. The "savage massacre" at Little Big Horn became the Battle of Little Big Horn and was balanced by the more recent inclusion of the "massacre" at Wounded Knee.

The single most glaring omission I found in every high school American history text I checked was the Holocaust. In most texts, a mere four or five sentences described the concentration camps and defined genocide. Nothing about the gas ovens or Dr. Mengele. No mention of the pervasive anti-Semitism that set the stage for the mass murder of 6 million Jews. No attempt to raise the question of how this could have happened? Why this cursory treatment of man's greatest inhumanity to man?

Santayana wrote, "Those who cannot remember the past are condemned to repeat it." Is it any wonder that the world fails to respond even today to genocide, whether in Cambodia, Bosnia, Rwanda, or Darfur?

My all time favorite historical concept came from Orwell's *1984*. "Whoever controls the present, controls the past; whoever controls the past, controls the future." Orwells's theory aptly applied to the front pages then as it does still today.

In 1989 the Berlin Wall fell and history was turned upside down. Heroes became villains in Eastern Europe; enemies became allies.

By 1991 we were at war in the Persian Gulf with a former ally.

More currently, the government's penchant for classifying record numbers of documents and in particular, reclassifying thousands of pages of previously declassified materials in the National Archives, is a classic illustration of Orwell's thesis. They have the power *presently* to control what can be accessed of *past* records, which in turn affects the research of historians writing to inform *future* generations. And there you have it!

Exciting current events dictated much of my social studies curriculum from 1988–1992.

Students protested and tanks rolled in Tiananmen Square.

South African apartheid was under siege. By early 1990, Mandela was a free man after almost 30 years in prison.

The Clarence Thomas appointment to the Supreme Court made the constitution, checks and balances, advise and consent much more exciting for kids. Sexual harassment became a hot topic overnight.

How could a social studies class be boring?

I was never shy about my passion for teaching. My face would often flush with excitement, laughter, and sometimes anger. A few brave students teased me with the nickname "Pinky," which I still hear occasionally when I bump into a former student.

Life was exciting on the Mt. Iron-Buhl home front as well. A school board election had changed the balance of power on the school board from a Buhl majority in 1988–1989 to a Mt. Iron majority for the 1989–1990 school year. The new majority promptly reversed the high school building closure, voting to close the Buhl building and reopen the Mt. Iron high school. What had been a complicated but remarkably successful consolidation unraveled overnight. Open animosity and bitterness dominated relations between the two communities over that single, high school issue.

Unfortunately for the Mt. Iron-Buhl District, the high school closure controversy coincided with the passage of Minnesota's Open Enrollment law, which phased in from 1987–1990. Unhappy parents could simply pull their kids out of their resident district and enroll them in a neighboring district. Mt. Iron-Buhl was surrounded by school districts more than willing to take these students in. Revenue followed students and more students meant more revenue for the neighboring school districts.

Hundreds of MIB students open-enrolled out of the district. Buhl students went west to Chisholm while Mt. Iron students went east to Virginia. It was enrollment blackmail for Mt. Iron-Buhl and windfall profits for its neighbors. Enrollment is revenue and Mt. Iron-Buhl was hemorrhaging both. More programs and positions were cut each year.

I had been opposed to the enrollment choice programs from the early days of discussion at the state level. These programs were supposed to improve public schools by introducing market competition. I wrote an article entitled "Myths of Choice: The Governor's New Clothes?" for the *Kappan* magazine in June 1989. I warned, "Open enrollment leaves a school board terribly vulnerable to single-issue pressure groups." With over 200 students leaving and producing a $1.5 million revenue loss, the Mt. Iron-Buhl situation was the worst-case scenario.

My 1989 article led to many speaking requests around the country. I became one of the "token" opponents to parental choice. Every panel or interview had a pro and a con, to provide the kind of politically correct balance that enlightens no one. I participated in programs from a two-hour public television forum at Penn State entitled, "Communities and Their Schools: Should Parents Choose?" to testifying before the joint education committee of the Kentucky legislature. I presented my positions at the EWA (Education Writers of America) conference in Seattle and was interviewed by Judy Woodruff on the MacNeil-Lehrer News Hour on PBS.

School choice reinforced one of my foremost social science principles. Simple solutions to complex problems and simple answers to complicated questions are usually wrong. They will often create more problems than they solve and should be met with real skepticism.

The pro versus con format of these forums finally convinced me that the brief exchange of one-liners shed far more heat than light. The issues were far more complicated, far less black and white, than these debates could convey. I decided it would be better use of my time and more effective to flesh out all the complexities of school choice in one place. My work was published in a book entitled *Myths of Educational Choice* (Praeger 1993). My fundamental premise is that free and equitable public schools are essential to our democracy. School choice programs threaten traditional support and commitment to both the free and the equitable criterion.

School choice is elitist because only those who have the means can exercise their choice. If you don't have a car, or extra money for gas, how do you bring or send your child to the neighboring school district? School choice is particularly destructive to smaller, rural communities where the school is the center of community identity. When parents chose to take their children out of their resident school district, what happens to the choices, programs, and services for the students who stay behind?

My writing and speaking provided a welcome transition following the stressful lawsuit and trial. But nothing relieved the anxiety over the financial storm clouds building in the Mt. Iron-Buhl School District. Once again, seniority and job security were eroding beneath me. My principal position was gone and now my teaching job was threatened.

With the additional financial trouble caused by open enrollment, I was laid off every spring and called back in the fall when the enrollment numbers and budgets firmed up, just like I had been 10 years earlier in Duluth. I was placed on ULA (unrequested leave of absence) again in the spring of 1989. Then in June 1989, Mt. Iron-Buhl Superintendent Duncan resigned to take another position. He picked a good time to leave. The deepening financial trouble and the continued animosity over the building closures left little incentive to stick around.

The school board asked me to serve as interim superintendent until they could hire a new superintendent. Even though I had been one of the two superintendents steering the consolidation process, I was surprised to be asked. The current majority on the school board was from Mt. Iron and the relations between the two communities had deteriorated over the high school closures. Board members even encouraged me to apply for the full time position, which I did.

I served as interim superintendent after Duncan left in June, struggling to get the schools ready to open in the fall. What a mess it was. Due to the newly elected board's reversal on which high school would be closed, all the furniture and equipment had to be hauled from the Buhl High School to the Mt. Iron High School. This included moving the entire industrial arts, home economics, and computer facilities. In addition, there was a huge remodeling project in the Mt. Iron High School to complete before moving the equipment in. On top of this, the budget for the 1989–1990 school year was anybody's guess.

The two decisions on high school closure had resulted in over half of the high school students open enrolling to other districts. Many Mt. Iron students had indicated they might come back to the district with the reversal, but there was no way to know until the first day. Two plans, two high school schedules, and two lists of teacher lay-offs were prepared, depending on how many students showed up. With the reversed building decision, now more Buhl students were leaving. The budget, the scheduling, and the staffing were all up in the air for the start of school, just weeks away. The enrollment numbers for the high school fluctuated daily.

I had already experienced a unique combination of educational experiences, but on August 15, 1989, I had one to top them all.

As we made final projections on staffing for the high school, it was my job as interim superintendent to recall the necessary teachers to fill the schedule. By licensure and seniority, I recalled myself to a teaching position in social studies. The recall letter is addressed to teacher Pearson and signed by Pearson, interim superintendent. It doesn't get any more unique than that. That letter's framed. Following my recall of myself, I requested and was granted a leave of absence from my teaching position until I finished the work as interim and/ or was hired for the full-time superintendency.

It was a race to be ready for the start of school. I was putting in sixty-hour workweeks and then working weekends to stay ahead of the workload. The contractors and maintenance staff hated to see me headed their way. I ran so I expected them to run. I pushed hard, even denying and delaying vacation requests, so we could get the work done. I didn't win any popularity contests that summer, but we were ready for school to open on time. On September 5, 1989, teachers reported to work for the opening inservice. I was there early to make sure the facilities, coffee, and rolls were ready.

After I welcomed the staff, made announcements, and broke for coffee, the school board chairman introduced me to Dr. Craig Bangston, the new superintendent.

I was floored! I choked back my surprise at this bolt out of the blue, shook his hand and sort of burbled out, "Welcome aboard."

That was how I found out that someone else had been hired, that I wasn't even being considered. It had all been done behind my back and out of the public eye. There had been no interviews conducted that I was aware of. Apparently Mt. Iron school board members Robert Swanson and Peter Heltunen had traveled to Wisconsin to meet with Bangston and recommended him to the rest of the board.

I had no access to his credentials, but the newspaper report of his hiring indicated that he had served several districts as superintendent and that he had two doctorates. So he was more qualified as far as I knew. I was still hurt by the lack of consideration from the board, especially springing it on me at the opening teachers' meeting. After that morning's inservice meeting, I cleared out of the superintendent's office and began preparations for the teaching assignment I had recalled myself to.

There may have been procedural issues with Bangston's hiring, but he appeared to be the more qualified candidate, so I never considered a challenge. I would have been more discouraged about the events of that summer if it weren't for the students and the teaching. The times were exciting and the students a joy. That combination always sucks me in.

When the Berlin Wall came down, "Dr. Strangelove" seemed a perfect celebration of the end of the Cold War. After we watched the Steven Biko story in the movie "Cry Freedom," I knew the students would never forget the definition of apartheid. Jack Nicholson and Nurse Ratchet intrigued my psychology class when we watched, "One Flew Over the Cuckoo's Nest" in preparation for the unit on abnormal psychology. I liked to use relevant films occasionally for their motivational value, but I always chose films that were a significant part of film history as well.

Hollywood was not necessary to motivate students to study the checks and balances in our Constitution such as the advise and consent role of the Senate for the President's Supreme Court nominations. Clarence Thomas and Anita Hill brought plenty of the drama to that stage without the benefit of a screenplay. Social studies boring? I don't think so!

While I was thoroughly enjoying the classroom, things were not going so well for our new superintendent, Dr. Bangston.

Two very talented and dedicated secretaries resigned abruptly.

Both worked directly for him in his administrative offices, one in the Buhl building and the other as the Superintendent's secretary in the Mt. Iron building. I had worked closely with both of them and asked them what was going on. They could not express exactly what the problem was but they both, "refused to work another day with Bangston." I asked them if there was some form of harassment or abuse going on and offered help and support if it was. They both assured me that wasn't the case, but neither one could find words to describe the behavior that caused their discomfort with Bangston. "Ishy" and "creepy" explain very little.

There was quiet talk among the other teachers that Bangston had trouble in his previous districts. A couple of teachers said they were looking into it. Somehow, he had provoked lots of hostility in a short time. I should note that I had several contacts with him which had not raised any issues as far as I was concerned. I had, in my own mind, closed that chapter and had no desire to revisit the insult, which wasn't his doing.

Some of the teachers inquiring into Bangston's past must have tracked down his troubles because on April 7, 1991, the headline in the *Mesabi Daily News* in Virginia read, "MI-B Official Falsified Past Reference."

The article reported that Bangston's contract had been bought out by his previous school district. He was, essentially, paid to resign. He had falsified letters of recommendation from previous school board members. The newspaper reported, "The six letters contain similar wording, information and spelling errors. 'Best superintendent I ever worked with...a financial genius...work-a-holic...works himself to death,'" were identical statements that appeared in several different letters. The newspaper contacted school board members from his previous districts and they stated they hadn't written or signed the letters with their names on them.

The newspaper article reported that Bangston had told the Mt.Iron-Buhl board members about the letter issue. "Both board members that hired me knew about the incident. I told them everything that occurred. They hired me knowing everything that had occurred."

Both board members?

A former board member was quoted, "The board went by the recommendation of Swanson and Heltunen."

How can two members of a school board legally hire anyone? Something was wrong with the process. In addition to the procedural issues, it was obvious they had hired a less qualified man for the job. The article raised questions about the rest of Bangston's credentials. "He has a doctorate from East Texas State University in Commerce, Texas, as well as a degree from Columbia Pacific University in California, a non-traditional, non-resident university whose credits are not recognized by all states." He had mail-order degrees!

I was astounded and mad as hell. I had served as interim that summer and worked my tail off to get the job done. Several board members had even encouraged me to apply for the full-time position. Eighteen months later I learned that the board (or two men on the board) had hired a less qualified man at the last minute.

What the hell's going on here? I asked myself.

Was it the Buhl connection, the informal blacklist from the lawsuit, or discrimination? I didn't think it could be the Buhl versus Mt. Iron building controversy, because the board vote to hire Bangston in 1989 had been unanimous and there were Buhl residents on the board.

I called the EEOC to see what recourse I had. They informed me that all timelines had run out and they could not process a complaint, even though I had just learned the facts. I was frustrated, yet relieved at the same time. For one thing, I was emotionally exhausted from the lawsuit that had concluded a few months previously. I had no desire for another round in the legal ring. Also, with Bangston so discredited, it was likely the superintendency would open soon. I hoped to get another shot at it.

Was I naïve or what?

At the end of that 1991 school year, I got a pleasant surprise that balanced the frustration. The dedication for the MIB high school yearbook read, "The 1991 Laurentian staff would like to dedicate this yearbook to Mrs. Pearson. For six years, she has been with our graduating class as a principal, a teacher, and most of all as a friend.

She has always been a very fair and honest person to each and every
one of us. She has not only taught us history, but also to realize what's
going on in the real world. She has always stressed the importance of
thinking for ourselves and making our own decisions. Mrs. Pearson
has also been one to listen and keep confidential any problems we
may have had and help out in any way possible. We will never forget
all of the good times we've had with her and all that she's done for
us. Thank you, Mrs. Pearson, for everything and we will never forget
you." It lifted my spirits considerably. Students reminded me again
about what really matters.

Bangston hung in there throughout the summer and fall of 1991,
but in January 1992, he disappeared, left with no notice. The board
hired a retired superintendent as interim and posted the permanent
job. In February 1992, I applied again for the position. So did former
elementary principal John Gornick, who had also been bumped back
into the classroom. Both of us had been laid off from our principal
positions beginning with the 1988–1989 school year. Gornick had
no experience as a superintendent and had only recently received
his administrative licensure. He had been working under a license
variance from the state department since 1979. By the March posting
deadline, the board had 24 applicants.

March 1992 was a stressful month on the job front. The March 19,
1992, *Cook News Herald* reported in the St. Louis County School Board
minutes that three principals would be retiring from the district. Two
principals would leave after the 1991–1992 school year and the third
would be leaving after the 1992–1993 school year. I only had one
school year left in the window of injunctive relief from the lawsuit.
One of those two retirements in June 1992 would have to produce a
principal position or I was out of luck.

I now had two possible administrative positions for the 1992–1993
school year, the Mt. Iron-Buhl superintendency or a principalship
in St. Louis County. I was skeptical about both. Mt. Iron-Buhl had
treated me shabbily in 1989 when they hired Bangston behind my
back. St. Louis County might find ways to avoid implementing the
injunctive relief or do so in a way I couldn't accept. For example, if

they transferred within to create the principal opening in AlBrook, I'd have to drive over 80 miles one way to get to work.

I hated to get involved with attorneys and legal bills again, but there was no choice. There was no one else looking out for my interests and my rights. There never is.

One of the opposing attorneys in the lawsuit had impressed me. Rick Prebich had defended Gary Albertson. I wasn't impressed with his client's honesty, but Prebich had been the most aggressive, persistent, and prepared of the attorneys I met. I called him and asked him to represent my interests for the injunctive relief of a principal's position in the St. Louis County School District. He agreed and contacted the St. Louis County School attorney, Scott Neff. He inquired about a position for me for the 1992–1993 school year. The district's responses proved I was right in getting legal help.

The county school district was closing remaining elementary schools and consolidating to six K–12 attendance sights. They would then have seven principals for six positions. They were considering the creation of an additional administrative position in the central office. Superintendent Mobilia could transfer existing principals to accommodate this new position. If one of those remaining principals left, Mobilia indicated they would simply cut the additional position. Creating and then eliminating administrative positions sounded suspicious to me, like a strategy to circumvent the court order.

Meanwhile, by April the Mt. Iron-Buhl School Board had selected eight of the 24 applicants for superintendent to interview. Both Gornick and I were included. In May, the board voted to hire Dan Brooks, an outsider to the district, as superintendent. I had no problem with that because the board had expressed a desire for an experienced superintendent and the papers reported Brooks had nine years of experience.

However, on June 3, 1992, the *Mesabi Daily News* reported that Brooks had turned down the position. The article continued, "According to Robert Swanson, board vice chairman, the board Tuesday discussed John Gornick, Mountain Iron-Buhl teacher and former elementary principal, as a possible candidate." No mention of me. This was the same Swanson that had recommended Bangston in 1989. All the gut-wrenching acid from the lawsuit gurgled up. Another dusk to dawn marathon of pacing.

Once again, students brightened the gathering gloom. As a classroom teacher, I had no direct responsibility for the Mt. Iron-Buhl graduation ceremony and did not plan to attend the June graduation. Max had a music performance at the Cook school that evening and I planned to be there. However, my seniors kept bugging me to attend their ceremony. I didn't see how it would make a difference whether I was in the huge crowd or not, but they were persistent.

I finally caved in and attended the Mt. Iron-Buhl graduation ceremony. Rick videotaped Max's performance so I could watch it later. Just before the presentation of diplomas, the class president walked to the podium.

"On a note of dedication, I would like to send out a special thanks to a teacher. I believe I can say I speak for the whole class when I say thank you to Mrs. Pearson for the different ways she some how found to teach us. To broaden our minds to the reality of the world. She has made us aware of what really goes on out there and prepared us with the knowledge to understand it and power to change what needs to be changed. She has been there to help us and listened when no one else cared to or thought our ideas important enough. She never criticized us on our answers or ideas and really cares what we think. Some of the things you've taught us will remain with us forever - so thank you, Mrs. Pearson."

Sneaky kids, so that's why they were all bugging me, I smiled to myself. I had taught those students for three years and their respect meant a lot to me.

At a special board meeting (that I knew nothing about) on June 15, 1992, the Mt. Iron-Buhl School Board voted six to one to hire John Gornick as the superintendent. The June 16, 1992, *Mesabi Daily News* reported on the meeting. The dissenting board member said, "Board members had agreed experience as a superintendent was a qualification for hiring...Whoever will be picked will be leading a high school and we know there's a lot of things that have to be done."

Gornick had no experience as either a superintendent or high school principal.

I had no problems with Gornick personally; we worked well together as principals for three years following the consolidation. But I knew he was not as qualified as I was to be superintendent.

The newspaper account of that board meeting shocked me! After the motion was made and before the vote was taken, the board took a recess. Board members talked individually with Gornick. One member said that after the motion, he had a talk with Gornick and that Gornick "convinced me he can run the district." Another said after the one-to-one talk with Gornick, "I could ask questions I wouldn't ask in an open forum, I don't have any problems with him." A third board member said he talked with Gornick. "I can't say he relieved all my concerns. I think I am flexible enough to work with anybody, even him."

These were hardly ringing endorsements for Gornick and the process described in the article was hardly open or fair. Something was rotten in the state of Mt. Iron-Buhl.

On the substantive issue of qualifications, the board was wrong. Again I had lost a job to a less qualified man. Everyone who knew the two of us knew that as well. On the procedural issues they were possibly illegal. They had not notified me or the other finalists of the special meeting or invited us to attend. All candidates should be treated equally. I did not get one-to-one interviews with board members. Those private discussions were a violation of the spirit if not the letter of Minnesota's open-meeting law.

I cried by night and paced by day. The loneliness and isolation that went along with challenging haunted me. How could this be happening again? I couldn't believe that one more time, I had no choice.

Why did I feel I had no choice? Was it ego, pride, reputation, or outrage at the humiliation? The local papers had carried my name in the list of finalists for months. The frustration was almost unbearable and doing something relieved the pressure. Doing nothing was not an option.

I called the EEOC office, explained the issues, and asked them to send the complaint forms. I was informed again that timelines dictated that the complaint had to be limited to the Gornick hiring even though I believed it was continuous discrimination since the 1989 Bangston hiring. I called Prebich and asked him to put the Mt. Iron-Buhl district on notice. I wanted to make certain that all documents and records were preserved.

On June 18, 1992, Prebich wrote to Scott Neff, the school district attorney. "If, while you are reading this letter, you hear a 'thunk', that is simply the sound of my jaw hitting my desk as I am reading the *Mesabi Daily News* front page article of June 16, 1992. To my utter amazement, the Mt. Iron School Board seems to have turned back the calendar to years when due process and equal protection were of little importance." He concluded by requesting that no notes, records, tapes, or other documents relative to the hiring process be destroyed.

Rick and I talked at length about what we were willing to go through and to risk again.

"What do you want to do?" Rick asked. "You can't let the bastards get away with this!"

"That's a definite. But damn, I don't want to put everything at risk again, racking up those kinds of legal bills. I was thinking about the last time. Remember when we had the option of filing the EEOC complaint and just letting them investigate?"

"That's right. We filed suit right away because the EEOC investigation would take too long. I forgot that part it was so long ago."

"Well, that seems like a better option this time. I'll let Prebich know that we're going to file a complaint and let the investigation run its course."

Even when you know that you are right, it's risky to assert it. I knew this, yet I was so mad I could hardly wait to file the papers. I received the intake questionnaire from the EEOC in October and sent it almost immediately. On December 31, 1992, I received notification that the complaint was accepted for investigation and assigned to the EEOC office in Milwaukee. My complaint had survived the first hurdle.

At the same time I lost the Mt. Iron-Buhl position, my injunctive relief window for a principal position in St. Louis County was closing fast. At the last minute, one of the remaining St. Louis County principals interviewed in southern Minnesota. By the end of July 1992, he had accepted a position and resigned from his position as principal of the Orr School in St. Louis County. The July 30, 1992, issue of the *Cook News Herald* reported that after accepting the principal's resignation on July 27, the school board met in closed session with attorney Scott Neff.

On July 29, 1992, I received a letter from Superintendent Mobilia indicating that they were obligated to offer me the position. I had five days to accept or reject their offer.

I accepted the Orr principal's position. It wasn't Cook, but it was the next closest high school to my home. Even then, I had to remind them that the Judge's order included Putnam's 1986 date of seniority. The school board that reluctantly hired me on August 24 included Chester Larson from Cotton, Bill Conger from Cook, Zelda Bruns from Orr, Larry Anderson, who had succeeded me as the Board member from Albrook, Calvin Bock from Toivola-Meadowlands, and Bill Kauppinen from Cherry.

I fell and broke my ankle just a few days before accepting the Orr position. Because I was hobbling along with a cast and crutches, Max drove me to Mt. Iron to pack up my desk and haul the boxes out of my classroom. As we were leaving the building, Gornick came down the hall. I introduced him to Max and then we leaded for the door. What Gornick said next just blew me away.

"Judy, do you have a couple of minutes? I really need help figuring out the FTE's and seniority for the high school recalls."

"Max has to get back to work, but I'll be in the Orr office next week, give me a call," I responded.

I couldn't believe he'd asked for my help, after beating me out a job I was more qualified for.

From our joint administrative meetings, I knew Gornick had never grasped the complexities of about high school licensure, seniority, and FTE (full time equivalent) calculations. For example, if the full-time workload for high school teachers is five classes a day, one class is .2 FTE of a teacher's assignment. But if a class meets for only one semester, then it's .1 FTE. Quarter classes calculated at .05 FTE. If a particular course met for a two-hour block of time, it was worth .4 FTE, unless it was a semester course. Then it was worth .2 FTE. It got even more complicated when classes met on alternating days for a quarter or a semester.

These calculations had to be accurate because they determined who worked, how much, and who got laid off by how much. These numbers also determined teachers' paychecks. There was no tolerance for mistakes.

I had done all of the licensed staff assignments, merging of the seniority lists, and FTE calculations for the first year of consolidation. Following that year, I did most of the secondary scheduling and assigning, including identification for layoffs and recall of licensed teachers. Through three years of administrative team meetings, reviewing the staffing levels for all schools, Gornick had never followed the details.

He called the next week and I helped. After all, it was the board that made the decision. To my knowledge, Gornick had never said or done anything against me in our competition for the job.

My first day as Orr Principal was six years plus a few days since I had met with the Cook chamber. After what had just happened in Mt. Iron-Buhl, I was convinced this was the only administrative opportunity I would get in the area. Who wants to hire a "litigious" woman?

The Orr School was about 35 minutes from my home on Lake Vermilion. I still had a commute, but it was half the distance I was driving to Mt. Iron-Buhl. I had missed most of Erik's school activities. He graduated from high school in 1990 and was already beginning his third year at college. Now I would miss the rest of Max's high school activites. The big exception with Max would come when the boys' basketball season started and Cook came up to play at Orr. Max had played basketball since 5th grade and was now a junior on the Cook varsity team.

"Hey, Mrs. P., who you routing for tonight, Max or us?" was the teasing query from the Orr players every time Cook was on our home schedule. I'd stay neutral as I supervised from the sidelines, silently rooting for Max to play well, but Orr to win! Ten years later, I would recall that "Max" dilemma as I support Max and the rest of our troops but remain opposed to our unilateral invasion of Iraq. *Logical to me, so why do so many people see those positions as contradictory?*

At least in Orr I was in the same school district and closer to home than ever before.

The August 27, 1992, *Cook News Herald* reported that I was hired as per court order. The editorial reminded readers, "A jury of seven women and one man found for Pearson. She is now the principal at Orr, so this case is history. And now on to more interesting things…"

The August 24, 1992, issue of the *Mesabi Daily News* carried a more detailed report of the lawsuit and my hiring. It included the fact that the district's insurance company, National Union Fire Insurance of Pittsburgh, had covered the district's fees and costs from the lawsuit.

Hooorrrray! After Albertson's obvious inferences in the Cook paper and the guilt trip laid on Max by the Cook board member, the fact that THE INSURANCE COMPANY PAID was finally in print—just not in the *Cook Herald.*

Chapter 7

1992–1997
INJUNCTIVE RELIEF

"Woman who won suit to be hired."
Mesabi Daily News, 8/24/92

WHILE I SETTLED INTO the Orr School for the 1992–1993 school year, the EEOC investigation on the Mt. Iron-Buhl superintendency had stalled out. I heard nothing from the EEOC until December 1994 when I received a letter indicating they were backlogged and the investigation had been reassigned to a new investigator. It was two years since I signed the formal complaint.

Bess Worden, the new investigator, flew to Minnesota from Milwaukee in early 1995 to conduct the investigation. I met with her one evening in her motel room, describing what had happened. She spent the next two days meeting with the Mt. Iron-Buhl board members. She called after she returned to Milwaukee.

"I have to tell you, Judy, that I'm leaning toward a finding for the district on your complaint," she announced.

"But Gornick was clearly less qualified," I responded. "And how did they explain the private meetings granted Gornick in the middle of a board meeting?" I asked.

"Well," she replied, "they gave a pretty good explanation for selecting Gornick. They said he would have a better chance of passing a voter referendum for additional revenue."

"They're blowing a lot of smoke!" I exclaimed to her. *It's pure bullshit,* I cursed to myself. "He's never had any responsibility for passing a referendum and I have planned and successfully passed two. Besides, under the new 1991 Amendments to the Civil Rights Act, doesn't the burden of proof fall on them? How can they simply assert an explanation like that with nothing to back it up?" I demanded.

She seemed caught by surprise when I referred to the amendments, but indicated that she would discuss the burden of proof issue with her supervisor. I had followed the progress of these amendments carefully, from their proposal in February 1990 through President Bush's veto in October 1990 to their eventual passage by Congressional override in November 1991.

The amendments were passed to overturn several Supreme Court decisions that had weakened civil rights. The new law strengthened civil rights in several areas, including shifting the burden of proof back onto the employers. The Mt. Iron-Buhl board should not get away with pulling some phony, hypothetical justification out of thin air. They should have to show evidence that their explanations for their decision are valid. They had none.

I faxed Ms. Worden the newspaper report and the official minutes of the June 15, 1992, meeting when Gornick was hired. The board minutes had no mention of the recess taken in the middle of the vote that allowed for discussions between Gornick and individual board members. Thank goodness the *Mesabi Daily News* was there to report the entire story. Nobody has to convince me of the importance of journalism and its watchdog role of holding elected officials accountable in a democracy.

As further evidence of the prevailing sexist attitudes on the Mt. Iron-Buhl board, I sent copies of two additional articles from the *Mesabi Daily News.* The April 27, 1993, issue reported on the Mt. Iron-Buhl board discussions about hiring a high school principal following Lucarelli's retirement. During the regular meeting, Swanson recommended a full-time principal at each building.

"Get yourself a real good man," Swanson was quoted in referring to the high school position. *Some people never learn,* I thought to myself.

*They already had an investigation pending on my discrimination complaint
on the superintendency.*

This was the same Swanson that led the hiring of Bangston for
superintendent behind my back in 1989. The April 30, 1993, *Mesabi
Daily News* reported on a special Mt. Iron-Buhl board meeting. A
letter from a previous employee (not me) was passed around. The
writer objected to Swanson's "good man" comment and demanded
a public apology.

"Swanson's remarks have set the district back 20 years," the letter
asserted.

This time the MIB board did not follow Swanson's advice. They
hired Carol Anne, the first woman to serve as High School Principal
in the Mt. Iron community. She was hired for the 1993–1994 school
year, one year after I filed the EEOC complaint on Gornick's hire for
superintendent. Maybe my complaint helped make a difference.

The EEOC decision on that complaint came six months after
Worden completed her investigation and more than three years after
Mt. Iron-Buhl hired Gornick. On August 11, 1995, the certified letter
from the EEOC Director read, "During the investigation, relevant,
available witnesses were interviewed and relevant documents were
reviewed. I have considered all the evidence disclosed during the
investigation and find that there is reasonable cause to believe that
there is a violation of Title VII of the Civil Rights Act of 1964, as
amended." "*There is reasonable cause to believe*"… precious words!

The letter continued with an explanation of the EEOC process for
conciliation. On August 24, 1995, I received a copy of their proposed
conciliation agreement. It included reimbursement for back pay and
benefit differences from July 1992 through June 1996. The timelines
did not allow for reimbursements back to 1989 when "Dr. Dr."
Bangston was hired, which was frustrating because both the 1989 and
1992 board decisions were about the same superintendent position.
I knew they were connected and part of a pattern of continuing
discrimination. But I agreed to the conciliation rather than file suit.

The agreement included a **Notice to All Employees** that had to
be conspicuously posted around the district. The notice restated

the federal laws against discrimination and continued, "Specifically, the Board of Education, Independent School District #712 will not discriminate against women in the consideration and hiring of persons for managerial and administrative positions. Federal law also prohibits retaliation against any employee who files a charge of discrimination, or who cooperates with the government's investigation of a charge."

This posting was a priority for me. I wouldn't have accepted the conciliation agreement without it. I did not want my acceptance of the conciliation proposal to allow the issue to be quietly swept under the rug. I wanted to establish the precedent that administrative positions were now open to women.

With the posting requirement included, I signed the conciliation agreement.

But the ISD #712 School Board had to accept the agreement as well and they weren't going to concede without a fight.

Nothing came easy. Three months later, on November 14, 1995, I received a copy of a letter sent to the Mt. Iron-Buhl district from the EEOC. "The EEOC will not make further efforts to conciliate this charge. At this time, we are forwarding the case to the U. S. Department of Justice for possible litigation."

The board soon changed its tune.

In January 1996, the Mt. Iron-Buhl School Board agreed to the conciliation agreement, including the posting requirement. It had taken three and a half years. I hoped this agreement and the posting requirement would finally make a difference, because my legal costs on this challenge and securing my injunctive relief with the Orr position made the financial settlement a hollow victory.

During the years it took to settle the Mt. Iron-Buhl complaint, I had settled in as K–12 principal in Orr. It was encouraging to find that with me on board as Orr Principal in 1992, three of the seven K–12 principals were women. Corrine Spector had been hired in December 1986 to fill-in at the Albrook School and Bonita Gurno had been hired in 1988 as principal at the Cotton School.

The job was more challenging and exciting than I expected. How could a small school take much time or effort? I had previously served as a junior high principal, senior high principal, and superintendent of schools. I thought I had sufficient experience to hit the ground running, without a steep learning curve. After all, Orr was a smaller program than those I had previously supervised. The Buhl district had an enrollment of close to 600 students before consolidation and the Mt. Iron-Buhl junior high had a starting enrollment of close to 500 students in grades 6–9. The Orr School K–12 enrollment was under 300.

Was I wrong! Enrollment was the only factor that was smaller in Orr.

Supervising a small, rural, and sparsely populated K–12 school was more difficult and challenging than I had imagined. K—12 building administration included a much larger and more varied number of responsibilities than any elementary or secondary school. A high school principal does not deal with pre-school screening and an elementary principal does not count credits toward graduation.

Ironically, Orr's small size was one of the largest challenges. For example, a grade enrollment of 34 was difficult to manage. It was too big for a single section, whether it was a self-contained 2nd grade or an 8th grade industrial arts class. But two sections of 17 doubled the staffing costs and forced cuts elsewhere. A high school physics class of eight was even more expensive per student.

Other budget issues were equally tough with revenue allocations based on the number of students. The Orr School was one of the three smallest K–12 schools in district. An $8,000 copy machine represented almost 50 percent of Orr's annual capital (large, more permanent items like furniture, computers, appliances, over $50 each in value) allocation. The same machine was only 20 percent of the capital allocation for the largest school in the district. Small schools have huge economy-of-scale problems.

The sparse population presented another challenge. Orr bus routes were some of the longest in the state. The Orr attendance area covered 800 square miles. In fact, comparison with Department of Natural Resources figures revealed that the Orr attendance area had more black bear per square mile than students. Many students rode the bus 90 minutes one way to get to and from school. Most roads were gravel and frequently in terrible condition, particularly in the long, cold winters. The buses carried early childhood through 12th grade students.

Discipline on the buses was the immediate responsibility of the drivers, but those issues regularly came into my office. Occasionally, resolving morning bus run complaints would consume the entire day.

The K–12 enrollment brought unique challenges. The issues that arose in 3rd grade were different than those that came up in the junior high or high school. This was true whether the issue was student behavior, achievement, scheduling, teacher supervision or curriculum. I realized quite soon that elementary and secondary teachers approach their students and teaching from very different mindsets.

Basically, elementary teachers teach the child and secondary teachers teach the subject. There's an ownership of the whole child with elementary teachers I would loved to have cloned in secondary teachers. However, secondary teachers taught five different classes or preparations to over 130 students a day compared to the 20-25 students assigned to elementary classrooms.

The disparity in high school grading and student evaluation philosophies drove me crazy. This was true in most secondary schools, but it seemed more pronounced in Orr. An "A" from one teacher would likely be a "C" from another. This even happened within the same department, between two English teachers. Some teachers gave almost no failing grades and others gave 30-40 percent failing grades.

My biggest frustration with teachers' grades hit every May. Seniors suffer from a recurring and predictable ailment, called senioritis, every year. In preparation for that epidemic, teachers routinely upped the ante on senior assignments as the year went along, just to maintain leverage. The counselor and I checked transcripts at the beginning of the year to make certain all seniors were enrolled in enough credits to graduate. We monitored their progress every quarter and intervened when they strayed off course. I notified parents, officially, at the first sign of trouble. I reminded senior teachers throughout the year to keep me posted and prevent any last minute surprises.

Yet invariably, at the last minute of the last quarter, just hours away from graduation, a teacher would decide to fail a senior. I suspected it was often an angry reaction to the blatant indifference that can be a manifestation of chronic senioritis. But it was too late to warn the parents, too late to take back all the money spent on class rings, graduation announcements, invitations, and party arrangements. Those were some of the toughest phone calls I ever made. I finally dictated that if teachers got to this point, they had to call and explain to the parents how this happened at the last minute, with no warning. Problem solved.

While some teachers would cooperatively adjust their assignments for special education students, others felt it compromised their standards to make any modification or accommodation. An accommodation maintains the same standard, but is an appropriate change in the setting of a test or assignment, like a Braille version of the regular test for a blind student or an extension of time for a student with a reading disability. A modification is an adjustment to an assignment or test that changes the standard or requirement, like 60% passing rather than 70%.

Laws require accommodations and/or modifications for students with learning disabilities, depending on the student's IEP (Individual Education Plan). In spite of the laws, I had to spend significant time and energy as administrative lead finessing the hard-liners to get the necessary changes for special education students. Essentially, a student with an assessed and documented learning disability should not receive failing grades for academic work related to their disability.

One EBD (emotional behavior disorder) student suffered from a severe anxiety/panic disorder. Among other problems, she could not complete a test in a classroom setting. When I insisted that the classroom teacher allow the student to take her exams one-on-one with the special education teacher, I was guilty of "compromising her standards" and "coddling the student."

Supervising early childhood through adult community education in Orr may have involved small enrollments, but it included a huge variety of supervisory tasks. The number of tasks remained the same regardless of the number of students. These tasks ranged from transportation to food service, staff development to supervision of extracurricular activities, kindergarten round up to high school graduation. Tasks involved day-to-day scheduling of facilities, students and staff, including the immediate supervision of all employee contracts.

The K–12 building principals were like mini-superintendents. We closed schools in bad weather and emergencies. We approved leaves of absence and signed payroll vouchers for all employees. We did the written observations and evaluations of all employees. We made the recommendations on all hiring and firing, from teachers to bus drivers, food service to coaches. We budgeted for all curricular and extra-curricular programs. We shopped for venders and requisitioned all supplies and equipment, from texts to desks, from computers to basketballs.

The sheer number of tasks dictated that we were jacks of all trade, masters of none. Mastering one task or initiating a new program often meant that some other responsibility got short shift. I craved more time to be proactive instead of reactive. I left work every night when I ran out of hours, not because the job was done. It never was. I'd make a list of the priorities for the next day before I left work. Many times, the next day started off with a bang from the buses and kept banging away all day. I'd never get the list out of my briefcase on those days.

I used to jokingly describe my posture as I got to work. As soon as I stepped out of the car, I'd bend my knees to stay flexible, ready to respond at anytime. The issue-of-the-day could come from any side, sometimes several sides at once.

For the most part, I think I thrived on this level of hustle. There was never a dull moment. I was a juggler of sorts and if I could keep three to four balls in the air without dropping one, it was a good day. However, never feeling the satisfaction of a job well done or mission accomplished weighed heavily over time. K–12 principals burned out more often than principals with more narrow, focused assignments.

Attendance, discipline, and conflict consumed the most time every day and there was never enough. The conflicts came from the playground, the hallways, the cafeteria, the buses, and the extra-curricular programs, etc. The majority of discipline issues came from the classrooms. I spent a lot of time back in mediator mode. I reminded teachers to think about how they would want their own kids treated, to think about how they'd like to be treated as parents, should–heaven forbid–their own kids ever misbehave.

I was most frustrated when teachers over-reacted to student behavior and then expected me to back them up. I did so publicly but those situations always took a lot of time to correct and resolve behind the scenes.

For example, Mike is an eighth grade student who regularly fails to complete his homework assignments. In exasperation and in front of the whole class, the science teacher tells him he's just lazy, to get out and not come back until he has written 500 times, "I will always turn in my assignments on time." Mike refuses, flinging the "F" word as he slams the classroom door on his way out. Now the teacher informs me, in no uncertain terms, that she won't take him back in her class.

Since I do not have an alternative eighth grade science class for Mike, my job is to negotiate with both of them to get Mike back into class with some chance of future success. This has to be accomplished without the teacher losing face or feeling like there is no administrative support.

Mike gets two days of suspension for his language (which he knows was out of line), writes his sentences, and is coached to apologize for his behavior. The teacher is coached to accept the apology, reduce the number of sentences to 100 and agree to work with the school counselor to explore other ways to get him to do his homework.

In another instance, a teacher demands that a senior remove his hat in the cafeteria at noon. When the student refuses, the teacher grabs the hat. Now it's a physical confrontation and they have to be broken apart by others. Threats are exchanged. This situation could have been de-escalated by the teacher. Instead, there is a career and a diploma on the line. It was a tricky finesse to keep charges from being filed against the teacher and to keep the student in school.

The most frustrating discipline issue was pressure from the school board for consistency in all the schools. This refrain echoed nationwide. Demands for consistency led to zero tolerance. Zero tolerance led to ludicrous instances of disciplinary abuse. The national media had a feeding frenzy with those stories. In one case, a kindergarten boy was expelled because he kissed a classmate. "Sexual harassment" said the principal, quoting the definition of sexual harassment and zero tolerance from their discipline policy.

In another instance, the police picked up a 4th grade girl from school, loaded her in a paddy wagon, took her to jail and put her in a cell. She had a scissors in her backpack that her teacher had told her to bring to school for an art project. The principal called the police because scissors were mentioned specifically in the zero tolerance policy on weapons. *Isn't this mindless enforcement of the letter, rather than the intent of the law? Making a mountain out of a molehill,* as my mother would say.

I experienced the dilemma of those pressures with a seventeen-year-old student. He lived 30 miles from school and played football. He was a bright student and had overcome many odds to be where he was in school. He lived for football and playing varsity ball was all that kept him in school. He called one Friday morning about 11 a.m. to tell me his mother was sick and he hadn't been able to get to school yet. He was worried about the policy that said he couldn't play in a game if he missed school on game day.

I asked him if his mother had been drinking again. After a moment of silence, "Yeah," he admitted in a subdued tone. I knew what that meant. He had gotten his younger brothers and sisters up, fed them breakfast and gotten them off to school. We had been there before with the family. I asked him why he was still home. He said he had been taking care of his mom and then calling around for a ride. He just found an uncle to bring him in. He called to check in and ask if his uncle could write an excuse for him so he could play that night, because his mom was still sick. That meant passed out.

Technically, following the letter of the policy, I should have said no. But I had seen too many casualties of consistent consequences. Which was most important, keeping the kid in school or blindly following the policy? I told him to bring in his uncle's note. I excused his absence and certified him to play.

Another football player and honor student accidentally dropped a Swiss Army knife from his jacket pocket in the locker-room. He said he forgot to take it out and leave it at home after hunting over the weekend. The zero-tolerance policy on weapons required a full year of expulsion from school for bringing a knife to school and left little room for discretion. However, his hunting story checked out so I confiscated the knife and kept him in school. Yet, when an unmanageable student repeatedly swung a baseball bat at a classmate on the field at noon, I expelled him under the weapons policy. The baseball bat wasn't listed in the policy, but his use of it made it a weapon.

Consistency and zero tolerance are no substitutes for judgment in disciplining students. Zero tolerance, equal and absolute consequences are not necessarily fair and equitable consequences. A wise professor once told me that, "A foolish consistency is the hobgoblin of little minds," quoting Emerson. It was my silent shield against the prevailing popular pressure.

One of the toughest jobs in Orr was recruiting and hiring teachers. Several factors combined to make it difficult. Orr's relative isolation and small size topped the list. I had to find teachers who desired the rural, rugged lifestyle. Three short seasons are filled with great outdoor activities like hunting, fishing, swimming, camping, canoeing, and hiking. But winters are long and harsh. Not everyone graduating with a teaching degree was interested in that outdoor lifestyle so far north from the rest of the world.

The small enrollments often meant that the secondary teaching openings came in fractions of full-time positions. I might have a part-time opening in science and a part-time opening in French. It was not easy to fill either position separately or to find one candidate with both licenses. Many teachers had to combine positions between two schools or teach outside their licensure area in order to hold full-time employment. One time I traveled 250 miles south to interview a teacher for foreign language.

It was desirable to have teachers live in the community, so I spent as much time trying to find rental housing for new teachers as I did interviewing and recommending candidates to the school board. I even had new teachers stay in our home for weeks at a time while we were looking or waiting for housing to open up. With the responsibility for interviewing and recommending new staff, there was no such thing as summer vacation. July and August were tense months as we struggled to fill the last positions in time to open school.

It was almost as difficult to keep teachers in Orr as it was to recruit them in the first place. The St. Louis County teachers' contract provided for district-wide seniority, not building seniority. In addition, the district was getting bigger. In 1993, two neighboring school districts—Tower-Soudan and Babbitt-Embarrass—consolidated into the St. Louis County School District. ISD #710 became ISD #2142 when the state issued a new number to the consolidated district.

The independent Tower-Soudan and Babbitt School Districts were experiencing financial difficulty like many of the school districts in Northeast Minnesota. The former Buhl and Mt. Iron Districts had experienced similar financial trouble several years earlier, prompting their 1985 consolidation. A decline in the domestic steel market combined with new automated technologies had reduced the number of jobs in the iron mining industry. The entire region was slowly but steadily losing population. School enrollments declined and revenues shrunk.

By 1994, the St. Louis County School District had seven K–12 attendance sites spread over 5,000 square miles with over 100 miles between the Orr School in the north and Albrook School in the south. The school district was now larger than the state of Connecticut or the states of Rhode Island and Delaware combined.

Between the bump system for determining lay-offs and the transfer policy negotiated in the contract, each spring a school could lose a substantial portion of its staff for the following year. Orr often took the largest turnover hit because it had the least senior staff and was over 40 miles from the larger range communities located in the center of the district. It was frustrating to work so hard at recruiting teachers for Orr in the fall only to lose many of the teaching staff in the bump process every spring.

The teachers I worked with in Orr were some of the most dedicated and professional I had worked with. I resented the newspaper and media reports of negotiating conflicts that only portrayed teachers as looking for more money and less work. The media seldom told the rest of the story. The teachers were in the building, preparing on their own time, weeks before school started in the fall. They put in longer hours than the public ever realized, graded and prepared materials at home, attended school events on their own time to support their students, subsidized their classrooms out of their own pocket, and consistently gave beyond the call of duty. I was proud to work for them and did everything I could to minimize the extraneous administrative interferences with their teaching.

Part of my supervisory responsibility for certified and non-certified staff was providing written performance evaluations. After hundreds of observations and evaluations, I've concluded that teaching is an art, not a science.

The most intriguing questions involve the difference between a good teacher and a bad teacher. You know one when you see one, but I challenge you describe the difference in behavioral terms. I've asked countless students and adults to do just that. Everyone remembers a favorite teacher, but finds it difficult to describe the specific behaviors that made the difference. Everyone says that good teachers care about kids, love their subjects, and earn rather than demand respect. But what do care, love, and earning respect look like in behavioral terms?

When there were performance problems, I would talk to the employee first, identify the area of concern, and request the change needed. If necessary, I would then write an informal note detailing the issue, documenting both the verbal and written notices. Rarely did it have to go beyond this.

On a couple of occasions, I had to proceed with progressive notices of deficiency, leading to termination of contracts for both teachers and non-certified employees. These were the toughest tasks I had to perform. It's tough because the legal protections provided to public employees require a rigorous and often lengthy process. It's tough because there is always union support for the employee. It's tough because once the formal process is engaged, most relationships in a small school are affected. These confrontations were stressful for all involved, myself included. I hated this part of my job. But the bottom line is what's best for kids. If employee performance, whether teacher, driver, coach, or cook, was bad for kids, I could not duck that responsibility.

The Orr School Community was very different from the Range communities I had served in Buhl and Mt. Iron. Due to the taconite mining economy, those communities were predominantly middle class. Orr had almost no middle class. There was a small entreprencurial class of resort owners, small business owners, and loggers. Except for a small number of folks that commuted north to the paper mill in International Falls or south to the mines on the Range, everyone else worked for the few local entrepreneurs for low wages.

The Orr student body reflected this economic structure. Over 50 percent of the students qualified for free or reduced lunch under the federal income guidelines. At least 70 percent of Orr students would have been considered "at-risk" in any given year. At-risk referred to potential failure in school and was a predictive term based on national trends and research. It typically included the categories of poverty, racial minority, learning disability, low standardized test score, family substance abuse, and single-parent family.

One can argue with each of those categories or any such categorization of students. However, the data was useful in understanding the big picture when it came to planning program needs and asset allocation. For example, the data might dictate that resources be shifted from French III to study skills or help with homework if 35 students had received failing grades but only four students were enrolled in the French III.

Orr's K—12 student body averaged between 35–45 percent Native American. Most of these students lived 25 miles west of Orr on the Nett Lake Reservation, one of two reservations that are home to the Bois Forte Tribe of Chippewa Indians. The Nett Lake School District is the only K–6 school district in Minnesota. Students living at Nett Lake attended the Nett Lake Elementary School in grades K–6. Nett Lake then paid tuition to the St. Louis County School District for their grade 7–12 students to attend Orr.

There were Indian students in the Orr School elementary grades as well. These students lived off the reservation and averaged about 20 percent of the elementary enrollment. After the Nett Lake students arrived in seventh grade, the grade 7–12 racial balance was closer to 50/50. I used the term Indian rather than Native American because that was the term the Nett Lake community leaders used.

I suspect this was due to the traditional nature of the Bois Forte communities. They had not participated in the more radical movements of the 60s and 70s. In fact, when the pressures rose for schools and sports teams to change Indian logos, we took a poll of Nett Lake students and parents. In 1993, over 93 percent of the Nett Lake parents and students voted against changing the Orr Braves logo. Written comments included,

"I believe the Indian people of our community are proud we use the name Braves."

"I believe the Indian logo is a symbol of resilience and perseverance."

"I am Indian and proud."

I was impressed with how well the Indian and white kids got along in the Orr School. The Indian students participated on and often captained the athletic teams. They were frequently selected as homecoming royalty. They were members of the high school band, choir, and honor society. Biracial dating was relatively common. I heard from many area administrators that the integration of Indian students at the Orr High School was unique and remarkable.

However, the biracial nature of the student population occasionally created special administrative concerns. Conflicts are a normal part of school life, but when a conflict involved Indian and white kids, it could quickly escalate. It was essential to get the issues resolved as fairly and quickly as possible. Entire communities could be mobilized in a short time if the perception of fairness was not clear and immediate. If I was accused of being too soft on Indians about as many times as I was accused of being too tough on Indians, I took that to mean I was doing a pretty good job.

A disproportionate number of Nett Lake students struggled academically when they came into our seventh grade. Addressing this issue was a top priority. Like most social concerns there would not be a single or simple explanation or solution. But I worked closely with the Local Indian Education Council (LIEC) on this issue and we made some progress. Lack of Indian parent involvement was one of the contributing factors we tackled. We knew that Nett Lake parents rarely came to parent-teacher conferences. They rarely came to the school for any reason other than for athletic events.

Relations between the Orr School and Nett Lake parents had been strained over the years. The reasons were complicated, but due in part to the fact that the only contacts the parents had received from the school were negative, either failure notices or suspensions. I began by encouraging teachers to take advantage of our mid-term notice process to send improvement and positive comments to all students whenever relevant. I quickly received feedback from the LIEC that Nett Lake parents who received such notices were impressed. One parent reported, "I always dreaded mail or calls from the school. This is the first time I ever got something positive from the Orr School."

The LIEC suggested and I agreed to have one night of the next round of parent conferences conducted out at the Nett Lake School, following a potluck dinner for the teachers and parents. The Nett Lake community prepared the meal and I brought the Orr secondary teachers on a school bus. It was 25 miles to the reservation and the bus was cheaper than paying mileage to every teacher.

This project was no meager feat. Many teachers complained and resisted. Neither the Nett Lake Superintendent nor the St. Louis County Superintendent supported the idea. *Why not?* I think most institutional leaders avoid tinkering with tricky race relations until there's trouble. Fortunately for us, neither superintendent vetoed our plans. However, I was clearly out on the limb all by myself.

It was a huge success, measured by the fact that we met with over 90 percent of the Nett Lake parents. We continued that conference format every year during my tenure as principal at the Orr School. It opened channels of communication and made cooperative work with parents possible. Calling parents had always been a primary strategy for me. Now when I called Indian parents, I was talking to folks I had met in their community and shared food with. The discussions were much more productive and successful in preventing the divide and conquer maneuvers that all students use so effectively between school and parents. The conference plan was dropped after I left Orr in 1999, but has been recently reinstated.

By 1993, 95 percent of Indian students graduated from high school. In 1994, 10 Indian students graduated from a class that included 10 Indian students in seventh grade. That's 100 percent. This high graduation rate for Indian students continued every year and was not common in other schools serving Indian students. Most Minnesota schools average a 50 percent graduation rate for Indian students and the national average has consistently been less than 40 percent. This success was due in large part to the improved communications between parents and the school.

In particular, truancy rates dropped dramatically. Indian parents felt more comfortable calling school to explain students' absences. Unexcused absences had been a big part of Indian students' failures. The strong and trusting relationship that developed with Julie Whiteman, the Indian liaison worker from Nett Lake, was also a huge asset. She had helped open the communication channels by coordinating Nett Lake's participation in the parent conferences. She worked several days each week to keep communications flowing.

Counselors and teachers also had a huge impact on the success of all students. We developed a very effective weekly child-study process in Orr. We picked up signs of trouble for students early in each academic year and divided our tasks so that we had time to involve parents and do the interventions that can make a difference before it's too late. These weekly meetings were a top priority for me. I scheduled everything around them and rarely missed one. I didn't have to say it was important. When the principal attends every meeting, the message is clear.

I had always been concerned about adolescent use of drugs and alcohol. It seemed every year I'd have to attend a funeral of a senior high student killed in an alcohol-related accident. But the alcohol abuse in the small rural communities that made up the Orr attendance area was the worst I had seen. I suspended more students from school and athletic programs for alcohol use in one year in Orr than I had all previous years as high school principal. When I discussed this with parents and students, the number one explanation was, "There's nothing else to do but party. If you don't drink, you spend the night alone."

Working with the LIEC from Nett Lake and parents from Orr, we decided to open the school on Saturday nights for teen recreation, so there would be something to do other than "party." In the small, remote town of Orr, there were no movie theatres, bowling alleys, roller rinks, or even pizza parlors. There were no places for kids to hang out, to gather and socialize on the weekends.

We called our project Saturday Nite Rec. I spent lots of time that first year making sure we had enough parent volunteers to supervise the programs and the clean-up. The LIEC provided transportation to and from the reservation. We managed to open seven Saturdays the first year. The gyms were open for basketball, the ITV (interactive television) room was open for movies, and the kitchen was open for pizzas and pop. And the students came in increasing numbers. Basketball was king in Orr and they loved to shoot hoops.

The program was tough sledding. District administration was not excited about the project. The district maintenance supervisor and the building custodians hated the project. The teachers were not very supportive either. In effect, they all saw the school as their property. However, the school belonged to the community and taxpayers. The community needed the resource to provide a safe and sober alternative for kids. With little administrative or staff support, I was out on that limb again. But we kept at it. It fit the concept that it takes a village to raise a child.

By the second year, I had secured grant money to pay a parent to coordinate the volunteers. We kept the program running for 12–16 Saturdays each year, depending on how the holidays fell. We averaged 45 students, grades 7–12, per night. I found grants each year and kept the program running until I left the Orr School. The program did not solve all the abuse problems, but at least students had a choice.

The Saturday Nite Rec program died after I left the Orr School. Supposedly the funding dried up. However, the total budget for the program in my last year of supervision was only $2,900, which included 15 nights of salary for two adult supervisors, who also coordinated the additional parent volunteers. I suspect if the commitment had been there, the money would not have been hard to find.

Orr had the highest percentage of at-risk students of any school I had served. At-risk students frequently have problems that originate outside of school. These could include poverty, dysfunctional families, alcohol/drug abuse, poverty, mental illness, or pregnancy. When these problems threatened school progress, it was frustrating to try to address the academic concerns with no way to influence the underlying problems.

In 1995, I was appointed to the Board of Directors of the first Family Services Collaborative in Northeast Minnesota. This was an exciting new program. It was funded by state and federal grants and designed to decentralize family services like public health, mental health, social service, and corrections. By using schools as outreach centers for these services, we could bring the services into our communities to help address many of the issues that blocked school progress for our students. Our child study team began working regularly with workers from these agencies. Now we could address many of the problems blocking student progress that originated outside the school environment.

I believe this coordination and integration of services for students was some of the most important work I did. I served on this Board and advocated for this kind of collaboration until I retired in 2001.

In addition, the collaborative mission was to develop community resources and assets. From the beginning, I had been working with the city of Orr and the district's community education program to keep the school open after regular hours for students. Many rural bus students who wanted to attend evening practices or athletic events simply stuck around town after school. However, they had to leave the building until their event started because there was no supervision in the school building. Kids locked out, just milling around with no place to go, worried me—particularly on a sub-zero afternoon in January.

Working with the city of Orr and the district's community education program, we began in 1993 by opening the school library two afternoons a week. Staffing for supervision was paid for with funds from the city and community education.

The addition of computers and Internet access in the school library meant that the school could provide a real service to the entire community. With the help of collaborative funding after 1995, the library was open more evenings for more hours. I had a vision that a community/school library could be a terrific asset for a small town.

Superintendent Mobilia agreed. By 1996, our Open Library program and the community/school library concept had generated so much interest and support that a partnership with city, school district, and state was created to secure funding for a new library addition to the Orr School. The new library addition was open for business in 1997. Our Open Library now had a real home, with a separate public entrance. I was very proud of the results that collaboration had brought to the Orr community. A small town now had a library!

In reality, the new library was "community/school" in concept only. It was still an addition to an existing school building and as such, was owned and operated by the school district. I worked to keep the new facility open for as many hours after school as I could. Every year, I sought funding for adequate supervision from several sources, including city grants, community education, and collaborative funds. During the 1998–1999 school year the library was open four nights a week until 10:00 p.m. and averaged 20 people in attendance. The budget for the year was $10,000.

In May 1999, a senior citizen wrote and requested that I keep the library open during the summer. Her letter illustrated how important the resource was to the community.

"Dear Principal Pearson,

"I would appreciate it very much, as would so many others, if you would approve the continuation of the "open library" for the summer. It has been a much appreciated program, not only for the students, but also for us previously computer illiterate adults, to access the computers. What a modern miracle to be able to "surf" the Internet Highway.

"We are all grateful that you have had the foresight over the years to fight for the Orr School to gain such state of the art computers. Being that Orr is in frontier country, we appreciate that the school library is considered a public library available to everyone."

Managing the facility was not always a breeze and often took as much or more effort than finding the funding. On several occasions I had to mediate and resolve conflicts between the outside, community supervisors and inside, district personnel. It seemed a small price to pay for such a significant community resource.

The open library and public access ended shortly after I left the Orr School. Legitimate factors like lack of funding or inadequate supervision are cited as the reason the program was dropped. The bottom line is that funding and managing the program required significant administrative time and effort, over and above the already heavy load principals have to carry. It was my vision, no one else's. With limited spare time available, principals would logically put any extra time into their own projects or programs, not spend it keeping someone else's programs going.

Challenging as the work in a K–12 school was, I loved the job. I worked hard at it; 50–60 hours a week was the rule, not the exception. I spent more than 60 evenings a year supervising extracurricular activities and attending evening functions. Principals can make the critical difference in school tone and atmosphere. I worked hard to make it a positive place to learn and work.

There were some "tricks of the trade" I had developed that helped create a positive atmosphere. I kept a coffee pot brewing in my office everyday. Our welcoming expression at home had always been, "coffee pots always on." Whenever someone came into my office with a concern, I offered a cup of coffee. It didn't matter if it was accepted or not. The offer was a welcoming gesture. It also had the added benefit of disarming the angriest visitors right off the bat.

The second strategy evolved over time with lots of experience. As I got older and found it more difficult to juggle five or six crises simultaneously, it became a matter of necessity. Whenever someone came in or called the office with concerns, I grabbed a piece of notepaper. Whether it was a student, concerned parent, angry teacher, driver, or secretary, I wrote a note. I kept a stack of notepaper on my desk and I'd start writing almost the moment someone walked through the door. I dated it, documented names, telephone numbers, concerns, and asked questions to fill in any blanks.

When my visitor left, I kept the note on my desk until it was dealt with. When the issue was resolved, I added the details and dropped it in a desk drawer. By the end of the year, it was a drawer stuffed with a chronologically ordered record of visits and issues.

I started taking notes to be more responsive in doing my job. In the first place, I didn't have to worry about forgetting the issue. I had the telephone number right there to respond if necessary. Drawer or desktop easily sorted resolved from unresolved issues. Some issues required more attention, generated more paper, or had long-lasting impact. They would be filed alphabetically in a cabinet for longer storage and retrieval.

I realized over time that there were significant collateral benefits to the note taking. It provided a buffer of activity and time to cope with the blasting anger that was often in my face. Even the angriest would pause to make sure I correctly documented their complaint. Most importantly, everyone felt they and their concerns had been validated. The nonverbal message conveyed was, "the principal listened, cared, and called me back." In July, I could dump the drawer and make room for another exciting year as principal.

In spite of the exciting administrative hustle, I missed teaching almost everyday—especially when I got reminders from former students who were now teaching. In 1994 a former student wrote:

"Dear Mrs. Pearson, I know that you probably don't remember much of me, but I came across your name the other day and thought I would write to thank you for something you did for me about five years ago. I was in your Senior Social Problems class in 1989–1990. Believe it or not, what you did for me as my teacher that year put the little spark of interest in me that it took to put me where I am now in my life. Needless to say, it has taken me many years to decide what to do with my life, but many times along the way I have looked back on that class with fond memories. Thanks to your wonderful attitude toward the social sciences and the exciting way you taught your class, I have chosen the social science field with a teaching degree. I am hoping to be able to teach in high school or college and hopefully have the same impact on at least one of my students that you had on me."

Another former student e-mailed in 1996:

"Hello Mrs. Pearson, How are you doing? You know, I've never really thanked you for the inspiration you gave me. When I left high school, I really had no idea what I wanted to do but eventually I came back to memories of you and what you did in the classroom. I knew that was what I wanted to be. You were one of the few at MIB who ever really pushed me. You make learning fun, made us think, and made us feel like you really cared and we had a friend in the school. I still model your style in dealing with students. You were (still are) a great role model and I really would like to thank you for that. See, sometimes we can't measure the impact we have on kids based on the grades we give them!"

That last comment was a dig, in case you missed it, because my pushing and nagging was rarely successful and his grades reflected his resistance. He had plenty of ability but wasn't ready to turn it on and consequently, did not get top grades from me.

I've advocated many times that you can get rich teaching, but the riches are not measured in dollars! Those notes proved my point.

Former students and staff gave me a poster that summed up many of my thoughts about teaching. It featured a powerful quote from Haim Ginott.

"I've come to a frightening conclusion that I am the most decisive element in the classroom. It's my personal approach that creates the climate. It's my daily mood that makes the weather. As a teacher, I possess a tremendous power to make a child's life miserable or joyous. I can be a tool of torture or an instrument of inspiration. I can humiliate or humor, hurt or heal. In all situations, it is my response that decides where a crisis will be escalated or de-escalated and a child humanized or de-humanized." *If you change the word classroom to school, it applies with equal relevance to principals.*

In 1997, several events determined the direction of my career for the next several years. They were all very positive, except one. On the positive side, I had returned to the professional secondary principals' organizations with my return to a principal position. In 1996, I was again elected to represent the Northeast Division of MASSP (Minnesota Association of Secondary School Principals) on the state board of directors.

I had been the first woman to serve on the state board in 1980 and now in 1996, women were serving as officers and president-elect of the statewide organization. In 1997, the state board members elected me to serve a three-year term as the region 4 (Michigan, Minnesota, North Dakota, South Dakota, Wisconsin, and Wyoming) representative on the NASSP (National Association of Secondary School Principals) Smaller Secondary Schools Committee. This was an honor and a terrific learning experience.

Before I could accept the national position, my superintendent and school board had to approve the three-year commitment because they would share the costs of my participation. The regular committee meetings were held annually in Reston, Virginia, outside of Washington, D.C. We also met every year at the NASSP national convention, from Orlando and San Diego to San Antonio and New Orleans. I served with principals from all over the country.

Committee members had similar concerns in spite of the differences in geography. Principals from around the country argued that it was getting more difficult to do a good job. State and federal mandates, particularly unfunded mandates, continued to add to the list of responsibilities for principals. No tasks or responsibilities were ever eliminated or reduced, just more added. Increased testing requirements, additional reporting responsibilities, ever expanding liability exposure for abuse, harassment, disability issues, graduation standards that changed every other year, and site-based management mandates were just a few of the common concerns.

In smaller schools, often with no assistant principals, it was becoming more difficult to be successful in meeting the increasing demands placed on the job. Many principals were leaving the job and fewer teachers seemed interested in stepping up.

Many principals raised concerns about the growing emphasis on high-stakes testing and its effects on both teachers and students. In some states, test performance was tied directly to professional salaries and tenure. In others it was tied to students' promotion and graduation. Poor and minority students and students with learning disabilities were hit the hardest with these tests and were dropping out in increasing numbers. Concerns about high-stakes testing were echoed nationwide in the early 90s.

That was years before President Bush's No Child Left Behind, which imposed additional levels of federal testing requirements with few resources to try to meet the new demands. The education business was becoming more about test scores and statistics than it was about kids. Real, live kids were being lost between the medians and the means.

By 2000, I was elected Chairman of the national Smaller Secondary Schools Committee. I had introduced our committee and its platform at two previous national conventions. I succeeded in getting cautionary statements about school choice and high-stakes testing into our platform. For the 2000 convention in San Antonio, I had responsibility for all the arrangements for our committee, from the menu for our planning dinner to the content of our presentations and the microphones and AV support required.

E-mail helped, but some of the committee members had no access or familiarity with e-mail. The technology index for principals around the country was a mixed bag. This surprised me because we had been using e-mail in our district for five years and interactive television to expand curriculum for 10 years. And we considered ourselves the boondocks!

In 1997, the NE Division of MASSP elected me as Principal of the Year. The nomination process for the state honor required letters of recommendation from several specific sources. I've included some of the observations from these nomination letters just to offset the pending disaster and the prevailing cynicism and disdain I would once again experience as a person who sues.

The Nett Lake Indian Parent Committee wrote in support of my nomination:

"For the past two years, in order to achieve a better parental participation at the fall parent/teacher conferences, the Orr High School teachers have come out to the Bois Forte Reservation for a meal followed by conferences with the parents in our local elementary school. This was a major undertaking for Mrs. Pearson, which involved selling the idea to the superintendent and the teachers, working cooperatively with our committee to insure community participation, and smoothing over the initial fears by all parties involved. It has been a highly successful way to cement relations with the Indian community which, in the past, have been strained."

An Orr parent wrote:

"One of the greatest problems that is always on the table in our school is the cultural diversity in our community. Judy is sensitive to this diversity and is always working to bring this diversity to the table to address the needs of the community and the school. As a Pastor I am always welcome in her office to address any problem concerning my children or children of our community. She treats everyone with the respect they deserve without partiality."

An Orr teacher wrote:

"She has always taken risks to improve student learning, often putting her own neck on the line to fight for what is best for our school and our students. She has personally taken a good deal of grief from the administration when she does battle with them to justify improvements in our curriculum and programs, building facilities, and technology. However, she nearly always wins those battles and the Orr school is without a doubt, a much better place because Judy Pearson cares enough to take risks in fighting for what she believes is best."

The Director of the Northern St. Louis County Family Services Collaborative wrote:

"Many of the initiatives we continue to support (such as Saturday Night Teen Rec) were implemented by Judy prior to our work, demonstrating her sense of vision and her willingness to take risks. At our most recent onsite state review, the grant manager for the MN Department of Children, Families and Learning had the opportunity to spend some time with Judy. At the end of our two days together, she asked Judy if she would be willing to serve as a mentor for her daughter and provide her with a job shadowing opportunity. Since she reviews over 20 collaborative sites throughout the state of Minnesota, I think this was one of the highest compliments Judy could receive."

Superintendent Dan Mobilia wrote:

"I cannot think of a principal more deserving of this award. In spite of her very involved workload, she also manages to participate in numerous activities outside the school setting. She has served in a variety of capacities in a number of educational organizations and functions in our area including her principals' association— both regionally and statewide. These experiences blended with her leadership abilities and personality, are part of the reason she is one of the first to be called upon to serve on committees or projects. Judy is an articulate person who can communicate as well as motivate. From what I have observed of Judy, she is well liked and respected by the educational community simply because of her ability to work so well with people in diverse settings. People respect her because they know she is not only knowledgeable but honest and sincere as well. Our region could do no better for its nominee."

Unfortunately, in January 1997 Superintendent Dan Mobilia announced his retirement, effective at the end of June. Dan and I had worked together for five years. We had not always agreed, but we had always respected one another. In my opinion, he was a strong superintendent. He cared about the kids, as well as our communities. He kept a tight reign on the budget, which accounted for some of our differences, but provided the district with a financial stability that was the envy of surrounding school districts. I had learned a lot from Dan and felt I could continue most of the policies and practices he had so successfully employed.

On April 4, 1997, I applied for the superintendent position.

Disastrous decision!

I had a good run in my career for which I will always be grateful because everything was about to change.

Chapter 8

1997

BEHIND CLOSED DOORS

"St. Louis County school board holds illegal closed meeting to discuss superintendent applicants." Timberjay, 9/13/97

FIVE MONTHS BEFORE SUPERINTENDENT Mobilia announced his retirement, Assistant Superintendent Rick Neuenfeldt had abruptly walked off the job. Neuenfeldt began his tenure with the district as the Curriculum Coordinator. Although he had no administrative training, he was a good people person and loved working with teachers on curriculum development. His unrequested promotion to Assistant Superintendent was a mixed blessing. It brought a higher salary, but added many administrative tasks that took him away from the staff and curriculum development that he loved. He was particularly frustrated with the district transportation responsibilities.

I did not apply for the Assistant Superintendent's position when Neuenfeldt left. I had several projects started in Orr that I wanted to complete. In some respects I was freer to commit extra time in Orr because our sons, Erik and Max, were no longer living at home. Rick groused a bit now and then, joking it would be easier to compete with another guy than with my job. However, his web work was taking off and he was soon busier than I was.

After 1990, Erik was away at school, Carleton College and then the University of Minnesota. He'd come home during the summer breaks to work on construction jobs to help pay for school. We took out college loans to pay for the rest.

We had some fascinating family table talks those summers. The boys' horizons were expanding and they were finding their own, independent voices. Max was finishing his last couple of years of high school, working summers as a dock boy at a local restaurant on the lake. On many weekends, Max would come home later in the evening, after the restaurant and bar closed, with his pockets filled with more money in tips than Erik had earned after a long, hard day on construction.

Max graduated from high school in 1994 and left weeks later for the Air Force Academy. In fact, it was Max's attendance at the academy that pushed Rick and I up on the Internet. During his first year at the academy, Max had very limited phone privileges. After that, he had the privileges but little time to call. The most efficient way for all of us to stay in touch was e-mail. Naturally, our tech genius Erik was only too glad to push, prod, and nag us along.

So after 1994, Rick and I were residing in an empty nest, albeit one that was fully wired and connected. As Max prepared to leave home, friends and colleagues issued dire warnings about how lonely and empty we'd feel after the last kid left home. Not us! Never happened!

Of course we loved our kids, but our lives were busy and full, independent of our kids. Our typical response to such dire warnings was, "We didn't raise them to keep them!"

Orr was a very busy place. In addition to the myriad of daily tasks and responsibilities, it often produced surprises that could blindside a prophet.

One such surprise I call the condom conundrum.

I got a phone call at home one night about 10:30 p.m. from the afternoon custodian at the Orr School.

"Mrs. P, we've got a big problem up here. The girls just got back from their volleyball game in Cotton," she said breathlessly. "They've all got condoms in their lockers!" she exclaimed. "They're in every locker."

"What in the world are you talking about?"

"When they went to their lockers to get their books and bags, they all found envelopes stuffed into their locker vents. Each envelope has a condom inside and there's a typewritten note with it."

"Better read me the note," I said.

"Dear Fellow Student,

"It has come to my attention that we are losing two to three students per class each year to teen pregnancy. Also keep in mind that STDs such as AIDS and HIV are found also in small communities like ours. This alarming fact doesn't even seem to interest our principal or community. I say this because I have not seen *any* movement to change the teen pregnancy rate around here. As you may or may not know, there have been requests made to Mrs. Pearson about putting a condom machine in the school. Unfortunately, these requests have been denied. I have therefore taken it upon myself to provide you with a safe option, for if and when you decide to have sex. This letter is not meant to pressure you into having sex, but to make sure that you are protected when you decide to make that *big* decision to have sex. This is not a practical joke.

A Concerned Student."

Oh, shit!

"What do I do with these?" she asked me.

"Better collect them from the girls and let them go home. Do it calmly, without making a big deal out of it. Then call in another custodian and take them out of all the lockers. Use bolt cutters when you have to, we'll replace the locks."

Good grief! I thought to myself. I knew we had just dodged a bullet that could have caused a community uproar. "60 Minutes" would have been next!

When I got to the office the next morning, there was a shopping bag full of 90 envelopes and condoms the custodian had tucked under my desk. I surreptitiously snuck them out of school—in a plain, brown, paper wrapper—at the first opportunity.

As luck would have it, I had set the stage for this little drama myself. A month earlier, I had arranged for county health specialists to come to Orr and present an AIDS program in a high school assembly. Of course, safe sex was part of their message. I watched aghast as one of the presenters stretched a condom over a baseball bat to demonstrate its proper use. Not in this lifetime would I ever have approved that bombshell had I known it was coming.

Man oh man, am I going to pay for this! Damned if I do, damned if I don't with this sex-ed stuff.

I paid big time. It took days for the dust to settle from the stampede of angry teachers and parents that stormed my office and reamed me out. Most accepted the message presented at the assembly, but objected to the method. I conceded, repeatedly, that I would never bring another presentation to school that I had not previewed ahead of time.

However, a couple of seniors had heard the assembly message loud and clear. They continued to push me to bring a condom machine into the school. In our rural and conservative community, it had been risky just to bring the program into the school. The first ever condom machine in a public school would have shut us down!

Don't you just hate it when kids learn their lessons so well?

I suspected who the condom culprit was. I knew if I did nothing and said nothing, I'd hear from him. Sure enough, by 10:00 a.m. a note was slipped under my door.

"Dear Mrs. Pearson,

"I am shocked and appalled (sp) by the fact that you encourage teen pregnancy! Your futile attempt to keep kids around here pure, naïve and innocent is not going to work. I don't know how you found out about the letters and furthermore, don't understand why you took them. What are you going to do with 90 condoms? At least I am trying to encourage a safe option for kids when they decide to have sex. You are doing nothing to stop or even prevent it. And, if you think you have kept me from getting condoms to kids, you are in for a rude awakening!

A Deterred, But Still Concerned & *Very* Upset Student!"

Hell, the little stinker won't even give me credit for bringing the program to school in the first place. Part of me wanted to drag him into the office, chew him out, and suspend him. After all, wasn't he being arrogant and disrespectful of my authority? The other part of me knew he had a point and chuckled admiringly at his spunk and initiative, his willingness to take a stand.

Besides, busting him would just keep the condom controversy alive and escalate it another notch. However, I knew that access to protection was almost nonexistent in our small town. The only place in town that sold condoms did so from behind the counter. You had to ask for them. That doesn't help teens in a small town when the clerk is related to half the community. So I discussed the problem with the local store/gas station and convinced them to put condom machines in their washrooms.

"So now what do I do with 90 condoms?" I joked to Rick.

"Well, I can tell you what I did with them once, but you're not going to like it," he teased.

"Let's hear it, just spit it out."

"A couple of us guys drove the old junior high principal crazy with condoms. We'd stretch them over the faucets on those ancient porcelain water fountains, fill them with water, and whip'em at kids down the hall. They made great water balloons! He raved and ranted, but he never caught us!" he said, laughing at the memory.

"Hmmm, I wonder if condoms have always been a bane of principals?"

On the district-wide front, after a five-month search process for an assistant superintendent, the board hired Dr. William Zitterkopf from Kentucky in December 1996. Zitterkopf was physically impressive, big and tall, with a neatly trimmed goatee. The February 13, 1997, *Cook News Herald* added, "He has great credentials. Supt. Dan Mobilia has a good assistant working with him." However, a careful examination of his credentials might have raised some questions. When he applied for the superintendent's position when I did in April, I took a closer look at his credentials.

Zitterkopf had moved around a lot in his career. From 1977 to 1996, he had worked in Wyoming, Colorado, Nebraska, and Kentucky, serving as teacher or administrator in nine different positions. Most positions were held for two years or less. *Haven't I heard this before, wasn't his name Putnam?* I thought to myself.

I was curious when Zitterkopf stated in his newspaper interview that he had earned his Ph.D. from Kensington University in California and was working on another one. No one who earns a bona fide doctorate casually goes back for another one. His Ph.D. was earned in 1994, while he was serving as superintendent in Colorado. The previous year he had been in Kentucky. California is a long commute from Colorado and Kentucky. *Is this another Bangston? More bogus, diploma-mill credentials?* I wondered.

The problem of bogus credentials was not confined to northeast Minnesota. In the May 19, 2004, issue of *Education Week*, an article headlined, "Federal Investigators Target "Diploma Mills." An investigator testifying before the Senate Governmental Affairs Committee said, "K–12 teachers and administrators are among the most common professionals to obtain such degrees." An article in the January 17, 2005, issue of *U.S.News & World Report* reported on a new book, *Degree Mills: The Billion-Dollar Industry That Has Sold Over a Million Fake Diplomas*, written by Allen Ezell, a former chief of the FBI's diploma mill task force.

In September 1996, Bonita Gurno left the K–12 Cook principalship to take an elementary principal position in another district. The board had hired Sidney Simonson as the new principal at the Cook School. Simonson had been serving as principal at an Indian alternative program in Minneapolis, after having taken several years off from education to work in the insurance industry. He had previously served as an assistant superintendent in southern Minnesota.

By mid-April 1997, the school board was considering 22 applicants for the superintendent's position. The list included 21 men and me. Zitterkopf and Techar (Babbitt Principal) were also internal candidates for the position. Simonson had applied as well, but withdrew his application before finalists were selected. On May 8, the *Cook News Herald* reported that the board had narrowed the field to three finalists. They were Assistant Superintendent Bill Zitterkopf, Chisholm Superintendent Bob Belluzzo, and Cook County Superintendent Don Langan.

After four months of working with Zitterkopf, I had serious concerns about his competence. He did not seem to grasp Minnesota's education laws and rules and our labor agreements. He repeatedly said he resented all the complexity and interference in our business. While many of us sympathized with his complaints, we paid attention to the details and followed the laws, rules, and contracts. He either couldn't or wouldn't learn.

Zitterkopf had worked closely with Superintendent Mobilia as the Assistant Superintendent for four months. Mobilia later indicated he had not been impressed with Zitterkopf.

"I questioned some of the decisions he made, whether he'd make a good superintendent or not. For example, he always did what I told him to do, but it was almost like you had to breast feed him through it."

Since Mobilia was assisting the board in the superintendent selection process, I assumed they were all aware of his reservations about Zitterkopf. Nevertheless, Zitterkopf was the favorite of Chairman Chet Larson and several others, so he had a strong chance.

Having learned a couple of bitter lessons about phony credentials, I decided not to take anything at face value.

Kensingston International University, Zitterkopf's Ph.D. institution, had one telephone listing. When I called to request information, the secretary handed the phone to the President sitting next to her. The information packet I requested included the 1996 Tuition and Fees Schedule. According to their packet, a full doctorate degree would only cost $4,195. It also indicated that upon application, credit would be given for experiential learning, including project involvement, conferences, colloquia, and continuing education courses.

It's another mail-order degree, just a couple of years after Bangston was splashed all over the local headlines. I fumed. *Don't they ever learn?*

However, I did not have to worry about challenging his credentials. In a May 19 letter, Zitterkopf withdrew his candidacy and abruptly resigned from the district. His letter stated, "I wish to continue educational studies and employment in Colorado, where I am more familiar with the legal and finance system as a whole."

The next day, he was gone, walked off the job in violation of his contract.

His abrupt departure was the fourth time (my predecessor in Buhl in 1979, Bangston in Mt. Iron-Buhl in 1992, Neuenfeldt in 1996) in my experience that men had simply walked away from their administrative positions. There were no consequences for these contract violations, even though their licenses could have been in jeopardy.

Zitterkopf actually sued the district over his loss of pay on the balance of his contract. The district filed a counterclaim. After the lawyers had made their bundles, the district finally settled with him three years later on August 28, 2000. The August 31, 2000, *Cook News Herald* reported on the meeting. "The Zitterkopf litigation, which involved a man who was hired as assistant superintendent in 1997, but after receiving a contract never showed up to work, was settled. The board finally agreed to a $3,000 settlement."

Albertson got it wrong, because the guy did show up to work, but only for four months. He also had it wrong in his ringing endorsement of Zitterkopf's hire in the February 13, 1997, *Cook News Herald.* "He has great credentials. Supt. Dan Mobilia has a good assistant working with him." Albertson never gave any of the women administrators hired endorsements of any kind.

Once again, the board paid for not having done a thorough background check.

The other two finalists for Mobilia's job had more years of superintendent experience than I had, so I rested easy. The board needed to act soon because within a month they would have neither superintendent nor assistant superintendent. I had a niggling concern that I wasn't being considered because of the previous lawsuit, but I had completed five years of good work and had no indication of any hard feelings from Chet Larson or Larry Anderson. Both were current board members who were on the board I sued in 1986 and prevailed against in 1990. As long as a more qualified candidate got the position, so be it.

My sense of ease with the selection process did not last long.

On Wednesday, May 21, the morning Duluth paper quoted an interview with school board chairman Chester Larson. "But with Zitterkopf's departure, the seven-member School Board will meet later this morning at the district's central office in Virginia to decide its course."

Later this morning?

The very next morning, Thursday, May 22, the paper quoted Larson again, "The board decided Wednesday to re-interview Langan. It appears Belluzzo is out of the running," Larson said.

The board decided? That would have been an unposted and illegal meeting. Any quick and unannounced or unposted meeting is "closed" by definition. The public can't attend what it doesn't know about!

Minnesota's Open Meeting Law allows public agencies such as school boards to hold closed meetings for only a few, very specific exceptions. Those exceptions are to meet with their attorney to discuss pending litigation, to consider preliminary charges against an employee, to evaluate an employee, to discuss student data, to discuss data relating to victims of abuse, and to conduct strategy sessions for labor negotiations.

Superintendent selection does not appear anywhere on the list of exceptions!

Minnesota law does permit school boards to call special or emergency meetings when necessary to conduct business. However, these meetings must be posted to the public according to stringent guidelines about what constitutes adequate public notice.

There was no notice for this May 21 meeting!

The *Duluth News Tribune* had essentially documented an illegal school board meeting. On Friday, May 23, the board re-interviewed Langan. At a regular board meeting on May 27, the board voted to amend the published agenda and offer him a contract. I was alarmed about the closed process, but I assumed, with what I knew at the time, that Langan was the more qualified candidate. He had Minnesota licensure, a doctorate, and years of superintendent experience.

Rumors of another issue were more alarming. On Wednesday, May 28, Cook teachers told me that recently hired Cook principal Sid Simonson had been offered the assistant superintendent position left vacant by Zitterkopf. By June 4, the talk was everywhere. That day, Simonson arrived two hours late to meet with me at the Cook School. We had scheduled a joint interview to hire a French teacher to serve Cook and Orr.

"What's up?" I asked him when he walked in.

"Mobilia called me to the central office this morning for a meeting with Langan (superintendent-select)," he answered.

"What about?" I asked.

"They just wanted to discuss my ideas for the district."

"I keep hearing that you've been offered the assistant superintendent position," I persisted.

"It was never mentioned," he insisted.

Simonson had been less than candid with me in the past on several issues, so I was skeptical. I called Mobilia the next day to get some answers. He was gone for the day so I left a message indicating I was concerned about the rumors I was hearing. Mobilia did not call back, so I e-mailed him with my concerns. Other principals, myself included, might be interested in the assistant position. Another school year had passed and I felt most Orr projects were on solid ground.

"Doesn't the position have to be posted?" I queried in my e-mail.

My main concern was Simonson. I liked him well enough, as did most everyone. He was a very personable guy with a great sense of humor. However, I had worked closely with him on several issues, including scheduling for shared staffing between our two buildings. I had not observed much attention to detail or the old-fashioned, roll-up-your-sleeves, follow through that produced solid results. Besides, ours was an extremely complicated school district and several of us had years of experience in the district, compared with his six months.

The week beginning Monday, June 9, 1997, was horrible. It began with a site-based leadership conference for teachers, administrators, and board members from each of the seven attendance sites. The three-day conference was scheduled for the exclusive Ludlow's Resort on Lake Vermilion and began on Monday evening, June 9, with a registration reception. I lived a few miles down the lake so I did not register for the overnights.

There was also a regular school board meeting scheduled that same evening in Tower, so several board members and administrators would not join the conference until the next day. This June 9 school board meeting was to be the last meeting for both Mobilia, who was retiring June 30, and board chairman Chet Larson, who had not run for another term on the school board. The newly elected Cotton board member, Arlette Krog, would take office on July 1.

I left the reception about 9:00 p.m. When I got home, Tower Principal Walt Fischer had left a message on my answering machine. He had not been at the conference reception because the school board meeting was in his Tower school building.

"Judy, you're not going to believe it, they hired Sid as assistant superintendent tonight," he reported. "I'll call back later."

When Fischer called later, he was still angry. He had applied and interviewed for the assistant superintendent position the previous fall, when Zitterkopf was hired. He held a superintendent's license, had several years of experience in the district, and a proven track record. He felt he was more qualified than Sid for the assistant job and had been summarily passed over.

"Mobilia tried to recommend that they post the job. He even handed out a revised agenda with his recommendation on it," Walt said. "But they just went right ahead and hired Sid anyway."

"Who pushed it through?" I asked.

"Chet was clearly pushing it," Walt answered. "Mobilia said Langan (superintendent-select) and Simonson had already met and discussed the position."

"Larry Anderson jumped in and said the whole world knows the job had been offered to Simonson," Walt continued. "Then Mobilia told the board that Langan wanted Simonson for the job."

Walt said that after the 7–0 vote to hire Simonson, the board served cake, presented plaques, and thanked Mobilia and Chet Larson for their service. Then they went into closed session to discuss Langan's superintendent contract.

I was stunned.

"So the jerk lied to you the other day when you confronted him about the rumors," Rick swore, referring to my meeting with Simonson on Friday. "They deserve what the hell they get. He just got here, they don't know him and he doesn't know the district."

That night was the first of many sleepless nights. I read our Principals' contract, which stated, "When a vacancy or newly created position occurs in an administrative area in the District, notice of each vacancy will be mailed to the president of the Association." I wasn't sure about the law at that point, but I knew the board's action violated our contract. The whole process stunk; illegal meetings, last-minute agenda changes, a superintendent-select picking the assistant superintendent, administrative positions filled with no posting or public input.

What the hell's going on here? This all had a nauseatingly familiar feeling to it.

It was about to get worse yet. When I got to the conference on Tuesday morning, I talked to Sid during the break. It only seemed fair to let him know where I was coming from.

"Congrats on the assistant position, Sid," I said as we walked the trail past the cabins. "But I want to let you know that I have a big problem with the process the board used. There was no posting to our association that's required in our contract. I'll probably challenge this thing."

"Well," he responded after some hesitation, without looking up or meeting my eyes, "I'm sorry you feel that way, but you do what you have to do. Just remember, I didn't ask for the job, they came to me."

I left the conference early that second day because we had to pick up Rick's mom in Gilbert to come up and stay with us for a week or so. She had broken her wrist and needed some time and help to recover. Albrook Principal Bob Larson called later that afternoon from Ludlow's.

"Mobilia called up here shortly after you left. He told Chet Larson that Langan had backed out of the contract offer. When he got off the phone, Chet announced the news to the conference," Bob explained.

"After Mobilia's call, Chet met with Sid and the other board members," Bob continued. "It was weird because the rest of us just milled around for over an hour while they all met behind closed doors."

"Who was in that meeting behind closed doors?" I asked, scrambling for pen and paper. *Not a good sign when I'm back taking notes like this,* I though to myself.

I had a sinking, sick feeling in the pit of my stomach.

I arrived at the conference the third day, June 11, about 10:00 a.m., after helping my mother-in-law with dressing and breakfast. I had been up most of the night, stewing over the closed way Simonson was hired as assistant superintendent and replaying Bob's description of the previous afternoon's drama.

Ten minutes after I got there, the conference presenter directed a comment to the "new Interim Superintendent, Sid Simonson."

I felt as if I had been socked in the gut!

The other principals soon informed me that Mobilia had already come and gone that morning. He met with Chet Larson, the other board members in attendance, and Sid Simonson. According to the principals, there were some loud and angry exchanges at those meetings. Right after Mobilia left, Chet Larson stood and announced to the conference that Sid would be Interim Superintendent.

The whole group was upset. Three of us had all applied for one or both of the administrative openings in the past several months. Simonson had not applied for the assistant position the previous fall (when Zitterkopf was hired) and he had withdrawn as a candidate for the superintendency. He had little knowledge of this district and he had no superintendent experience.

This was another decision made illegally, at an unposted meeting behind closed doors, without a quorum. I couldn't believe what was going on. For the last five years, I had watched Mobilia and the board follow rules, laws, contracts, and policies to the letter. Now it seemed all attention to contract, law, and professional process had been tossed aside.

Maybe the version of events I heard had been overstated or maybe Chet had misspoken? But the June 12 *Cook News Herald* had an announcement for a Special Board Meeting four days later, on Monday, June 16, at the Cherry School. The Cook paper is a weekly that comes out every Tuesday or Wednesday, so that meant the notice was sent to the paper by the first or second day of the conference. Is somebody pushing this thing behind the scenes or what?

Then the Saturday, June 14, *Duluth News Tribune* quoted board chairman Chet Larson, "Sidney Simonson, recently hired as assistant superintendent may be named interim superintendent at Monday's meeting, scheduled for 6 p.m. at the Cherry school."

"Jude, calm down or you're going to blow a gasket," Rick warned me.

"I just can't believe this shit!" I swore, kicking the counter stool halfway across the kitchen floor. "When are they going to stop suckering for the good looking, smooth talking guys who can't administer their way out of a paper bag?"

"What the hell's wrong with Mobilia, how come he's letting them ram Simonson through like this?"

"Either he wants out so bad he doesn't give a damn or he's so lame-duck he can't stop it," I said, trying to figure it all out.

About 3:00 a.m. I figured it out.

Chet's behind this. It's retaliation for the conspiracy verdict. He wants to ram someone through before he leaves the board so I have no shot at the superintendent's position. But what's with the rest of the board? I wondered.

A June 12 *Cook News Herald* article about Chet's retirement from the board provided some insight. "Larson has been the backbone of the board for 21 years." Chet had been Chairman most of those 21 years. Mobilia described Chet's chairmanship, "Anybody that knew Chet knew that he pretty much knew how to run the board."

Besides Chet, there were two other board members who were on the board I sued in 1987, Albrook board member Larry Anderson and Cherry board member Dave Clement. Chet wouldn't have any trouble convincing them to push somebody, anybody, else but me. I rehashed that lawsuit and the players all night.

By the time we left the conference at Ludlow's midday on Thursday, June 12, the principals' group had discussed our growing concerns about the closed and illegal process several times. Jim Techar (Babbitt principal) and I were current applicants for the superintendent's position when Langan was selected. I indicated to them that if the closed and illegal process continued, I was going to file a complaint and challenge the process. They were all supportive, but in a quiet, noncommittal way. Just the word challenge sends everyone running for cover.

If the conference week was a bummer, Monday, June 16 was pure hell. I suspected that the special board meeting that night had been called to rubber-stamp Chet's decision to make Simonson interim superintendent. My sense of foreboding escalated exponentially after a phone call I received that morning from a colleague in the Range Principals' group.

"Judy, I just read about your new Interim Superintendent. Your district better check on Simonson," he said. "There's something wrong with his license. I'm not sure what it is, but we found it when he applied here a few years ago. He may be a dresser and a talker, but I think his license was suspended or something. Better check it out!"

I immediately called the State Department to check on his license. All they would tell me at the time was that he did not have continuous licensure. There was a two-year period during which his license was suspended, but it was reinstated in 1994. I was told that the Data Privacy Act prevented release of any more information. It was just enough information to make my head pound. Apparently my buddy knew what he was talking about.

Suspended license! How can this be true? Mobilia's smarter than that. Didn't he and the board check him out when they hired him for Cook last fall?

I wondered.

The hurt I felt compounded the anger. It cut to the quick to think that they didn't want me so bad that they promoted someone with a license suspension. That's a huge red flag in our business. Rage reigned again.

I didn't feel well when I left work that day. Dizziness or light-headedness had been bugging me for a couple of days. I stopped at the clinic to get a blood-pressure check. A nurse took it twice and then told me to stay seated while she went to get a doctor. The pressure was 220/120. The doc came in and asked what was going on. All I could say was that I had been in a week long, round-the-clock rage and it didn't look like it would end soon. I left with my first prescription for blood pressure medication.

Rick was furious when I got home. "You should just quit this damn district," he hollered. "The bastards don't deserve your commitment. How many extra hours, nights, and days have you given them? They don't appreciate what you've done, so screw them, get the hell out! This anger and frustration will kill you."

Once again anger had become the elephant stomping and trashing around our living room and it wasn't good for either of us.

Cindy Jindra, the Cherry principal hired in 1996, called that night after the special board meeting.

"The meeting lasted less than ten minutes," she reported. "They hired Sid as interim superintendent. There was no discussion on the motion."

The next morning, the June 17 *Duluth News Tribune* reported, "Simonson's selection ends a somewhat bizarre superintendent's search. It's not clear how long Simonson will remain interim – or if he'll eventually be hired as the district's permanent superintendent."

Later that day, I called the EEOC and asked them to send the complaint forms. Then I called Rick Prebich, the attorney who had helped me on the Mt. Iron-Buhl issue and the court-ordered job in Orr. I asked him to call Scott Neff, the school district attorney, and warn the board to check on Simonson's licensure. I did not want the district to make the kind of mistake that would leave me no option. I knew I was a more qualified candidate and naively thought I still had a shot at the permanent superintendent's position. However, I also told Prebich to start the clock because I was also skeptical and suspicious of the way the board had been making its decisions.

Whether it was the medication or the call to Prebich, I slept well that night for the first time in over a week. Doing something, anything, relieved the rage and the utter helplessness over the retaliation I knew was in play.

Rick and I had great walleye fishing that evening and that also helped. During the long days and nights of the cold, chaotic winter basketball seasons, I would dream of ice-out and fishing. Those dreams had pulled me through many long winters. Now fishing became my refuge from the rage.

Fishing is quiet, relaxing, peaceful, beautiful, fresh, and unpredictable. The random reinforcement is addictive. Every cast can produce a trophy, or at least, dinner. Fresh, fried walleye is a gourmet delight. Whenever other fishermen asked how we were doing, our standard reply was, "Fishing's great! Catching is a bonus." The joy of fishing is the concentrated anticipation that leaves little room for anger and anxiety. It's better than any tranquilizer. The old axiom, "A bad day of fishing beats a good day at work" was gospel for me. It would become more so as the number of good days at work diminished.

Even the bomb dropped in the next day's *Mesabi Daily News* failed to rekindle the full rage. The June 18 issue quoted retiring Superintendent Mobilia, "Simonson could be named permanent superintendent at the July 1 meeting." *He's not even a current applicant like I am. How can this be? Those three board members I sued are pushing these decisions. This has to be part of what's going on.*

I think part of me knew at this point that I had no chance at the superintendent's position. The biggest frustration was that I knew the district, its history, its staff, its communities, its strengths, and potential weaknesses better than most. After all, I wrote the book on school choice, the biggest enrollment threat to the district. It would be a tough job, requiring constant attention to the tiniest details. I had observed Superintendent Mobilia closely for five years.

With a district this large and complex, there is very little margin for error. The district's buses traveled more miles than any other school district in the state. The slightest increase in some marginal aspect of the transportation costs could have a big impact on the bottom line. Our seven high schools maintained full academic schedules, but graduated only 260 students from those seven high schools. There are harsh, "reverse" economies of scale buried in those numbers. Worse yet, in five years, the graduating class would drop below 200.

I had no doubt that I could manage the district, keep it out of the financial trouble that was perennially posed to strike and provide the vision and leadership necessary to take it forward. I had seen nothing from either of the board's two recent favorites, Zitterkopf or Simonson, to inspire that kind of confidence. In spite of the growing realization that my candidacy for the superintendent's position might be predestined to fail, I resolved to stick it out. Hopefully, I could function as the lowest common denominator, guaranteeing that the district would end up with a qualified and competent superintendent.

Prebich called after talking to the school district's attorney about the possible problems with Simonson's credentials. He told me to get a copy of Simonson's license suspension report. I called the state department again. I learned that the license had been suspended from February 1993 to November 1994 for allegations regarding district employees. The department spokesman told me they could not send me a copy of the suspension report, that only a school board member or a school attorney could request it.

Perhaps Prebich's call to the school attorney had some effect, because the board did not push ahead as the newspaper article had predicted and hire Simonson as permanent superintendent at the July 1 meeting. *Of course, Chet Larson's no longer chairman to ram it through,* I thought to myself. However, Larry Anderson was elected Chairman to replace Chet. With Dave Clement on the board that was still two from the board I had sued. It still didn't look good.

On July 7, I received a letter from Interim Superintendent

Simonson stating that the permanent superintendent's position was reopened, "due to unusual circumstances in the initial selection process. LETTERS OF CONTINUED INTEREST SHOULD BE SUBMITTED ON OR BEFORE *FRIDAY, JULY 18, 1997.*" I sent the letter with another complete set of credentials. *Maybe there's still a chance,* I thought. *At least there's a posting and what appears to be some process in place again.*

On August 11, the board assigned Jane Marconett as interim Cook Principal to take Simonson's place. She was an elementary teacher at the Cook School and fully licensed as K–12 principal. With Jindra and me, there were again three women principals in the district.

The August 28 *Cook News Herald* editorialized, "The search is still going on for a superintendent for ISD 2142. Interim Supt. Sid Simonson is apparently doing a good job, but the board feels they have to follow certain steps to make sure everyone is happy and no one will file a lawsuit because they felt that proper procedures weren't followed." *I wonder who he's writing about, what procedures he's worried about?* I chuckled to myself.

Simonson called me at the office on August 28, 1997.

"Judy, what do you know about an emergency meeting of the board tomorrow?" he asked.

"I haven't heard a thing," I responded. "You mean the board's doing this on its own? What's going on? Isn't this a violation of the Open Meeting Law?"

"All I know is that Chairman Larry Anderson called me and asked if I was still interested in the superintendency." Sid said. "Then he told me to call Scott Neff and get him to set an emergency meeting for the board. It's set at Neff's office tomorrow at 1:30 p.m."

"I have no idea, but Zelda Bruns (Orr board member) stopped in my office this morning as well, also asking if I was still interested in the position," I explained. *Now what's going on?* I wondered. *Could the meeting be about my candidacy and the previous lawsuit?* I was just paranoid enough by this time to assume I was the "emergency." It would be four years before I understood the substance of that "emergency" meeting!

Proper procedures became critical two weeks later on September 8, 1997. The school board held a study session at the Cook Country Supper Club to discuss the candidates for the superintendent position. A reporter from the weekly *Timberjay* was barred from the meeting. The next *Timberjay* headlines screamed, "St. Louis County School Board Holds Illegal Closed Meeting To Discuss Superintendent Applicants." The editorial title read, "Newspapers must remain vigilant of Open Meeting Law violations." Board Chairman Larry Anderson apologized for closing the meeting and was quoted saying, "I made a wrong interpretation of the advice I got from our attorney."

Between the "emergency meeting" on August 28 and the illegal, closed study session on September 8, my paranoia knew no bounds.

The September 10 *Mesabi Daily News* carried the names of the four finalists selected at that illegal closed meeting. In the next few days, all the other area newspapers carried the names. The finalists announced were Judy Pearson, Orr Principal; Sid Simonson, interim superintendent; Kenneth Rodgers, Assistant Superintendent from Osceola, Wisconsin; and Patricia Weaver, curriculum director in Sante Fe, New Mexico. After all my suspicions, I was surprised to be named a finalist.

In the September 11 *Cook News Herald,* Albertson couldn't resist adding his two cents. "Cook's new principal, Jane Marconett is doing a good job. Of course, she's been a teacher here for years so she knows everyone and won't even get lost." *How condescending can you get,* I thought to myself. "Her predecessor, Sid Simonson, is putting in a lot of hours as interim superintendent. The board has expressed thanks to him for the job he's doing. There is still no word on a permanent superintendent. The board met Monday at the Country Supper Club to go over the applicants. By law they don't make any candidates' names public until they reach the finals. Simonson should have the inside track though."

Surprise! Surprise! Albertson's not supporting me for the job! Anyone but me was more like it.

In his next issue, Albertson listed the finalists. "The ISD 2142 board now has four finalists. They are being very fair too; they have two women and two men. No one can say they aren't an equal opportunity employer." *Is that defensive,* I asked myself, *or just plain offensive?*

When family, friends, and colleagues expressed support for my candidacy, I jokingly responded, "Well, at least I've established the lowest common denominator for the position. They'll have to find a more qualified man and that's good for the district." I didn't want to get any hopes up, my own included.

I knew it was a long shot, but if there was no shot at all, why would they select me as a finalist? Anger levels at home had subsided and Rick quit cursing the district in every conversation. Rick's new business enterprise also provided a healthy distraction from my district stress. His syndicated radio business had dwindled due to the deregulation of the airwaves, the ensuing consolidation of smaller, independent stations, and the automation of programming.

Erik was studying computer science at school and had been bugging Rick about the world-wide-web. "Dad," he insisted, "everything you're doing is going to be done on the web before long. You got to get with it." He bought Rick a book called *Learn HTML in 21 Days.* Rick disappeared into that book and several others. He read, experimented, and began writing HTML, the language of the web. He still jokes about the false advertising of those "21 Days," as he works every day to stay on top of the technology.

In short order, he had registered the domain www.lakevermilion. com and built a preliminary website. Who says you can't learn from your kids?

The learning curve is an exciting place to be and the excitement is infectious. He dragged me along on the gentlest slopes of that learning curve with him. It was fun to brainstorm together about what could be done on the web. However, he still teases that his worst nightmares begin when I ask, "Rick, I got an idea, why can't you do this on the website?"

Soon Rick was developing and hosting other websites for clients. The business grew by leaps and bounds. After a couple of years, Rick added a live camera to his comprehensive www.lakevermilion.com website and the daily looks skyrocketed. By 2004, his site was receiving over a million looks a year and earning income that replaced the syndicated radio production. The learning curve is a healthy, hopeful, energizing, and positive place to be. It gave us a positive balance to the conflicts with my job.

The four finalists for the superintendent's position interviewed with the school board on October 6, 1997. We were all asked the same questions from a prepared list of questions. The final question asked of all candidates was, "Is there anything in your background that would embarrass the district?" Sid answered "No" to that question. *Did the board ever check out his license? What did they find out?* I wondered.

On October 15, former superintendent Mobilia called about an upcoming hearing on a lingering personnel issue we were both involved in. During the conversation, he volunteered that Chet Larson had been the "spoiler" for me in the first round, when Langan was selected. While that didn't surprise me, it was a bitter confirmation of what I had suspected. He also told me that the board knew about Simonson's background when they hired him in 1996. This shocked me. *Why in the world did you hire him?* It would be years before I learned that they knew only a fraction of that background at the time they hired him.

I was neither shocked nor surprised when the October 16 *Cook News Herald* reported that Bill Conger, the former Cook school board member, had spoken up at the recent school board meeting in favor of Interim Simonson for permanent superintendent. This was the same board member who had laid a guilt trip on my son Max right after I won the lawsuit seven years earlier. It was another reminder of how long those hard feelings could last.

The next shock came when Board Chairman Larry Anderson called my office on Friday, October 24. He told me that Don Langan was back in as a candidate. Shortly after Anderson hung up, Simonson called on his cell phone.

"Judy, Larry just called and told me that Langan is back in the race," he said. "I was so mad, I just walked out of the office."

"Yeh, I just got off the phone with him too. After all the interviews and publicity about us 'finalists,' it a little suspicious at this late date."

The board had a study session scheduled for 2:00 p.m. Monday, October 27, followed by a regular board meeting at 7:00 p.m. at the Cotton School. These study sessions, legally open to the public, were rarely attended by anyone unless invited and never by the *Cook News Herald*, the official newspaper of the district.

Walt Fischer was now the principal at Cotton. He had requested a transfer from Tower to an open spot Cotton to be closer to home. Simonson had approved Fischer's transfer shortly after becoming Interim Superintendent. Gary Friedlieb was hired in August for the Tower position following Fischer's transfer.

Fischer called me right after the meetings adjorned.

"You're not going to believe it, but they just hired Langan. Motion made, seconded, and passed unanimously, with no discussion," Walt announced. "Everyone was shocked, Sid most of all."

"What happened during the day with the study session?" I asked.

"Well, the study session lasted most of the afternoon."

"Who attended?" I asked. "Were you there?"

"Of course I didn't attend. We're not welcome and you know we never attend unless we're asked. But Mel and Joe were there, and Sid of course." (Business manager, maintenance supervisor, and interim superintendent.)

"Did they stay for the whole study session?" I asked.

"That's what's so interesting," he responded. "During the last part of the session, Sid, Mel, and Joe were just wandering around the building. Apparently the board asked them to leave the study session."

"The superintendent's position wasn't even on the agenda, was it? And no discussion on the motion? It had to be all worked it all out ahead of time, at the study session?"

"That was obvious," Walt responded. "Larry Anderson asked for a motion to amend the agenda and then they hired him. Bing, bing, bing! No discussion at all. Zelda told us afterwards that Langan was all set to go, that he already had an interim in place in Cook County."

"Did any one say anything about how Langan got back in the

process before tonight, at the last minute? There's been no board meeting at which they could have made that decision."

"Nobody said a word about that and it was never brought up, about how he got back in," Walt answered.

"But one of the teachers at the regular meeting asked Arlette, the new Cotton board member, after the meeting why they didn't hire Sid," Walt continued. "She told him that they had found something in his past."

"That's all, no mention of a license suspension?"

"That's all he told me," Walt answered.

Damn! Another illegal decision had been made at the closed study session earlier that day. By now, I was numb from anger and frustration that had been brewing since June. My head ached from banging it too often against that "glass ceiling!" *Can you get a concussion from an abstraction like that?*

Langan wasn't even a finalist in this second selection round. He had not reapplied, as the rest of us were required to do. *Wasn't that requirement CAPITALIZED AND UNDERLINED?*

Simonson called me the next day and said he was so pissed he'd like to tell them to stick the interim business, but couldn't because he'd need letters of recommendation. He probably felt a lot like I did in Mt. Iron-Buhl, when I was interim superintendent and the board pulled the rug out from beneath me when they brought Bangston in at the last minute.

I had little to say in response to Sid. I was angry for my own reasons, some of which had to do with him. Although I had never told him that I had learned about his license suspension, he knew I had concerns about the process from the beginning back in June.

The board had a wouldn't-couldn't dilemma, I figured out. They wouldn't hire me because of the lawsuit and they couldn't hire Sid because of the license thing or that vague "something in his past." Both realizations burned to the core. My wouldn't/couldn't hypothesis explained why they brought Langan back in and hired him illegally at the last minute. There was a lousy, rotten logic to it all.

The next morning, the *Duluth News Tribune* reported on the story.

"St. Louis County's long search is over. Langan's selection ends a prolonged and somewhat bizarre superintendent's search." The November 1 *Timberjay* reported on Langan's selection, "The search for a superintendent has been long and more than a little strange." Bizarre and strange are not terms customarily used to describe the hiring a superintendent.

Of course this crap's strange and bizarre, I cursed to myself. *Hidden agendas and dilemmas will do it every time!*

Chapter 9

1998

RETALIATION INTIMIDATES

"The Chilling Effect of Retaliation"
EEOC Guidelines on Retaliation

S O NOW, WHAT'RE YOU *going to do?* The night the
board hired Langan, I had an intense running argument with
myself. The argument raged on after the sun came up.

"Sue the bastards! Nail their ass for this shit!" my angry self said.

"Not so quick! Think about it. Do you really want to go through it
all again?" my wiser self reasoned.

"What choice do I have? I'm not caving in to this crap and nobody
else will hold them accountable."

"Just shut up with that 'nobody else'll do it bullshit.' What is it with
you anyway? Why you all the time? You paid your dues, let it pass this
time."

"But it can't be that bad this time. I've been through it all, know
what to expect, can do a better job of keeping it together."

"You forget what it did to you the last time. You changed. You
dropped out of almost everything and went into hiding. For five years.
You're still not your old self."

"That's the point, I can't be hurt any more than I was and besides
nothing will catch me by surprise this time. I know what to expect."

"Sure you do, you dumb shit, except this time you'll be working for the guys you take on—and you don't think that'll make a difference?"

"Yeh, but the jerks should never have selected me as a finalist if they were never going to consider me in the first place. What a rotten thing to do. They played games with me, humiliated me."

So, what're you going to do? The serenity prayer had always seemed like great guide to life's dilemmas. I was willing to fight to change the things that needed to be changed, but did this instance require the serenity to accept what I couldn't change? Would I have the wisdom to know the difference? Those are the tougher questions.

Wise or not, win or lose, I greeted the sunrise with a certainty this was retaliation and that I was not going to let them get away with it without a fight.

"This is unbelievable! Ten years and it's the same damn script all over again!" Rick's anger was directed at the district and the fight ahead. "'We'll just have to drag them to the woodshed one more time."

Rick's determination was never in doubt, but he'd rather have taken them on face to face and punched their lights out! Our only discussion concerned how best to fight back. No arguments, no disagreements, just dug-in resignation that the whole thing sucked big time. After the Cook and Mt. Iron-Buhl battles, this conversation was getting really old. The dark doubts and fears from the lawsuit still haunted us. If we had not won, we would have lost our home, the only "savings" we had, to pay the legal bills.

We decided, as we had in the Mt. Iron-Buhl challenge, to file the complaint and let the EEOC complete its investigation. Hopefully, if we got a favorable finding, we'd be able to settle short of going to court.

I already had the EEOC filing information. I had requested it right after Simonson's two rapid-fire promotions in June. I had held off filing at that time because I was still a candidate for the permanent superintendent position.

I called attorney Prebich the day after Langan was hired and explained that I was going to file a formal EEOC complaint on discrimination and retaliation. I wanted him to review the complaint before I sent it out. He needed to be in the loop from the beginning, in case the EEOC process did not work out.

Rick and I met with him a few days later. We both felt comfortable with Prebich. Like us, he was a Ranger and understood the area. He was easier to talk to than Williams had been. For one thing, he actually listened. He was not as high priced and was not part of a big firm with fancy offices, but we felt from the beginning that he believed we were right. That made a world of difference. Trust and comfort level are as important with an attorney as they are with a doctor.

I worked on the complaint most of November. All my introspective conclusions that this fight would be easier, that I was more prepared were wrong. The tension notched up day by day. I was smoking over a pack of cigarettes a day and consuming Tagment, Rolaids, and Tums like they were candy. I felt like I was being eaten by acid from the inside out. It's a good thing we didn't drink much, because the setting was ripe for abuse.

More than anything else, I hated the subtle changes creeping in on me. I could hear an impatience and bitchiness in my voice. I caught myself interrupting folks talking to me in order to hurry it along. I always hated that. The temper perched just below the surface, which was becoming paper-thin. I may have been older and wiser, but it wasn't any easier.

Prebich called in December to ask how the complaint was coming. I told him that I did not want to file the complaint until after the holidays. He said he was worried about the timelines, which mandate that a complaint must be filed with the EEOC within 180 days of the alleged discriminatory act. Although the last action was October 27, the first had been either May 27 (Langan's first selection after an illegal meeting) or June 9 (Simonson's hire as Assistant Superintendent).

I explained that I had just talked to the EEOC and was told that since I lived in a state that had an anti-discrimination law and state agency, Title VII provides a timeline of 300 days from the latest action. I also asked if I had to file with both state and federal agencies. Both federal and state agencies confirmed the 300 days and the fact that once I filed with the EEOC, I would be cross-filed with the state. I wanted to be certain about the timelines because timelines had closed me out of a challenge on the Bangston hiring in Mt. Iron-Buhl in 1989.

The reasons for holding back were complicated. I dreaded going through it all again. I was still wrestling with the wisdom question. I kept putting it off, knowing that I had 300 days from October 27, 1997. In addition, I had negotiated our last Principals' contract, for 1995–1997, and was working on the next contract for 1997–1999. It was already many months past its expiration of June 1997. I hoped to get the contract settled before I filed the complaint.

I did not want my complaint to sour the process for the entire group. Perhaps I had a premonition that challenging from within the district, which I had never done before, might be more difficult. I had no idea just how difficult.

However, Superintendent Langan's style of negotiating was convoluted and progress was slow. Our first meeting with him was out-of-this-world. Literally. He had only been on the job in the district a month when we met in early January 1998. Instead of exchanging proposals about salary, benefits, and contract language, he wanted us to develop and sign what he called a "covenant" of rededication and commitment. Basically, any attempt on our part to begin negotiations without it would get little traction. We pressed repeatedly for a definition of terms, some sense of just what he was looking for. He remained vague on specifics, but indicated clearly that the document was a prerequisite for moving ahead. He even said if done well, this "covenant" could mean the difference of several percent on our salaries!

"Is he for real? He's a little spooky don't you think?" we discussed after Langan left the meeting. "Never heard anything like this before! Did we just walk through a time warp or something? This is like the old loyalty oaths. Wonder if he wants a commitment to himself, the district, or the kids and communities we serve? He never answered that question, did he?" If he was looking for a statement of blind loyalty and commitment to him personally, we agreed that wasn't gong to happen.

We were uncomfortable with Langan's strange request, but we finally agreed to work on some sort of innocuous document that simply stated what we believed were our primary goals anyway. He was our new superintendent and no one wanted to get off on the wrong foot. Over the next few weeks, the rest of the group sent me their thoughts and I put them together. We discussed and amended it several times, finally coming up with a document we called, "Statement of Commitment." I faxed it to Langan on January 23, 1998, asking if we were in the ballpark.

After several inquiries to Langan, we still had no response on our document by the first of March and no progress on contract negotiations. On March 4, 1998, when it became apparent that my complaint would have no bearing on our contract negotiations, I mailed my complaint on the three administrative positions (assistant superintendent, interim superintendent, and superintendent) to the EEOC. I couldn't wait any longer; I was running out of time.

It's a good thing I didn't hold out for a contract settlement before filing the complaint. By July, we were one year past the expiration of our contract and we had reached an impasse in negotiations. Every time we met with Langan, he changed the rules of the game. Offers he made one day were gone the next, never to appear again. We could not establish a solid base to negotiate from. We finally filed for mediation and met with the state mediator on August 5.

After a long day of negotiation, with the mediator shuttling back and forth between the two sides, we reached at an agreement. Fischer, our association president, sent me e-mail the next day. "Just wanted to say thanks for the hard work at yesterday's mediation session. Thanks for all the preparation material. Without your input and suggestions, we would not have accomplished so much. You helped the process immensely." A second e-mail from Friedlieb, our other negotiator read, "For what it's worth, I want you to know that not only do I appreciate your knowledge and experience, but I also admire your tenacity and candor. It is a privilege and a pleasure to be a colleague of someone with the intellect, expertise, and integrity you possess and demonstrate."

At the mediator's request, Langan agreed to have the new contract typed up and ready for signature. Inconceivable as it might seem, when we met to review and sign the contract, Langan had reduced the annual salary figure. We were dumbstruck. It was another one of those, "This can't be happening!" Langan moments. The dollar difference was an insignificant $73. We had copies of the agreement with the state mediator's initials and could have pushed the issue. However, after much discussion, we decided, one more time, to give him the benefit of the doubt and sign it. We went out of our way to avoid an adversarial relationship within the administrative team.

In early April, the EEOC responded to my initial complaint. It was accepted for investigation and assigned to Bess Warden, the same investigator who had worked on my Mt. Iron-Buhl challenge. The EEOC indicated that the school board would be notified of the charge within 10 days after they received my revised complaint. I knew this was coming, but the reminder renewed all the stress and anxiety.

Do I really want to do this?

Friends and colleagues asked continually about the strange and bizarre process by which Langan had been hired as superintendent. My name had been all over the papers as a finalist. They all asked, "How could they get away with it?" That question was probably the tipping point for me. If I did nothing, they would certainly get away with it. I signed the final complaint on April 7, 1998.

The board was notified of the charge 10 days later or about April 20. I steeled myself for the public exposure, but there was no notice or mention of the charge in the board minutes or newspapers for almost a year. I was grateful for the reprieve from publicity, but surprised that it was never discussed at a board meeting. Langan would have received the formal notice and I assumed he informed the board at one of their frequent study sessions.

These study sessions were seldom posted to the public. The meeting times, locations, and agendas were also unavailable to the public. No minutes were kept or published. This practice was documented several times by the *Timberjay*. On April 14, 2001, the editor reported,

"School District Violates Open Meeting Law." The article referred to similar incidents as far back as 1998.

"The unposted meeting, which was illegal under the state's Open Meeting Law, was not the first improperly-conducted study session held under Langan's watch. The *Timberjay* has previously reported on unposted study sessions by the district, and following one such incident in 1998, Langan personally promised the *Timberjay* that he would post all study sessions along with an agenda, prior to the sessions."

Study sessions were a devious way to circumvent the Open Meeting Law. Board discussions of issues were kept out of the public eye. That way, all differences or controversial issues the public might have an interest in were hammered out before the regular, public board meetings. Then motions would be passed with little or no discussion at regular board meetings. Most votes were unanimous. Illegal "straw votes" were taken at many of these study sessions to guarantee consensus in public. The *Timberjay* article documented above continued, "In other study session action, the board rejected the proposed school calendar on a 4-3 straw vote."

A straw vote is an unofficial vote taken to indicate the relative strength of opposing opinions. When it is taken at an unposted public meeting where no minutes are kept, it is illegal by definition. Minnesota law requires all governmental actions to be taken at posted, open meetings, the votes recorded and published.

In March and April 1998, just three months into his new job, Langan made several decisions that were at odds with the principals in the district. As a result, we got our first indications that Langan did not tolerate independent opinion or dissent of any kind. Our first clues came at his principals' meetings, where our input was never solicited, as Mobilia had done on a regular basis. Any input we did offer was curtly dismissed. We just sat and listened for hours.

One of his most disturbing directives involved site-based budgeting. Langan proposed to budget all building-level expenditures on a per pupil basis. This per pupil allocation had only been done with capital (facility repair, purchase of equipment and books) expenditures in the past. There were good reasons why it had never been done with general fund allocations for personnel and salaries. Smaller schools could not maintain programs and services under that formula.

When I compared Orr's current year's expenditures with Langan's proposed 1998–1999 budget allocation, Orr was in big trouble. Further analysis indicated that the trouble was the same for the Tower and Cotton Schools, the other smallest schools in the district. Under Langan's proposed allocation system, the four largest schools would benefit and the three smallest would suffer.

Per pupil allocation worked only for those expenditures directly tied to the number of students. For example, more students in a building meant more art supplies, textbooks, desks, workbooks, and food in the cafeteria. But per pupil allocation did not work for those personnel expenditures that are the same for all schools, regardless of the number of students. These expenditures were set by the school board and fixed for all schools. Each school had a principal, a secretary, a head cook, a head custodian, a head bus driver, and the same numbers of extracurricular coaches. These fixed costs took a much greater percentage of Langan's new per pupil allocation in the smaller schools.

I shared this analysis with Langan and other administrators at a principals' meeting. I was told we would just have to learn to live within our means. I explained it to the business manager who echoed Langan's argument that equal dollars per student was an equal and fair system. I put together a budget analysis of all seven schools, showing the disparate impact of the fixed costs on the three small schools.

The small schools would have to dramatically cut programs and services while the four larger schools would have significant surpluses. No one challenged my figures or my conclusions, but I got nowhere. It was frustrating that the two principals from the other small schools did not speak up. However, few of the principals spoke up at meetings on any topic. There was little reward for anyone who spoke up at administrative meetings. All you did was expose yourself to criticism or ridicule. Better to say nothing and let the boss target someone else.

The other principals would call or e-mail me with their concerns, often urging me to speak up. Then in the meetings, they would say nothing.

Why me? Personality I suppose. On the assertive/passive continuum, I was probably born on the assertive end of the scale. Besides, I had always believed that dissent and discussion produced the best results. I was also a skeptic and questioned when things did not make sense to me. How else do you learn?

I also made it a practice to keep informed. I read several education publications regularly and closely followed the legislative and rule-making activity at the state and national level. I paid close attention to the laws and rules that affected our profession and public employment in general. I often asserted how important it is to know your rights and the rules of the game you are in. I was frustrated with other teachers and principals who had not even read their own contracts or any of the laws that govern collective bargaining for those contracts.

I read current books about education. I got blank looks when I referred to significant books like Kozol's *Savage Inequalities* (Crown 1991) about inequities in public school funding. Kozol describes how the rich get a better education and the poor get less and how so many schools in America remain segregated and unequal decades after *Brown v. Board of Education*. No one else had read Berliner and Biddle's *The Manufactured Crisis* (Addison Wesley 1995). Their research and statistical analysis debunked the politically popular and sensational myths about America's failing schools.

Former superintendent Mobilia offered some perspective on my role within the principals' organization in a performance evaluation. "Judy is well read and keeps current with educational issues. This is obvious during administrative discussions. Judy has a lot to contribute based on her knowledge of the literature. Judy is a very articulate, knowledgeable individual who does very well with oral presentations. She is an active, participating member of the administrative team, always has something to contribute to discussion and debate during administrative meetings."

On Langan's new budget allocation system, the principals from the other two small schools, Fischer from Cotton and Friedlieb from Tower, agreed with me. Principals from the larger schools were more ambivalent because they would receive large surpluses. That was to be expected I suppose, but I was disappointed in their lack of commitment to the district as a whole.

Does Langan just not get it or is he trying to starve the smaller schools? I wondered. *Deliberate or not, that will be the outcome!* In retrospect, I don't think he or anyone else really grasped the magnitude of the impact on the smaller schools at that time. There was no hint of any malevolent motive regarding the small schools.

I was far from being done with his per-pupil budget directives. There's more than one way to skin a cat.

I first asked if the board members of the small schools were aware of the consequences for their communities. I indicated that they should be fully aware of any huge cuts proposed for their school's programs. No one responded to my question. *They have no idea what's coming!*

After trying several times to get some modification in the process, I sent letters to the board members from the three small schools, outlining my concerns. I received no response, but Langan must have heard directly from them. They couldn't openly support the troublemaker who had filed a discrimination complaint against the district, but they obviously advocated for their small schools behind the scenes. Apparently my message finally hit home.

Langan made it clear he resented my going over his head. At the next principals' meeting, he chastised, "Principals who took their concerns directly to board members have introduced discord into our budget process." But I wasn't done and this wasn't over yet.

As a last resort, I met with my entire faculty on the last day of school and walked them through the current expenditure report and the new budget process for the next year. It was evident to everyone that something had to go—hell, lots of things would have to go. I gave them all the numbers I had been given and showed them specifically how each budget cut would affect various programs. Teachers normally disinterested in any talk of budgets were now on board. These were deep cuts in major programs.

In order to continue even minimal support for academic programs, we would have to cut athletic programs. We could afford the teacher aides that provided supervision for duty free lunch periods and preparation time for teachers or we could afford coaches. The numbers were clear. We could not afford both. These figures and realities shocked the teachers, particularly the coaches.

As I expected, the coaches took the message to their boosters and supporters. The news spread like a wildfire. They went public in a big way. I found it ironic that I could not get any traction on the pending budget crisis until athletic programs were threatened.

I have always supported a full range of extracurricular activities for students, including basketball, football, golf, music, speech, drama, and many others. Both our sons benefited from participation in a wide spectrum of activities, athletics included. However, it was often frustrating to see the priority given exclusively to athletics, often at the expense of academics and other activities. Any content analysis, column-inch and photo count, of educational coverage in local newspapers in small towns will reveal the preeminent place of athletics. This was the magic button to push to get attention to the issue.

Why this obsession with athletics? In most small communities, athletics are the only game in town. They provide the only regular, secular, social event. The athletic teams, colors, and logos become part of the community identity. In addition, most people are friends, neighbors, or relatives of the players or the cheerleaders or the band members.

The prominence given to athletics was one of the reasons I instituted an Academic and Fine Arts Letter program at the Orr School. Students who excelled in something other that athletics could also receive a letter, buy a letter jacket, and wear the school colors. Once we agreed that the new letter would not duplicate and dilute the status of the block style athletic letter, everyone was pleased with the program. We used an Old English style chenille letter to differentiate the Academic and Fine Arts letter from the athletic letter.

On Langan's new budget system, either my letters to the board members or the athletic finesse worked. Something made the difference.

On June 4, 1998, Langan backed down. He reluctantly presented new budget allocations for the buildings, including major modifications. This one took into account the impact of the fixed salary costs on the small schools and eliminated them from the per pupil, site-based allocations.

I had won.

I had prevailed in getting revised budget calculations. Apparently Langan had not appreciated my input in the process. He presented the new allocations with no explanation for his shift from his adamant position. When I asked a simple question about the one of the new budget columns, he brusquely shut me up. *That's okay by me,* I thought, *as long as it doesn't shut down the small schools.*

Langan's next action violated our contract and the way hiring had been done for years. In compliance with state laws and rules, the district had long-standing policies and practices of hiring properly licensed employees. In fact, Mobilia had lobbied successfully to get a law passed in 1991 allowing principals with either elementary or secondary license to supervise K–12 buildings. This had enabled the district to consolidate attendance sites, supervise them with fewer personnel, and do it legally.

Back in March of 1998, Superintendent Langan and Assistant Superintendent Simonson put significant pressure on Jane Marconett to decide if she was going to stay in the Cook principal position or return to the classroom for the following school year. She had complained to our group and to the district that she found the job too much for one person and requested a part-time dean of students be added for the Cook School, which had the largest enrollment in the district.

Marconett called and described the pressure being put on her to decide. I assured her that she was under no contractual or legal constraints to decide this early for the following year.

The pressure put on her was anything but supportive. Neither

Langan nor Simonson gave Marconett any encouragement to stay in the principal position.

What's not said is often louder than words, I thought to myself. We principals encouraged her to stay on, or at the very least, take ample time to consider all her options. Regardless, by March 31, she decided to return to the classroom for the 1998–1999 school year.

Two weeks before Marconett had made her decision, Langan took a Cook teacher and Larry Salmela, the Cook board member, to a southern Minnesota school district to visit a potential candidate—for a position that wasn't even open yet! On March 13, Langan's group interviewed Kevin Abrahamson, a teacher at in the Win-E-Mac school district, where Langan had worked previously. Then he asked principals Walt Fischer and Bob Larson to interview Abrahamson the following week, on March 23.

After our principals' group discussed the issue, Walt Fischer, Association President, sent the following e-mail to Dr. Langan. "The position of the Association is that members should not participate in selecting a non-licensed-principal candidate until all means of finding a person with a Minnesota Principal License have been exhausted. We will honor your request for our participation but wish to express our concern about the process."

Both Fischer and Larson called me following the interview. They were upset because Abrahamson was a personal friend of Langan's and did not have a principal's license. In fact, he had no administrative training, had never even applied for an administrative degree program. His only claim to fame was that he knew Langan.

Abrahamson's letter of application was particularly intriguing. It was dated June 16, 1997, almost one year earlier. The first sentence referred to his conversation with Langan one week earlier. That conversation had to take place during the short, two-week period that Langan was superintendent-select, between May 27, 1997 and June 10, 1997. *How could Langan have known that Simonson would be out of Cook and Cook would be open?* Obviously, he knew because he had recruited Simonson for the assistant superintendent position in a closed and secret process.

Did Langan select Simonson in June 1997 specifically to open that position for his friend Abrahamson whose parents lived in Cook? Did he push Marconett out of Cook a year later, in 1998, to give Abrahamson another shot at the job? Aren't the dates in Abrahamson's letter further evidence of the closed recruiting of Simonson for the assistant position and Abrahamson for Cook? While these were frustrating scenarios to consider, Abrahamson's letter was strong evidence for the EEOC investigation of my complaint.

On Friday, April 24, 1998, the district had an inservice meeting for all teachers and administrators at the Cherry School. During a principals' meeting that afternoon, Langan informed us that Abrahamson would be hired as site administrator for the Cook School at the regular meeting on Monday night at the Orr School. When we questioned Abrahamson's lack of licensure, he brought up our lack of K–12 licenses.

"I'd be very careful if I were you about criticizing someone else's license when none of you are properly licensed for the K–12 jobs you hold," he threatened.

Our jaws dropped to the floor!

"Maybe you're not aware of the special law Mobilia lobbied for in 1991?" I asked. It specifically allows either a high school or an elementary principal to supervise K–12 buildings like ours."

"Oh, I'm well aware of the law, but the state department is not recognizing the law anymore."

After Langan left the meeting, we discussed his threat. We all knew Langan was trying to intimidate us for challenging him. Jindra called St. Cloud State University and asked about the process for updating our licenses to the recently adopted rules for K–12 licenses. Although we had state law on our side and were grandfathered in under our existing K–6 or 7–12 licenses, Langan had successfully intimidated the group.

"My college advisor told me Langan was a vindictive person," Marconett shared with the rest of us. "She told me that there were lots of grievances against him in Grand Marais by teachers and parents. That's one of the main reasons I decided to go back to the classroom.

I don't need this kind of hassle."

Langan pushed ahead with his Abrahamson agenda. He changed the title of the position on the board agenda from Principal to Site-Administrator. At the board meeting in Orr on Monday, April 27, I spoke, on behalf of our principals' group, in opposition to hiring an unlicensed person with no administrative training to run our largest school. Most of the other principals drove up to Orr to present a united front.

Several Cook teachers were present and presented a petition against the hiring of an unlicensed principal. The petition had been signed by the entire Cook faculty. A long-time former board member and board chairman spoke as well. The *Cook News Herald* quoted her, "This is hasty work. Do not vote on it tonight." She also criticized the lack of publicity given this new job and the timeliness of the board agendas coming out.

Langan told the board that he was not pleased with the other, licensed applicants. In spite of the significant opposition, Cook board member Larry Salmela made the motion and the board followed Langan's recommendation to hire Abrahamson.

The May 9 *Timberjay* carried an editorial on the board's failure to publicly post the date, time, or place for the April 14 "study session." In addition, agenda items for the study session did not include anything about the hiring of an unlicensed administrator. The editorial also referred to a "straw vote" taken at that study session on the hiring of Abrahamson.

When asked about the vote to hire Abrahamson, board member Arlette Krog told several teachers at the Cotton School about the straw vote. She indicated that she had reservations about hiring an unlicensed person, but felt bound by the straw vote taken at the study session. Krog was the newest board member and not in a position to challenge the superintendent. *What about the rest of the board? Why follow so blindly?*

In retrospect, my 12 years (three as a board member and nine as a K–12 principal) with the unique St. Louis County School District have provided some perspective on that question. The district is unique in several ways. It is the largest geographically in the state. After the 1993 consolidations with Babbitt and Tower-Soudan, it covered close to 5,000 square miles. It included seven K–12 schools, each with several different telephone exchanges. It was one of the few school districts in the state with board members elected by precincts, rather than at-large. Board members lived miles apart in separate communities, rarely socialized or met at public functions other than board meetings, and were a long distance call from other board members.

As a consequence, this isolation of board members from one another made it relatively easy for a superintendent to get his agendas adopted. That isolation also made it more difficult for board members to challenge a superintendent's agenda. If lay board members don't visit with one another except at board meetings, it is unlikely that any questions or opposition for a professional superintendent will be initiated or successful. Unfortunately, the district's unique geography and governance structure made it vulnerable to administrative abuse and to a control freak like Langan.

Webster defines a "control freak" as a person whose behavior indicates a powerful need to control people or circumstances in everyday matters. The Encarta World English Dictionary defines control freak as somebody who feels an excessive need to exert control over people. We were just beginning to understand the concept in very real terms. We had a lot more to learn.

Langan's use and manipulation of language was a major control tactic. In the first place, his speaking and writing were often unintelligible. His communications were full of needless syllables and obscure terminology. I thought at first he was just trying to impress everyone with his vocabulary. I later concluded there was a more sinister motive. Control! It was very effective with the lay school board. Who was going to speak up and say they couldn't understand one of his reports or recommendations? Langan's jargon and multi-syllabic obscurity keep everyone in their place. Eventually it became known around the district as "Langanese."

One example of Langanese picked at random from his e-mails to principals is illustrative. In March 1998, to a very simple question, "Can we grant high school credit to students auditing college courses?" we got, "I am confident that we will get this straightened out. However, it is essential that alternatives to the current "college course" model be identified and analyzed. The notion that what we have is the best alternative available to St. Louis County students is untenable and illogical until and unless analysis proves it to be so." *So what's the answer?*

In the second place, if he didn't like the clear terms, policies, or regulations we were accustomed to, he simply changed the language.

Langan's recommendation to hire Abrahamson read, "It is my recommendation to offer Kevin Abrahamson a contract for school site administrator for the 1998–1999 school year, with wages and benefits in accord with those established in the principals' agreement." "Site-Administrator" was a new title for the district. Langan used it in spite of the fact that the Cook posting for this position had specified an opening for a K–12 Principal, requiring Minnesota licensure appropriate for the position.

Langan simply changed the title from Principal to site administrator so he could hire Abrahamson. Langan's terminology would change again under oath in arbitration, when he referred to Abrahamson's position as a Dean of Students. In fact, the only principal's activity that Abrahamson did not perform was writing teacher evaluations.

The second part of that board motion involved salary. Although Abrahamson was not a principal, he was paid the full salary and benefits under the principal's contract. A year later, the district would begin hiring teachers part-time as Deans of Students. However, none of the those deans received compensation comparable to what Abrahamson received when he served as something other than a principal for two years.

Teachers serving as full-time Deans are paid based on their base salary plus additional pro-rated days and one extra hour/day. The range of compensation for Deans depends on their base salary, which is determined by years of experience and additional college credits beyond their bachelor's degree. By 2001, full-time deans received annual compensations averaging $35,000 less than a principal, less than Abrahamson earned from the beginning.

In addition to giving Abrahamson the full principal's salary and benefits, the district paid the tuition costs for Abrahamson to get his administrative license over the next two years. *Is this just Langan taking care of his friends, is he pulling in loyalists to consolidate control, or is something else going on?* I wondered. *Without some other explanation, this whole thing makes no sense.*

I was particularly incensed about Abrahamson's hire when I considered what I gone through to get my K–12 principal's position. I never even contemplated applying for an administrative position in Duluth before I left because I was missing a few credits for the license. We borrowed to pay all those tuition bills to get every last credit required. I missed the family many nights, weekends, and summers to get every last, damn credit. Hell, I went through five years of hell suing to get my job and now Abrahamson just waltzes in because he's a friend of Langan's?

Another friend Langan took care of was attorney John Colosimo. One of his first actions after being hired was to recommend to the school board that Colosimo replace Scott Neff, the school district's attorney for many years. That way Langan could insure that the board got the legal advice that he wanted it to get, rather than the advice the board needed to hear. Not long after bringing Colosimo on board, Langan recommended that Colosimo be allowed to buy into the district's group plan for health insurance. Langan, indeed, took care of his friends.

Our local principals' group and the state MASSP organization filed a grievance on the hiring of a non-licensed person for the Cook position and took it all the way to arbitration. It was a violation of our contract, which had internal posting requirements and exclusive representation for anyone spending more than 50% of their time in building administrative work. Langan's hiring of an unlicensed person was also a violation of state rule and law. I wrote and filed several complaints with the State Board of Education and the State Board of Teaching.

Following our grievance and inquiries from the State Boards based on my complaints, Langan took quick action to cover his back. He stated on the required, state licensure reporting forms that he was the supervisor of grades 7–12 at the Cook School, using his own 7–12 principal's license to cover the secondary programs. What about the elementary grades? On October 12, 1998, he raced up to the Cook School and had Jane Marconett sign a Notice of Assignment for Elementary Administration. Having left the Cook principal position after the 1997–1998 school year, she was back teaching full time in the Cook 4th grade.

Marconett was assigned to Elementary Administration in Cook for .167 FTE, over and above her full-time elementary teaching load. She was paid over $8000 for the assignment. She complained many times during that year that she was not given anything to do by either Abrahamson or Langan. When she tried to offer administrative input, she was ignored. Langan simply bought her license to cover his actions. She was also hurt in this process because other elementary teachers on the Cook staff resented her taking the money for doing nothing.

Langan never informed the school board about this new assignment or compensation for Marconett. Grievances and formal complaints require time, but by May 2000, we had lost on all fronts with the Abrahamson hiring. It was impossible to document and keep tabs on Langan's shifting rationale, maneuvers, and terminology. He posted the position for K–12 principal, hired Abrahamson as a site administrator, but told the arbitrator and the state complaint investigators that Abrahamson was functioning as a dean of students.

No on-site investigation was conducted in response to my written complaints to the state offices. They simply called Langan about the complaints and sucked up his glib and shifting fabrications. They never discovered who was actually doing the administrative work in Cook. It wasn't Langan and it wasn't Marconett. It was Abrahamson, acting without a license of any kind.

Langan got away with it because such deliberate obfuscation and deception are uncommon and unexpected in the profession. They are also difficult to prove against a master manipulator like Langan.

I have always been puzzled by Langan's hiring of Abrahamson. Langan had only been in the district a few months when he hired Abrahamson and risked lots of political capital to do so. Nothing in Abrahamson's credentials warranted the risk. He had no administrative training. His two letters of recommendation were mediocre at best and totally unrelated to administration. Why would Langan go out on a limb like this? He pushed an illegal "straw vote" at a board study session, ignored the Cook faculty, alienated the principals' group and their state association, and was less than candid with state investigators and an arbitrator. It didn't add up.

Meanwhile, the district had been informed by the EEOC of my complaint of discrimination and retaliation on the assistant superintendent, interim superintendent, and superintendent positions. In October, we received the district's response to the EEOC, which was required within 30 days. It was dated May 1998, but we did not receive it until October 1998. Months had vaporized.

The district's response argued that I had no basis to challenge on the assistant and interim superintendent positions. "First, and most importantly, it is undisputed that Ms. Pearson did not apply for either of these positions."

Unbelievable! Of course I had not applied; neither did Simonson. How could anyone apply for positions that were never posted? Their argument distracted from the real issues by blaming me for not applying. *How can they get away with this?* That became my mantra. They also argued that the first lawsuit was too old to prove a casual relationship for failing to consider me for the two promotions.

On the superintendent's position, the district argued that I was not qualified because I only had two years of superintendent experience, not the five years required in their posting. However, Simonson had no superintendent experience and he was given two quick promotions and later made a finalist for the superintendency.

Granted, Langan had more years of superintendent experience. But they used his experience repeatedly to distract attention from the closed and illegal meetings. Those procedural issues were the basis for my EEOC complaint on the superintendent position.

By the end Langan's first school year in the district, I was *persona non grata.*

I had filed the EEOC complaint, challenged Langan's budget process, and led the grievance process and the official complaints on the hiring of Kevin Abrahamson. The school board's retaliation for the lawsuit closed me out of any administrative promotion. That was passive retaliation by omission, the failure to do the right thing or follow proper procedures. I would soon experience aggressive retaliation of commission. Langan was a master retaliator.

Langan's retaliation against the principals for their challenge Abrahamson's hiring was swift and effective. He had warned us at the meeting on April 24 at the Cherry School that we should not be so quick to challenge Abrahamson's lack of license when most of us did not hold K–12 licenses for our K–12 jobs. When I reminded him of the 1991 statute on that issue, it was clear he intended to ignore the law.

The possibility of retaliation against us first entered our discussions after Langan left that April 24 meeting. By April 29, there was no doubt!

All principals got e-mails from that morning from Langan, with the agenda for a principals' meeting the next day. The e-mail read, "What will be the recommendation of the principals regarding K–12 licensure in accord with State Board Rule? It will be imperative that closure be reached on the issue." *Imperative* sounded ominous to all of us.

Our group caucused after the April 30 principals' meeting with Langan. During a general discussion of Langan's tactics on the licensure issue, it became evident that in addition to coming after our licenses, he was stepping up activity against individuals as well.

Tower principal Gary Friedlieb complained about a written evaluation he had received from Langan the day before. Langan wrote that Gary was immature and that, "Gary has no clue about budget process." Albrook principal Bob Larson had received a nasty write up from Langan on April 25 about the custodians in his building. Langan had just written up Cherry principal Cindy Jindra about her handling of a district-wide music program in her school.

On May 4, principals received a formal memo from Langan. He indicated that that he had talked to the local press about our principals' licenses. "It is unfortunate that the issue has become public at this time. However, when the specific State Board Rule (3512) is brought up at a public meeting, the only response to make is one of candor and fact. I know each of you are approaching licensure from the basis of your own prior training. I will need your specific plan to me by May 8, 1998, so I may better respond with specifics, if this becomes necessary."

Several principals called me in a panic. Most had either elementary or secondary principal's licenses, like mine. But, as I stressed to them, the 1991 law covered us; our licenses were grandfathered in. However, several of our principals were non-tenured and very stressed by Langan's directives.

The next day I contacted the Minnesota Association of Secondary School Principals and the Minnesota Department of Children, Families and Learning (CFL) for help. CFL personnel director Donald Krukow wrote to Langan. "This letter is intended to clarify a distinction between Minnesota Statutes 123.34, subd. 10 allowing the use of either elementary or secondary principals in K–12 schools and the requirements for a license as a K–12 principal under Minnesota Rules 3512.0200."

Langan scratched a note on the bottom of Krukow's letter, "From the tone of Don's letter, either a K–6 or 7–12 principal license will suffice."

On May 7, I got an e-mail from Cindy Jindra. "Thanks for the update. I really admire your tenacity and knowledge in all of this. I can see why you were successful in your suits in the past—you do get your ducks in a row. Thanks for being such an articulate spokesperson."

But Langan wasn't done with us. On May 14, the buildings received bundles of 10-page packets addressed to all teachers and principals in the district. The cover letter read:

"The primary function of any administrator is the support of the professional staff in the performance of their professional responsibilities. Unless we make some sort of effort to determine how well the professional staff perceives this support, as administrators we will simply wander around in a cloud of our own speculation.

"Attached is a survey form that is based upon specific knowledge, skills, and abilities for K–12 administrators as established by the Minnesota State Board of Education. Please complete the survey, place in the attached envelope, seal, and return to your building administrator by Friday, May 22, 1998. The surveys will then be delivered to my office where I will open them and do the data summary. A report will be generated for each building principal, with strong encouragement to share the report with building faculty.

"The only identification will be area of assignment – either 'elementary' or 'secondary' or 'K–12' and building assignment."

This was a first. It came out of the blue with no warning or discussion. After discussions with the rest of the principals' group, I e-mailed a response to Langan's "shot across our bow." I indicated that while we had no trouble with the concept, we had many concerns with its proposed implementation. It was a spur of the moment directive. It was a long document, with 90 items for evaluation. Teachers were in their last 10 days of school, their busiest time of the year. They would be rushed to finish it and would not have the time for serious consideration.

We also wanted an outside source to do the receiving, tabulating, and summarizing. *Obviously we did not have a trusting relationship with Langan.* We wanted to know what would be done with the results. We suggested that a similar process be used for central office administrators as well. We were certain Langan's purpose was intimidation and retaliation for our challenges on the hiring of Abrahamson.

He succeeded.

Without some assurance of how the results would be used, we were very vulnerable. Just doing their job, principals should have some staff members unhappy at any given time. At that time we were writing end-of-the-year evaluations, delivering layoff notices for the following

year, or cutting budget requests. We felt like we were being set up,
another tactic in his campaign to bring us under control.

I had personal reasons to worry about Langan's retaliation. I had
a personal leave request waiting for his approval. Max was graduating
with honors from the Air Force Academy at the end of the month.
Rick, Erik, and I planned to attend. Both sons had been out of the
home for four years and we had little opportunity to get together. Max
had limited leave from the Academy and Erik was constantly battling
deadlines on his software design projects. This would be a great
celebration and reunion. I needed Langan's approval on my personal
leave request. After a few stalls and hurdles, he finally approved.

Erik had to bail on the trip at the last minute due to another
deadline, but Rick and I flew to Colorado Springs for the ceremonies.
We participated in a full week of more pomp and circumstance than
we had ever seen, including parades, concerts, Air Force fly-overs,
parachute jumpers, and a thrilling performance by the Air Force
Thunderbirds. Max won several awards, graduating twelfth in his
class, with Academic and Military Distinction. He was also awarded
a fellowship to study in France for the next two years. We were very
proud of him.

I was just back from the celebration when for some reason, Langan
dropped his teacher evaluation of the principals project. It was never
implemented and no explanation was ever given. Perhaps Langan's
only goal was to demonstrate what he could do if we didn't come
around on his unethical hiring of Abrahamson.

I use the term "unethical" in reference to the permanent rules
relating to a Minnesota Code of Ethics for School Administrators.
This new set of rules specifically addressed the Abrahamson/Langan
issue. It stated, "A school administrator shall not knowingly falsify
or misrepresent records or facts relating to the administrator's
qualifications or to the qualifications of other staff or personnel." It
further stated, "A school administrator, in filling positions requiring
licensure, shall employ, recommend for employment, and assign only
appropriately licensed personnel."

The consequences for violating the Code of Ethics included

suspension or revocation of licensure. *Why would Langan take such risks to hire an unlicensed administrator?* I wondered again.

Langan's hire of Abrahamson made even less sense when Langan recommended John Metsa for the open principal position in Babbitt on July 28, just three months after hiring Abrahamson. Metsa had been an applicant for the Cook position (one of the licensed applicants Langan had told the board he was unhappy with when he recommended Abrahamson). The recommendation to hire Metsa read, "Mr. Metsa is a currently licensed elementary principal." The elementary license recommendation contradicted the hassles Langan was giving our group on the lack of K–12 licensure. Several principals held the same elementary administrative licensure as Metsa.

On August 10, Langan recommended Lisa Nelson as principal for the Albrook School. In his recommendation to hire Nelson, Langan said, "I called her references and with no exception received exceedingly high comments on her ability to work effectively with staff, students, and parents. Based on her excellent academic record (straight 4.0), her successful professional experience in demanding assignments, the review of her references, and the strength of her interview, I have no hesitation is giving the school board a recommendation for hire."

Lisa Nelson had also applied and interviewed for the position in Cook (another one of the licensed applicants Langan had told the board he was unhappy with when he recommended Abrahamson). So by August, Langan had hired two new, licensed principals he didn't like in April, when he hired unlicensed Abrahamson. Apparently for Langan, what was true one day was not true the next. For Langan, truth was relative to time, circumstance, and his hidden agenda.

Nelson replaced Bob Larson as the Albrook principal. Larson was the most senior and experienced principal in the district. Larson and I had negotiated the last two principals' contracts and led the complaints against the hiring of Abrahamson. Larson had angered Albrook board member Larry Anderson by sending his children to a private school in Duluth. Langan and chairman Larry Anderson put significant, negative pressure on Larson and he opted to go back in the classroom.

Langan's inducements to Larson included the additional assignment of Community Education Director for the district, with compensation set high enough to keep his salary at the principal's level. These were additional tactics in Langan's control arsenal. He rewarded his friends and got rid of his opposition, one way or the other, carrots and/or sticks.

When Lisa Nelson told me that her February 23, 1998, application had originally been for the Cook position, I urged her to file an EEOC complaint and challenge Abrahamson's April 27, 1998, hiring. Abrahamson was unlicensed and clearly a less-qualified man. Nelson had known Langan before he hired her, so perhaps she understood the price of crossing him. In addition, she was new to the principal's job in Albrook and did not want to rock the boat.

Langan added a part-time dean of students to assist Nelson after she was hired. Yet three months earlier, Langan had denied Marconett's request for a dean of students at the Cook School, which was 100 students larger.

With Langan, some received and some did not, depending on his control agenda.

Chapter 10

1999

INVOLUNTARY TRANSFER

"Judy Pearson Reassigned to Tower-Soudan School" Timberjay
August 14, 1999

IN LESS THAN A year, Langan had pushed out two
principals.

Albrook Principal Bob Larson and Cook Principal Jane Marconett
had left their administrative positions by the start of the 1998 school
year as a result of pressures brought to bear by Langan.

Now Langan started in on the other principals.

On November 5, Cindy Jindra received a letter of reprimand from
Langan. It concerned the fact that one of the three major candidates
for governor had called and offered to stop and talk to students at
the Cherry School. She called Langan to seek permission. He was out
of the office, but Assistant Superintendent Sid Simonson took the
call and supported the idea. As a result, Jindra allowed Jesse Ventura
to speak to any students who were interested. A large majority of
students attended the assembly.

Langan was angry about Ventura's visit. He took it out on Jindra
in a letter of reprimand.

Langan's letter read:

"It is my judgment that your decisions regarding this event demonstrated a complete disregard for the notion of a political forum, and the doctrine of protected and limited forum as this relates to public schools. It further demonstrated a complete disregard for the political realities surrounding the 1998 governor's race in Minnesota.

"We have discussed several times the need to assess any and all decision making prior to implementation. It is my judgment that you too often execute poorly framed decisions in several areas of your administration. The above incident, although significant in and of itself, is in my judgment indicative of an absence of decision making skills essential for successful school administration."

Jindra called me after receiving the letter. She was angry and demoralized. It was a scathing and devastating general assessment. It was full of undocumented and unsupported assertions and sweeping generalizations. Langan's pen cut like a samurai sword. I assured her that as grievance chair for our principals' organization, I would help her file a grievance to have it removed from her file.

On November 23 we met with Langan in a grievance hearing. On December 7 Langan sent Jindra a memo stating that the reprimand would be removed from her file. She felt vindicated on that specific issue, but remained concerned about his general evaluation of her performance. Those kinds of comments from a supervisor are guaranteed to eat away at one's self-confidence. Removing them from a personnel file doesn't remove them from one's memory.

Peter Jurkovich was also a principal in our district and in our bargaining unit. He was not assigned to a building, but had several district-wide responsibilities. He had joined the St. Louis County School District with the Tower-Soudan consolidation in 1993. Jurkovich had an unfair labor practice lawsuit pending against the Tower-Soudan district and the St. Louis County School District inherited the lawsuit at the time of consolidation.

The December 17, 1998, *Cook News Herald* announced that the Jurkovich lawsuit was settled. If Jurkovich agreed to retire immediately, the district agreed to pay him $63,000 and pay his full family health insurance until age 65. With that settlement, Langan had disposed of another principal.

Cindy Jindra had good reason to remain worried about Langan. So did I. In January 1999, Langan had completed six-page written evaluations of all principals. Jindra and I received the lowest ratings. Gary Friedlieb, non-tenure principal at Tower-Soudan, received the highest ratings.

Langan's written comments on my evaluation were astounding. In reference to district priorities, he rated me low and wrote, "You must either adapt to them or "leadership" becomes "sedition.""

This was a first. In thirty years, I had never received less than an excellent evaluation from my supervisors. I had certainly never been called seditious. Sedition is defined as the prompting or urging of resistance to lawful authority. *What if the authority is wrong? Doesn't that obligate resistance?* I mumbled to myself.

Langan gave no specifics in any of his comments, but I suspected this referred to our budget disagreements, as did his next item. "You have a strong understanding of the use of data in decision making. However, your decisions too often are made contrary to these understandings." *No specifics, so that must refer to my victory for the smaller schools with my fixed cost analysis and the "discord" I had sown in his new budget process?*

No doubt he held a grudge about losing our budget battle in his comments on resource allocation. "This is your weakest area. Your performance in managing fiscal resources and requisite procedures is unsatisfactory. Your comments relevant to this standard, and your attitude as perceived by district office staff are counterproductive."

Whoosh, his samurai pen swings again.

However, I was stunned by his comments on legal and regulatory applications. He rated me "very low" and wrote, "You have a tendency to adhere to those rules and statutes (usually regulatory federal and state statute), and an equal tendency to either limit or ignore the importance of policy when these are contrary to the course of action you have deemed most appropriate." I couldn't believe it. *I get a low rating because I adhere to state and federal laws? Which laws? I wondered. Federal laws against discrimination? State laws and rules on hiring licensed personnel? Open Meeting Laws?*

Of course I refused to sign the evaluation and wrote a response to this evaluation, requesting specifics to all his sweeping generalizations. In truth, I was not terribly upset by his harsh words. I found his negative comments somewhat flattering. You can judge a person's character as much by their critics as you can by their supporters. Some enemies you have to be proud of because you earned them the hard way.

Langan's tactics of deception and subterfuge, of rewarding friends and punishing adversaries were becoming well known throughout the district. He tolerated no dissent and disliked anyone who stood up to him. I had zero respect for his integrity. Had a supervisor I respected written those harsh comments, I would have been very concerned.

Former Superintendent Mobilia, whom I did respect, called my office on January 13, 1999. He had been contacted by the superintendent's secretary and asked to get in touch with Colosimo, the district's attorney, "about Judy Pearson." He called me to find out what it was about. I explained that I had filed a complaint on the way Simonson and Langan had been hired and that might explain the call he received.

The rest of the conversation was remarkable. He had told me earlier that Chet Larson was the spoiler for me in the first round of superintendent selection. Now he volunteered more of the story.

"The deal was cut at Ludlow's," he said. "You know, Chet supported Zitterkopf and was angry with me when I questioned Zitterkopf's competence. He voted against Langan, you know. When Langan pulled out, Chet pushed Sid."

"What kind of deal?" I asked, grabbing for more notepaper.

"Chet was pushing at Ludlow's to hire Sid as permanent superintendent after Langan turned it down. Chet pushed Simonson right after Zitterkopf left. He told me to set up the meeting with Simonson and Langan. He had the assistant deal cooked for Simonson before the Tower meeting. Rolland (Fowler, board member from

Babbitt) made the motion right off the bat, before I could recommend posting the position," Dan said. "They never listened to me."

"Then Jim (Techar, principal from Babbitt) called me from Ludlow's and warned me they were meeting behind closed doors," he continued.

"Who was meeting?" I asked.

"Chet was meeting with Sid for sure, maybe Rolland and other board members," Dan responded.

"But didn't you go up one morning and meet with them?" I asked.

"Of course I did. I got a call the night before from the Duluth reporter and he told me Chet told him Sid was going to be the superintendent. So I got in my car first thing and drove up there to stop them. They weren't going to have a closed meeting on my watch."

"What happened," I asked, frantically scribbling notes.

"We had words. I told them Sid wasn't very competent and he had a bad history. They wouldn't listen and I was really hurt by the way they treated me. They agreed to hold a special meeting for Interim so it would be official board action."

Most of my suspicions were confirmed. But I had more questions about the sequence of events. Before I could ask, Dan brought Sid up again. Other superintendents would joke with him about having Sid on his staff.

"He's useless," Dan said. "He's a womanizer, he's still doing it. I could tell you stories that would curl your hair," he declared.

"Please don't bother," I said jokingly.

"How did Langan get back into the process in the second superintendent search?" I asked, trying to keep the sequence going. I was learning a lot about what had happened.

"That's an interesting story," Dan chuckled. "I met the pig farmer, Clement, at the casino on my way back from an IRRRC meeting in Bloomington. He told me that Salmela had found out bad things about Sid and they had to get rid of him. He asked me to call Larry Anderson, the school board chairman. Larry confirmed that they couldn't hire Sid as superintendent. I suggested he call Langan and make a more generous offer."

What about me? The words screamed silently in the back of my mind. *Why didn't you recommend me?* I wanted to ask but was afraid it would shut down the conversation.

"Did he call Langan?" I asked.

"Well, Larry asked me to make the call and asked if I would consult in the process. I told him that it could cost between $8,000 and $10,000 for a consultant but I'd help them out for $3,000. I was looking for some name recognition and credentials in the consulting business so I could do some work for other districts."

"So you called Langan?" I asked.

"I talked to him and he was interested." Dan said. "The next thing I knew, the board had hired Langan. They cut me out of the process," he said bitterly.

"I'm not doing anything for that board again unless they pay me," he concluded, ending the 45-minute conversation.

It was no surprise that Mobilia had tried to use the district's dilemma to get in on the consulting business. No one survives two decades working with lay boards as superintendent of schools, without becoming skilled at looking out for number one. Mobilia was very good at it. *But why is he volunteering all of this now? Didn't I just tell him I had filed the complaint? Obviously, he's angry with the board and using me to get back at them. Fine, works for me too!*

I wonder what his answer would have been to the *why not me* question if I dared to ask it? Sure, I didn't want to interrupt the dynamic of the conversation, but maybe I was just afraid of his answer. What if he'd said he didn't think I could handle the job? His opinion mattered and that would have hurt too deep to risk? What if he'd said no way, no chance because of my previous lawsuit? I wish I had asked.

I also wondered what he'd have said if I'd had asked his opinion before applying for the superintendent's position back when I first applied in 1997. What would I have done if he had answered candidly and told me Chet and the board would never consider me for any promotion because of the lawsuit? Would I have reacted to that information and challenged on the spot? Any chance I would have had the serenity to accept what I couldn't change? What would have been the wise thing to do? Just questions, no answers.

Cotton Principal Walt Fischer called me in the Orr office on February 1, 1999, regarding additional copies of the 1997–1999 Principals' contract. We had finally settled in December, a year and a half late and just months from beginning negotiations for the 1999–2001 contract. In the course of the conversation he told me that someone–he refused to say who–had gotten a copy of an eight-page license report on Simonson and turned it over to the school district's attorney.

I called CFL immediately. This time I was told it was public information and it would be sent to me. It came the next day. The department had stalled me twice in June 1997, so I was surprised to get it. It was a shocking read!

The document was a stipulation agreement between Simonson and the Minnesota Board of Teaching and the State Board of Education. The facts described in the agreement included the October 8, 1990, Glenwood School Board action proposing immediate discharge of Assistant Superintendent Simonson under MS 125.12, subd. 8. Grounds for immediate discharge under that section include immoral conduct and conduct unbecoming a teacher. Simonson requested a hearing as provided by statute, but resigned before any hearing could take place.

There were allegations by three separate district employees in the document that Simonson had "exposed his genitals." There was an allegation that Simonson appeared "naked" to a district employee in his home. There were two complaints by a district employee of physical assault. A Temporary Harassment Restraining Order was issued by the Pope County District Court against Simonson in 1991.

As a result of these allegations, the state Board of Teaching, the Board of Education, and Simonson agreed that he would have to produce three separate opinions from independent licensed and practicing psychologists and/or psychiatrists that he was fit to teach or he would lose his license. The opinions had to be from professionals trained and experienced in evaluating sexual perpetrators and persons with impulse control disorders. His license was suspended in February 1993 and not reinstated until November 1994.

I was devastated.

Mobilia had referred to stories that "would curl my hair." Was this what he was talking about? Did he and the board know this stuff when they hired him for Cook in 1996? Did they know this when they pulled him up secretly for the assistant superintendent and then interim superintendent positions? Exactly when did the district's attorney get this report and did the school board ever see it?

What's so wrong with me that they pass me over to hire a guy with this history? Am I the problem or is it women in general? The lawsuit alone couldn't be responsible for this kind of humiliating snub, could it?

I spent hours in brutal self-examination trying to figure out why I kept losing jobs or consideration to less qualified men. Putnam, Bangston, Gornick, Zitterkopf, and Simonson. And after one year, I had doubts about Langan's qualifications, at least on the issues of integrity and judgment. I had often joked that my application for superintendent would at least establish the lowest common denominator. *Guess I didn't realize how low that denominator would be,* I chuckled bitterly to myself.

The only people I showed this document to were Rick and Prebich.

"This is incredible," Rick blasted. "I can't believe this bullshit. You've got to get the hell out of this damn district. Stop taking calls from everyone who wants your help. If I take the call, I'm going to tell them all to go jump in the lake! It gets you nowhere. Quit putting in all the nights and weekends. If they'll hire a jerk like this instead of you, they don't appreciate what you do anyway."

Rick and I had been married for over 30 years and long ago learned to resolve any differences by talking things out. There was little tension in our relationship or in our home except from my job. Rick would explode over these things. Even though his anger was always directed at the district and in my defense, it introduced an element of stress at home that was difficult to escape. At least the boys were gone and we didn't have to worry so much about keeping the anger under wraps.

The only good thing about getting the license report on Simonson related to my EEOC complaint on the assistant and interim superintendent positions. This report strengthened my argument that the board had hired a less qualified man for both positions. I sent a copy of the report on Simonson to attorney Prebich.

We had heard nothing from the EEOC since receiving the district's response to the complaint months ago. Prebich was as astounded as I was to realize that the district had made Simonson a finalist for the top position with this stuff in his past. Prebich agreed that my *wouldn't/couldn't* hypothesis explained the board's bringing Langan back in at the last minute.

I had also found a fascinating document on the web. Every so often I checked the EEOC web site and other resources to learn more about the current status of retaliation precedents. The document I found on the EEOC site was Section 8 of the new Compliance Manual on Retaliation. It downloaded to 22 pages of fascinating reading. It described to a "T" everything I had experienced, from applying for a promotion to the negative evaluation.

The document explained the importance of legal protections against retaliation. "Voluntary compliance with and effective enforcement of the anti-discrimination statutes depends in large part on the initiative of individuals to oppose employment practices that they reasonably believe to be unlawful, and to file charges of discrimination. If retaliation for such activities were permitted to go unremedied, it would have a chilling effect upon the willingness of individuals to speak out against employment discrimination or to participate in the EEOC's administrative process or other employment discrimination proceedings."

When I shared the document with Prebich, he said it was as if they knew exactly what was going on here. *How could the EEOC have it so right?* I wondered. Unfortunately, I suspect the answer is because retaliation in one form or another is so common. It's too often the employer's first line of defense against complaints by employees. Retaliation is also easy, cheap, and effective.

I had yet to learn just how effective.

At 1:05 p.m. on Friday, March 5, 1999, I received an interesting e-mail from Langan. It was addressed and sent to all the principals, but written only to me. In response to a budget question asked by one of the other principals at a meeting the day before, Langan wrote, "Judy, I want you to prepare a brief report at our next administrators meeting depicting the FTE reductions Orr has made in both regular and special education using 1996–1997 as your base year up through and including your recommendations for 1999–2000 school year. I am hopeful that your data will aid in providing a clearer picture of how the district has responded to the need for staff reductions."

Eight minutes later, he sent another e-mail to all the principals directing us to review those sections of our contract that addressed principal assignments and transfers.

"I asked the question at the February 16, 1999, meeting if any principal would wish to be considered for a reassignment for 1999–2000 school year. I have received no response to this date. Given the fact that there does exist more than one or two factors that would impact on 1999–2000 assignments, I will be making my recommendations to the school board for 1999–2000 assignments at the first school board meeting in May. I would encourage principals to review Article III, Section 1; Article IV, Section 1; and Article XIII, Section 1 of your master agreement to familiarize, or re-familiarize yourself with the procedures and basis for principal assignments."

Before I left the office for the weekend, I got e-mails or calls from most of the other principals. They concluded from the timing of the two e-mails that I was on Langan's mind and I was likely to be transferred. Jindra's e-mail subject line read, "Go Gal!" She wrote, "So, Jude: Is there an underlying message in the latest messages received from the district office? My sense is that we are being warned that there will be some unpopular transfers made within the principal ranks for next year? What is the intent of gathering the data on reductions at Orr? Have a nice weekend! CJ"

I brushed their concerns aside. I could not conceive that Langan would transfer me involuntarily. I had an EEOC complaint pending and it would clearly be retaliation. Over that weekend, I spent hours reviewing Orr's staffing for the past four years, calculating FTE's, and writing the report. Rick was not a happy camper that weekend, because we had to put our plans to visit family on hold.

All for nothing! I was never asked to give the report at that next meeting or any other meeting. After that next meeting, several of the principals asked me why he hadn't asked for my report. All I could say was, "Ask Langan." I suspected that it was nuisance harassment, to keep me off balance and on the defensive. Knowing this did not relieve my frustration however. I had spent an entire weekend pouring through records and compiling the report.

Shortly after those two e-mails, Jindra decided to leave her principal position at the Cherry School. The negative evaluations and the veiled threats of transfers were clearly factors in her decision. Langan offered her part-time status doing curriculum work out of the central office to carry her over into her retirement benefits. Langan was a master of using carrots and sticks to get what he wanted.

I was sorry to see her leave because she was one of the few principals that would speak up at our meetings and stand her ground. But I think she felt she had lost the support of her supervisor and that can make the already difficult K–12 principal's job almost impossible.

My good luck in keeping a low public profile on my EEOC complaint was blown on March 20, 1999. Apparently a relative of the Orr board member was talking about it all over town. A reporter from the *Timberjay* came in to see me on March 15 and asked about the lawsuit I had filed against the district. He had heard about it downtown. I said it was not a lawsuit, just a complaint filed with the EEOC. The top headline on March 20 read, "Principal files job bias complaint."

Both the district and I declined to provide the newspaper with a copy of the complaint, so the publisher called the EEOC. He was told that the Minneapolis office handled over 1,100 complaints every year and most were found to be without merit and were not accepted for formal investigation. I had already overcome that hurdle.

On April 14, 1999, Rick Prebich called and told me that Bess Worden, the EEOC investigator assigned to my complaint, was beginning her investigation. She indicated that she hoped to have a decision within 30 days, but she had several witnesses to contact. She told Prebich that former superintendent Mobilia would be an important witness to interview. Finally, there was some movement. The events had occurred June through October 1997, almost two years earlier. Many board members, principals, and other witnesses had already left the district. *Same issues as the first lawsuit.*

On the afternoon of May 25, I had driven from Orr to the central office in Virginia for a collaborative board meeting.

As I left the meeting about 4:00 p.m., Langan stopped me in the hall and asked if he could see me for a few minutes in his office.

When I entered his office, he came out from behind his desk, shut his door and sat in another chair facing me.

"This is one of those conversations that never happened," he began. My stomach knotted and dropped like a lead balloon. *Now what,* I worried.

"You know, I'm getting a lot of pressure to transfer principals for next year, there's a lot of pressure from Orr."

"What or who is the pressure from Orr," I asked.

"Well, there's a significant number of folks in Orr that are unhappy with you."

"Who are they? How many are you talking about? What are their concerns? Why is this the first I'm hearing about it?" I pressed.

He ignored my questions and asked me if I was aware of the tentative arrangement made with Cindy Jindra. I indicated that I was and asked if the board would approve her deal. He said that they were positive on the concept and would approve.

"I'd like to go back to your comments about the complaints from Orr," I interjected. "You said there were significant numbers. I'd like to know how many, was it five or 30 or what?"

"One doesn't tend to quantify that kind of thing, but there's a lot."

Again I asked, "But were there as many as 30?"

"You know how these things work, you get the 11th call and they call the next person who becomes number 12 and so on." he evaded.

"Was it one issue with those 11 complaints you're referring to or eleven different complaints? What's the main issue?"

He paused. "Just what are your plans, your present thinking about retirement?" he asked, ignoring my question.

He just sat there, cool and relaxed with his legs crossed, twiddling his thumbs and not meeting my eyes. My heart was pounding as I struggled to match his calm, nonchalant decorum. I consciously sat back in my chair, trying to appear as relaxed as he was.

"I'm still frustrated by your references to complaints from Orr. If I don't know what the issues are or who has concerns, then I can't do anything to resolve things. That doesn't make any sense," I interjected.

"Are you familiar with the arrangements made for Pete Jurkovich?" he said, again ignoring my questions and moving his own agenda. "The provision he got for full family health insurance until age 65 might be doable for you. I did a rough calculation for you, in my head you understand because one doesn't want to put these kinds of ideas into a computer, and it would be about an $87,000 value."

I just sat there listening, thinking. Of course he'd never put any of this in writing because it's all a violation of our contract and state rules and laws.

"That amount of money by itself would never be acceptable, but as health insurance, which many districts have and Pete got, the concept might be acceptable. And this provision could be separate from the contract provision for severance," he pushed ahead.

"The health insurance is only one issue," I responded. "I have to make sure my pension is not hurt by retiring so early. That's what will make the biggest difference over the years."

"Some sort of arrangement like Jindra's might be worked out to increase your current earnings for pension calculations. If we adjusted your work calendar to indicate that you had your 219 contract days in by – say May 10 – then any days worked after that would be pay above your annual salary. It can be done, like the deal made with Mobilia where he got his final salary up to $98,000. That way, TRA (Teachers' Retirement Association) will accept it as salary and use it for your high-five pension calculation."

"Are you talking about right now, this year?" I asked.

"Yes, but I'd have to have such arrangements in place very soon so all the money can get appropriated before July 1. Why don't you think over what you'd need to go this year, something reasonable, and get back to me as soon as possible," he concluded.

I was just as shell-shocked leaving his office as I had been driving away from the Chamber of Commerce interview at Smitty's in Cook back in 1986, where it all began. Life had now flipped a full 180 degrees. In a year and a half, I had gone from glowing evaluations and Principal of the Year to "seditious" and a buy-out proposal, the kind reserved for incompetents that are too difficult to terminate.

Obviously he really wants me gone, I thought to myself. If I won't intimidate, he'll buy me out. He'll do anything to get his way, remove opposition, and consolidate control. As I drove home, I realized that there had been no mention of dropping my EEOC complaint, no *quid pro quo*. If his proposals were not part of a settlement, then most of what he suggested was illegal, fraudulent, or in violation of our contract. No wonder he had called it a "conversation that never happened."

I shared the conversation with Rick when I got home. We just laughed. I typed up my notes quickly before I forgot the specifics of his comments and suggestions. I faxed a copy to Prebich. He called the next day and asked, "What are you going to do?"

"Nothing," I answered. "Absolutely nothing. When I retire it will be my decision, not his. Besides, there was no deal or settlement proposed, so isn't most what he proposed illegal or unethical?"

"Well, maybe if you responded, dropping your complaint would be tied to the deal. Are you interested?"

"The most important issue for my retirement is the pension and nothing he suggested really addressed that. I'm not giving him the satisfaction of a reply. The meeting was an insult and I won't dignify it with a response. I won't be bought off," I replied angrily.

"Okay, okay," Prebich said, "I should have known. Forget about it. I agree that's the right thing to do anyway, but I had to ask. We'll notify the EEOC about this 'conversation that didn't happen.'"

Two days later, Langan struck again. This time his samurai pen was directed at one of my teachers. She lived in the Orr district and had complained to the Orr board member about some of Langan's hiring decisions. She was also an officer in the teachers' union. Distrust of Langan had led the teachers' union to have someone in attendance at every board meeting, to monitor his actions. She specifically asked about the elementary supervision and salary added to Marconett's assignment in Cook and the new dean of students position at the Albrook School. School Board approval of those two expenditures had never appeared in the published minutes. The board member knew nothing about them.

On May 27, Langan wrote to her, "Your action with regard to taking unfounded claims to a school board member without benefit of discussion through communication channels that we had hoped would be positive and open is certainly unprofessional, and does not reflect the mature and professional judgment I deem essential with a tenured faculty member. Should I be made aware of similar breaches of professional conduct in the future, you will be subject to disciplinary actions which can include suspension and dismissal."

She came into my office almost hysterical. I calmed her down and had her call the union president. He assured her that the union would grieve the letter and have it removed from her personnel file. *Who does he think he is? You can't fire someone for talking to her elected representative.*

Several months later the letter was in fact removed, but it had its desired effect. It doesn't take many shots like this to shut people up. It closed off all communication between board members and professional staff. To the question, "How can he get away with this?" that's part of the answer. The board doesn't know!

On June 2, 1999, principals received a notice from Langan. Once again, he was after our licenses. I assumed that the issue had been resolved a year ago when state personnel director Krukow sent a letter to Langan stating that state law allowed either elementary or secondary licensed principals to supervise K–12 schools. Langan's notice referred to a report from the state department that identified those principals that did not have K–12 licenses under the new state rules. It was another law versus rule, bureaucratic snafu for Langan to take advantage of and use against us.

Langan ignored the clarification he received the year before and used the recurring state confusion to threaten us again. A simple phone call to the state would have straightened it out. Instead, he wrote, "It is certainly regrettable and unfortunate that current members of the principals' bargaining unit have been identified by the Department of Children, Families and Learning as being inappropriately assigned to a K–12 Principal position. I will have no alternative but to declare these positions vacant and will notify you as required by Article III, Section 1 of the principals' agreement."

He spends so much time harassing us, I wonder if he ever gets any productive work done?

This time he was threatening our jobs. Langan had us fighting on several fronts simultaneously, constantly on the defensive. He was a master at these games.

Actually Langan was not threatening all our jobs this time, just mine. I hadn't responded to his buy-out, so this was his next step. There were only two secondary licenses remaining on the erroneous non-compliant list—his and mine. Langan had reported himself as the high school administrator in Cook, using his license to provide paper cover for Abrahamson's lack of any license. He could easily change that by assigning someone else, like he used Marconett's elementary license the year before.

I was the only one left.

The other principals had either left the job or spent the additional time and money to get the K–12 license.

We sent Langan's notice to the MASSP executive officer and asked for help. Fischer was our local president and on June 11, he received a response from the MASSP attorney. The letter read, "The June 2, 1999 letter from Superintendent Langan is astonishing. I think the letter may constitute an unfair labor practice and may give rise to a claim for damages. I would like to start an action on behalf of the unit against the district for the behavior of Superintendent Langan and the board in this matter."

It was reassuring to get such a quick and strong response from our state association. However, I was the only one at risk and I already had enough complaints and actions pending. I asked that they hold off doing anything until I got a response to this issue from the state department. I had already written, again, to director Krukow, asking specifically if I was appropriately licensed to supervise a K–12 building.

Meanwhile, the EEOC investigator was coming to town. Bess Worden called to say she would be coming to the area to interview witnesses June 21, 22, and 23. She wanted to meet with Prebich and me on the 21st. The school board announced a special closed board meeting on that same day to discuss threatened and pending litigation.

Prebich, Rick, and I met with her on June 21. I gave her a copy of the license report on Simonson, evidence that a less qualified man had been hired for assistant superintendent and then interim superintendent. I shared my notes from the telephone conversations with Mobilia about Chet Larson's role in keeping me out of the process and the deals cut at Ludlow's. We gave her a copy of the judge's ruling from the lawsuit that found Chet guilty of discrimination and conspiracy to discriminate. I made copies of the newspaper articles that documented the closed and illegal meetings that took place during the superintendent selection process.

I provided my notes on Langan's attempt to buy me out and the threatened transfer and license hassles. I brought a map of the district to help explain the geography and structure of the large school district. There was so much complexity to explain. I also referred to several parts of the EEOC retaliation guidelines. I warned her that witnesses still working in the district might be reluctant to talk, given the current retaliatory atmosphere in the district.

I quoted the guidelines that read, "Direct evidence of retaliation is rare. The most common method of proving that retaliation was the reason for an adverse action is through circumstantial evidence. A violation is established if there is circumstantial evidence raising an inference of retaliation and if the respondent fails to produce evidence of a legitimate, non-retaliatory reason for the challenged action, or if the reason advanced by the respondent is a pretext to hide the retaliatory motive."

Worden told us that she had already interviewed former superintendent Mobilia. He confirmed much of what he had told me about the events at the Ludlow retreat. When she asked him if I was kept out of the process because of the lawsuit, he remarked that, "Old wounds don't heal well."

Before leaving, I asked her if there would be any help from the EEOC if I got transferred. I thought it was all bluff, just more intimidation, but I was curious about her answer. She said if that happened, we should notify her right away because injunctive relief was possible. An injunction is a court order to stop an action, to guard against future injuries, rather than one that provides a remedy for past injuries. In other works, the district could be ordered not to transfer me.

In spite of the volume and complexity of information we had to convey, I felt that the interview had gone well. Worden followed along well and asked pertinent questions. She indicated that she would complete her interviews in the next few days. A finding should be issued within 30 days, but no longer than 60 days.

Hurray, finally!

I was so busy trying to keep up with Langan's current and harassing maneuvers, I seldom thought back to the events of 1997.

By July 1999, rumors of principal transfers were all over the district. Some principals heard I was going to be transferred to Cherry, to fill Jindra's spot. Others heard I was going to Tower. Two of the principals, Nelson at Albrook and Friedlieb at Tower, had requested transfers to Cherry, both to be closer to their homes. On July 27, Langan sent a memo to Friedlieb, Fischer (association President) and me.

The memo read, "The school board has approved hiring Steve Reznicek as an administrator within our district for the 1999–2000 school year. I am now in a position to make formal principal assignments. I want to meet with you in my office on Monday, August 2, 1999, at 10:00 a.m. to discuss potential assignments prior to any final decision on my part."

I did not want to leave the Orr School. The memo indicated that no final decisions had been made. I hoped to convince Langan to leave me in Orr.

At the meeting Langan indicated that the new guy, Reznicek, was a rookie and he didn't want a rookie in Cherry. He said he was planning to put Reznicek's K–12 license in Orr, me in Tower, and Friedlieb in Cherry, but wanted our input. He used the licensure issue and my lack of elementary principal licensure as a major part of his justification for the transfer.

I reminded him that Abrahamson was a rookie when he was hired with no licensure for Cook, the largest school in the district. Nelson was a rookie when she was hired for Albrook. I also indicated that it was just days before we reported to work, very late to make the transfers. Our contract provided that transfers would be made by June 15.

Distance was another issue in the transfers he proposed. While Friedlieb's transfer would bring him closer to his home, my transfer would add over 20 miles to my commute due to the roads I'd have to take. I suggested transferring Friedlieb to Cherry, but assigning Reznicek to Tower, much closer to his home in Hoyt Lakes. Orr was at least 50 miles further than Tower from Reznicek's home. Why add that additional drive time of more than an hour each way to the job for a rookie? It made no sense.

Langan indicated he'd think it over and make his decision by the end of the week. As he concluded the meeting, I asked him to reconsider and let me remain in Orr. Involuntary principal transfers had seldom been done in our district. I indicated that if I were involuntarily transferred, I would consider it retaliation for filing the complaint and would contact the EEOC. I wanted to preempt and deter the transfer and the battles that would follow.

Langan remained behind his desk as we left. He made no comment or reaction to my closing remarks. I had hoped that logic and reason would prevail, but I had a sinking feeling as I walked out. *His mind is made up and there's nothing I can do about it.*

I left the meeting to join Rick, Max, and Julie for a trip up the north shore of Lake Superior. When Max graduated from the Air Force Academy in 1998, he had been awarded a fellowship to study at the Sorbonne in Paris. He was home for a week with his fiancé, Julie Baldovini. Julie was studying veterinary medicine at a school near by and they had apartments in the same building. Talk about romantic, they met taking out the garbage.

Max had talked endlessly about her when he was home for Christmas. Erik even said at the time, "Sounds like this is the one. It's all over but the wedding." Erik was still baching it, but was as excited for Max as we were.

This was the first time Max had been able to bring Julie home to meet us, so the weekend had special significance for all of us.

We had a beautiful weather and a great day together. We walked the trails and took pictures at Gooseberry Falls for Julie to take home to show her family. We stopped at our favorite market, bought smoked salmon and trout, crackers and cheese, and had a wonderful picnic on the shores of Lake Superior. I worked hard that day to stuff the anxiety and prevent the threat of transfer from distracting us.

On Friday, August 6, I was waiting out at the mailbox when the mail truck arrived.

Langan's letter of assignment was in the mail and even as I read the convoluted document, I couldn't believe it!

I've included it in its entirety below because it is otherwise impossible to make clear the degree of Langan's manipulation on the license issues.

August 4, 1999

TO: Principals
FROM: Dr. Donald Langan, Superintendent
RE: 1999-2000 Principal Assignments

The following are principal position assignments for the 1999-2000 year.

AlBrook School   Lisa Nelson, Elementary Principal and
                            K-12 Student Management, Faculty and
                            Program Support (See Note "A")

Cotton School   Walter Fischer, K-12 Principal (See Note "A")

Cherry School   Gary Friedlieb, K-12 Principal

Cook School   Steve Reznicek, K-6 Principal with specific
                            responsibilities for evaluation of probationary
                            elementary faculty, if any; and Level I K-6 faculty
                            grievance response under Master Agreement
                            between ISD 2142 and EdMn.
                            Sid Simonson, 7-12 Principal with specific
                            responsibilities for evaluation of probationary
                            secondary school faculty, if any; and Level 1
                            7-12 faculty grievance response under Master
                            Agreement between ISD 2142 and EdMn.

Tower-Soudan School   Judy Pearson, 7-12 Principal and K-12 Student
                            Management and Faculty and Program Support.

Babbitt-Embarrass School John Metsa, K-12 Principal, and K-6 Principal
                            for Tower-Soudan School with specific
                            responsibilities for evaluation of probationary
                            elementary faculty, if any, and Level I K-6 faculty

grievance response under Master Agreement
between ISD 2142 – and EdMn.

Orr School   Steve Reznicek, K-12 Principal, and K-6
                          Elementary Principal for Cook School with
                          specific responsibilities for K-6 probationary
                          teachers, if any, and Level I K-6 faculty grievance
                          response under Master Agreement between ISD
                          2142 and EdMn.

Note "A"

AlBrook School will require a secondary licensed person to provide essential evaluation for probationary secondary faculty, if any; and level 17-12 faculty grievance response under Master Agreement between ISD 2142 and Ed Mn. This position is still undetermined until I can discuss it with Mr. Fischer. Either Mr. Fischer or I will assume these duties with the cooperation of Mrs. Nelson.

The above assignments are designed to (1) place professional personnel in those areas of assigned responsibilities which best reflect my judgment of the District's needs, and (2) achieve the license appropriate coverage for each site as has been determined by the Commissioner of Education, and (3) to keep all principals within the St. Louis County Principals Association whole.

It is understood that all assignments will be carried out with complete professionalism and in accord with school district mission, district policy, and contract obligations.

cc: School Board

I was transferred to Tower! Our contract year began August 9, so this transfer was effective on Monday—effective in two days!

It was the longest weekend of my life. I was in shock the whole time. Two days and report to Tower. I knew what had to be done, but I just couldn't believe it. Seven years of giving my all to the Orr School was completely down the drain. Worse yet, seven years of my work, my files, my personal and professional stuff was still sitting up in Orr.

That weekend was absolute chaos. Max and Julie were flying back to France early Monday and they wouldn't be home again for another year. We were hosting a huge family gathering Saturday, for folks to meet Julie and wish them bon voyage. It was supposed to be a happy celebration, but Langan's retaliatory transfer had soured even my personal life.

We all canceled our plans for the rest of that Friday and got the truck ready to go up and pack me out of Orr. Max and Julie interrupted their packing and took a big shopping list to Virginia for us. The list including files, folders, and hanging file boxes so I could organize the work stuff that was coming home. I was most concerned about my computer at work. The computer and software belonged to the district, but the hard-drive was full of my e-mail, files, and confidential work.

I put in a crisis call to Erik in Minneapolis. He's the computer wiz in the family. He said he would head home earlier than planned that day, pick up a new zip drive, zip disks, and bring his computers with extra cables so he could pull my files off the computer.

Before Rick and I drove to Orr, I called Prebich and told him about the transfer that was effective on Monday. He said he'd call Bess Worden at the EEOC and try to get an injunction. She had indicated an injunction was possible if there was retaliation for filing the complaint.

Rick and I headed up to Orr.

Once we were alone in the truck, Rick exploded.

"I can't believe that son of a bitch," he yelled at the top of his lungs. "I'd like to get my hands on him right about now!"

"Hopefully, the EEOC will come through with an injunction," I said. "In the meantime, let's please don't talk about it. With all the family stuff this weekend, we just have to put our head down and do what we have to do. We'll deal with it after Max and Julie are on their way. You've got to help me here or I'll never hold it together."

In Orr, there was no time to organize or sort anything. We tossed everything in boxes and left. The truck was jammed. I told the head custodian that I was taking the computer home to copy the files, but would have it back by Sunday night. When I showed her where I'd leave my keys on the desk for the new guy, I found mail on the desk from the district office for the new principal, Steve Reznicek. It had arrived in Orr on Wednesday, two days before I got my notice of assignment. Very interesting. Obviously everyone else knew about the decision before I did.

It was also obvious that our meeting with Langan to discuss "potential assignments" prior to any "final decision" was just smoke and mirrors, more of his control games.

Erik got home about 8:00 p.m. Friday night. He, Rick, and Max started working on the computers. It was chaotic. Our home computers were Macintosh; my office computer was a Gateway PC. Fortunately Erik brought his PC laptop with the drives and extra cables so he could do the job. But programs crashed, new installs took forever, and the night wore on. By 2:00 a.m. we crashed as well, with the work unfinished.

Erik worked all day Saturday, no visiting or socializing with the family. He stopped just long enough to join us for dinner. I think the family gathering went well. Everyone liked Julie and wished them well on their return trip. I remember almost none of it. I have no idea what I prepared for the dinner or who showed up. I had deliberately numbed down to get through the weekend.

Erik worked again Sunday, finishing about 5:00 p.m. He checked the district software to make sure it was ready for a new user and it was ready to go. Erik left right away because he was late to pick up his rider for the drive back to Minneapolis, where he had left all his deadline work to rush up and help us. We would have never retrieved my files without his help. We had lost some of my work and files in the process, but the Gateway from work was clean.

That night, while Max and Julie packed for their return to France, Rick and I drove to Orr to return the computer. Rick was so angry I was worried about him. We had held everything inside as much as possible at home. It's physically enervating to stuff that much anger and emotion. When we left the building for the silent drive home, I never looked back. I couldn't. I fought tears all the way home. I tried not to think about all the great people I'd worked so closely with in Orr. I knew if I let go, I'd ruin our last few hours with the kids. I was hurt, heartbroken, and humiliated. I was also furious and bitter.

I vowed I would never invest so much in my job again. I'd never be such a sucker again!

When we got home, we unloaded the boxes of Orr stuff we had packed and jammed in the truck on Friday. We moved the cars out of the garage, piled the boxes on the garage floor, shut the door, and left the mess. The boxes covered the entire floor of the two-stall garage. We were leaving early in the morning to drive Max and Julie to the airport. We needed to get back in time for me to report to the Tower-Soudan School. It would be days before I could get at the boxes and begin sorting.

Late that Sunday night, after everyone else had turned in, I wrote and faxed a grievance on the transfer to Langan's office. I didn't finish it until the early morning hours, so it was dated Monday, August 9. That was frustrating because every day counted. I wanted to get the process moving as fast as possible. If the request for an injunction failed, I'd have to try to get a reversal through the grievance process with the school board. I hoped to reverse the assignment before school started in three weeks.

Our contract provided a grievance procedure for disagreements involving interpretation of the contract or for an employee who has been treated inequitably. The grievance process had four levels. Level One was a hearing with the Superintendent, Level Two was a hearing with the school board, Level Three was mediation, and Level Four was arbitration.

Each step in the grievance had timelines of five to 30 days. I knew that the process would have to be expedited if there was any chance of a hearing with the school board before school started. I concluded my grievance by requesting that the grievance be moved directly to Level Two with a hearing at the next school board meeting.

I drove that first Monday afternoon to meet with Gary Friedlieb and local board member Andy Larson in Tower. It was the longest drive of my life. I was exhausted from the lack of sleep and emotional turmoil. I bitterly resented the loss of quality time with family over the weekend. I was so frustrated, hurt, and angry, I couldn't even cry. There was no release from the emotional pressure building. I knew if it boiled over or I broke down, I'd be lost. I had to just keep going, one step at a time.

When I got to Tower, Gary Friedlieb and Andy Larson (Board member from Tower-Soudan) were waiting for me. Gary was packing up for his move to Cherry.

"Hey Jude, I'm sorry about the way this worked out for you," Gary greeted me. "If I'd have known my request for a transfer to Cherry would do this to you, I'd have never done it."

"I didn't think it was going to work like this either," Andy Larson added. "Langan told me that the licensure issues were the reasons for the transfers, that he needed someone with K–6 in Orr to cover Cook for Abrahamson. The last I heard, Gary was going to stay here and you were going to Cherry."

Oh really! How is it that Abrahamson is not even mentioned in the letter of assignment? I raged to myself. *How ironic—or deliberate—that I had been pushing the challenges to Abrahamson's hire and now his lack of license was used to justify my transfer!*

"I don't think your request had anything to do with it," I responded to Gary, struggling to keep my composure. "Be happy, it's a great move for you, lots closer to home and to your kids' activities. Langan should have assigned the new guy, Reznicek, to Tower and left me in Orr. Orr's so far for Reznicek to drive, he'll never stay there for long and Orr will have another principal turnover."

"What are you going to do?" Gary asked.

"I filed a grievance this morning and asked to skip Level One. I'm hoping that I can get a hearing with the school board before school starts. The best resolution for all is to reassign Reznicek here in Tower and me back to Orr. You keep your transfer to Cherry."

Larson left and Gary invited me into the library where the secretary and custodians were having a going away party for him. Obviously they were going to miss him, although they knew he had requested the transfer. His wife and kids had come up to join in. Introductions were made and I made a hasty exit. Talk about feeling like a duck out of water. I needed to explain to the Tower staff that I was challenging my assignment to Tower, but that my challenge had nothing to do with Tower. I had nothing against Tower. I was challenging because it was deliberate retaliation. Gary's going away party was not the time or place for all that.

As I drove home, regrets flooded in. I never had the chance to say goodbye to all the folks I worked with and served in Orr for years. No going away party for me. I was definitely feeling sorry for myself. How was I possibly going to go to work the next day as the enthusiastic new leader for the Tower School? How could I convey my ambivalence about my new assignment without letting them down? What a nightmare! I kept telling myself, *You can do this, one day at a time, you can get through this.*

I've learned over the years that the school secretary is the center of the school universe. She lives in the community. An experienced secretary knows everyone and everything, past and present. She's the one continuity in a school as families, board members, teachers, superintendents, and principals come and go. After the principal, the secretary does more to set the tone in a building than any other employee.

The next day, I spent time with Priscilla Mickle, the Tower school secretary. She was one of the most senior employees in the school. We both smoked and the smoke breaks we took outside provided a more relaxed and informal setting to get to know each other. She was very bright and quick to grasp the complexities of my position when I explained why I was challenging the transfer.

She had experienced some tough harassment from a supervisor

years before and as a consequence, understood more than most what I was going through. I was very fortunate to have Priscilla to work with in Tower. Her understanding and support had a lot to do with my making it through, one day at a time.

She introduced me to her brother Terry Driscoll, the head custodian, for a tour of the building. He was as gracious and supportive as Priscilla. I will always be grateful for their understanding and supportive welcomes in those first tough days. Terry had been in the Air Force and was still in the reserves, so with Max serving in the Air Force, we had a common bond. Terry admitted to me just before I retired that he never believed he'd like working for a woman, but I had changed his mind. That's a compliment I treasure.

On August 10, I received an ominous memo from Langan in response to my grievance. It read, "Insofar as I find our Agreement silent on the issue of bypassing grievance levels, I am reluctant to abridge the grievance procedure. With this in mind, I would meet with you and a representative of your bargaining unit immediately following the administrative meeting on Monday, August 16, 1999, as approximately 4:00 p.m. in my office." Any chance of getting back to Orr before school started was out the window.

I received Langan's written explanation for my transfer two days later. A written explanation for such a transfer was required in our contract. "In my judgment the issues and needs of the Tower-Soudan School require a mature and experienced administrator. An assessment of the administrative resources available to the school district has led me to the conclusion that Mrs. Pearson, with her experience working with a racially diverse students population, her understanding of the complexities of organizational change, and her demonstrated commitment to success for small schools, would be the appropriate principal to be assigned to the Tower-Soudan School." *Interesting to compare with his negative comments a few months ago in my evaluation. And what about all the license bullshit in his letter of assignment?*

I knew I was sunk. Coming from Langan, this letter was pure Langanese. He would do anything or say anything to get his way.

First he used the rookie issue, then licensure. His convoluted letter of assignment to the principals had licensures assigned all over the district (see letter p. 251). That no one followed through on his contrived licensure assignments didn't seem to matter. He had repeatedly told board members and principals that licensure was the reason for the transfers, specifically an elementary principal license in Orr to cover Abrahamson in Cook who still had no administrative license of any kind and didn't even appear on the assignment letter for the Cook School. Another masterful job of Langan obfuscation.

Five months earlier in my performance evaluation, he referred to my leadership as "sedition." He also wrote, "Your vision of the goals and priorities of the school do not reflect the goals and priorities of the district. Your consistent use of the 'uniqueness' argument is counterproductive to your effectiveness as a school leader and you have a tendency to politicize too many aspects of a school's operations." Now I'm mature and experienced, understanding the complexities of organizational change, and have demonstrated commitment to success for small schools. *Which is it, asshole?* I fumed to myself. *You can't have it both ways.*

Meanwhile, word of my transfer had leaked out. Although teachers and students would not be back in the schools for another couple of weeks, my phone rang off the hook. Orr teachers called. They all knew it was retaliation and demanded, "How can he get away with this?" They wanted to know what they should do. Some threatened to withhold support from the new principal. I told them that would be absolutely the wrong thing to do. He was an innocent in this mess, a first year principal who did not deserve any undo hassle. I reminded them that the students come first and any kind of chaos with the start of school just hurt the kids.

They wanted to petition the school board. Parents, students, and former students called to work on the petitions. I explained several times that I had filed a grievance and that we should let the process take its course. I did not want any public display, meetings, or petitions. Such pressure would only serve to undermine the new principal and would not help my grievance process. It fact, it could backfire with the board. So while I really wanted to see Langan hung in effigy in the public square, I told them to do nothing.

The calls and expressions of support were hard to handle. I ended up consoling others while I seethed inside. There was one exception.

Totally out of the blue, on August 13, I received a copy of an amazing letter sent to Langan and the school board members. It was from the Nett Lake superintendent and school board. The letter read in part, "We understand that Mrs. Pearson has been rotated from Orr to another position. The board strongly feels this would not be in the best interest of the Nett Lake students attending Orr and respectfully request that Mrs. Pearson remain as principal at Orr. Mrs. Pearson has established an excellent rapport with the Nett Lake Community. However, it should not be overlooked that this has been accomplished over a course of years. The board feels the continuity that made this possible should be maintained. They also feel that, due to the high percentage of Nett Lake students attending Orr, their voice in support of keeping Mrs. Pearson should be given proportional weighting in the final decision."

I don't know how they found out about the transfer so quickly. The unsolicited letter was remarkable because it was so unlike the Nett Lake community to speak up so forcefully and with one voice like that. It reminded me of a naive question I was frequently asked. Knowing that I worked with an Indian community, colleagues would ask, "What are the Indian students like?" or "What do the Indian parents want?" I chuckled as I answered the same to each such query. "Which ones?" Indians are no more "of one mind" than are women or blacks.

The Nett Lake letter was the only bright spot in those dark days. I wasn't feeling well, but that was no surprise. I wasn't sleeping much. I was on edge all the time, even snapping at Rick. To his credit, he let it go, gave me space to get it together. He took over more of the cooking and shopping chores for the next few months. The good news is he enjoyed the cooking. The bad news is we ate only popcorn, chili, and venison stew.

My sadness over the loss of Orr competed with the stress of getting my administrative bearing in Tower. I spent hours every night sorting through the boxes and files in the garage, trying to get organized. I needed some of my work right away at Tower. Why reinvent the wheel on forms or formats I had reworked many times. Lots of stuff could be thrown out. Some I wanted to save. My personal stuff, pictures, posters, coffee pot, cups were mixed throughout the boxes.

I stopped to see the doctor on the way home on August 13. Of course my blood pressure was up again, so the medications were increased. I asked about some sort of pain reliever to ease the pain in my neck and shoulders. This resulted in a discussion of my stress levels. The doctor said if I couldn't quit the job causing it, I could try regular massage for some relief. The muscles had tightened into hard little knots, causing the pain.

In addition, the doctor gave me 10 little pills referred to as "astronaut pills." Apparently the pills were used by astronauts to make sure they got the necessary sleep they needed before a launch. They were called Ambien and they worked like a miracle. In fact, they worked so well, I only used them for a few nights and then tucked them away. If something is too good to be true, it's probably is—neither true nor good for you.

The brief respite I had enjoyed from publicity on the EEOC complaint was over. The area newspapers all covered the transfer. On August 14, the *Timberjay* had an article on the new principal in Orr. Assistant Superintendent Simonson told the paper I was transferred to Tower because there was a need for my experience and expertise in dealing with students from a variety of racial and cultural backgrounds.

In reference to my leaving Orr, the home school liaison officer for the Nett Lake School was quoted, "She was very instrumental in establishing a good working relationship between Nett Lake and Orr. Tower-Soudan is very lucky to get her. I hope her replacement will work with us to establish the same kind of relationship." The newspaper quoted a non-Indian parent of three sons, "She takes a strong stand on the uniqueness of each student. She doesn't coddle students; at the same time she'll challenge them and stand up for them."

On August 20, *The Tower News*, another local, weekly newspaper, wrote, "Ms. Pearson has had an enviable career in the field of education. The *News*, on behalf of the community, welcomes Ms. Pearson and wishes her much success and happiness here." That welcoming tone in Tower was repeated as teachers, parents, and community leaders stopped in to meet and greet me. They were also quick to share their concerns, many of which would have to be addressed in the months to come.

After a few weeks of better sleep, the sun was a bit brighter, the days a bit better. Tower was a new challenge. There were lots of problems to get a handle on. The learning curve is a healthy place to be. The old work ethic kicked in, in spite of what I had vowed leaving Orr. I needed to figure out what was working in Tower and what wasn't. I knew it would take time, but the issues were sufficiently intriguing to get me back on board at Tower.

Chapter 11

1999–2000
INTRANSIGENCE

*"The Commission has determined that its efforts to conciliate
this charge have been unsuccessful."*
EEOC Notice November 8, 1999

PREBICH AND I HAD both called Bess Worden, our
EEOC investigator and described the involuntary, retaliatory
transfer. We requested injunctive relief before school started. She
said she'd check out the circumstances and agency practice on
injunctions.

Within a few days, she called back and said the determination
was that the potential harm of the transfer was not great enough to
warrant an injunction. It's a good thing I didn't know that when I
got the transfer notice or I'd never have held it together over that
family weekend.

Worden said I'd have to file a separate complaint on the transfer.
She sent more forms, but I decided to hold off until I had a chance
to present my case to the school board. I hoped the board would see
the logic and switch Reznicek and me.

I had discussed the transfer directly with Reznicek, as well. He privately confirmed he would prefer the Tower assignment, which was 50 miles closer to his home in Hoyt Lakes. Hopefully the logic of that geography and the Nett Lake school board letter would convince the board to overrule Langan.

I was scheduled to meet with Langan for the Level One grievance meeting on August 16. He cancelled it without rescheduling, so I had to call the next day to reschedule. *He'll push the timelines any way he can,* I thought to myself. I pushed back and we met later on the 17th. I stressed the importance of continuity in the principal position, particularly in schools with high at-risk populations. The principal sets the tone and atmosphere in a school and at-risk students benefit from that stability more than most students.

I reminded Langan that I would not qualify for early retirement pension benefits for two years, until after my birthday in November 2001. Orr would benefit from my continuing there for at least two more years before I retired. Reznicek would not be interested in any long-term commitment to a school that was over two hours of drive time from his home. If Langan stayed with his current transfers and assignments, Orr would probably have three different principals in as many years.

Although he promised to reconsider his decision, I was not optimistic. On August 20, I got his response. "I have given the assignment issue major consideration over the past several weeks, and am compelled to recognize the fact that your service as principal to the Tower-Soudan site is the most appropriate assignment considering the needs of the specific site and the skills, abilities, and training of the principal available to address those needs – namely you." *More of his "baffle them with bullshit" routine.*

I had specifically requested in the original grievance that if necessary, the Level Two school board hearing be placed on the agenda for the next school board meeting. However, after denying my request at Level One, he did not schedule the board hearing until September 13 at the Cherry School. That was two weeks after the start of school. Timelines worked against me again.

I finally got a response on the license issue from Krukow, head of the state licensing department. On August 26, he wrote unequivocally, "The statute means that any one of the principal's licenses – an elementary license, a secondary license, or a K–12 license, would be appropriate for supervision of a K–12 building. If you hold one of these licenses, then you are properly licensed for assignment in a K–12 school building in the State of Minnesota." Unfortunately for me, this response was too late to prevent Langan from using licensure to justify my transfer to Tower—and screwing up licensure assignments throughout the district.

I knew that license had nothing to do with my transfer, except to obscure Langan's retaliation. If Krukow's letter had been received before August, Langan would have just invented some other smoke screen. It still felt good to have that precise language to shove in his face. And this was precisely what I intended to do at my school board hearing.

Almost breathless with excitement, Prebich called my office on August 27, 1999. He had just received the EEOC's Final Determination in their investigation of my complaint on discrimination and retaliation in the denial of promotions to Assistant Superintendent, Interim Superintendent, and Superintendent in 1997. He began reading it to me. I heard, "there is reasonable cause to believe there is a violation of Title VII." He kept reading, but I heard nothing after the words "reasonable cause." I finally stopped him and told him to fax it to me so I could read it carefully when I got home.

It was rewarding reading.

The EEOC found reasonable cause on discrimination and retaliation for both the Assistant and Interim Superintendent positions, but made no finding on the Superintendent position. No finding on the superintendent position was better than a dismissal. While I was disappointed in the lack of finding on the superintendent position, I felt vindicated and validated. Of course, there was no reference to the transfer. I hadn't filed that separate complaint yet. I was still hoping that the school board would overrule Langan's principal assignments.

The proposed conciliation agreement attached by the EEOC was remarkable. It contained seven items:

1. Back pay differential for the Assistant and Interim positions.
2. A permanent increase in my salary to that of Assistant Superintendent beginning on September 1, 1999.
3. Reimbursement for car allowance that the Assistant Superintendent received.
4. $100,000 in compensatory damages.
5. The same term life insurance as the Assistant Superintendent.
6. The same family health insurance coverage as the Assistant Superintendent.
7. The same retirement benefits as the Assistant Superintendent.

This was huge! The agreement included significant compensatory damages, forward pay, and benefit increases. Forward pay and benefits were rare even as jury awards in civil lawsuits. The relatively innocuous sounding phrase, "find reasonable cause," was amplified ten-fold by the broad and tough conciliation provisions.

However, the conciliation proposal contained no provision to pay my legal costs. I had already paid Prebich a thousand dollars and still owed over four thousand. Rick and I hashed it over and discussed it with Prebich. We decided to accept the conciliation agreement. I would be glad to have it all behind me. I had no desire to fight these issues any longer.

Chester Larson was off the board and his retaliatory behavior had faded from my memory. Chet's retaliation was frustrating because it had denied me equal opportunities. Langan's current retaliation was fresh and raw. He was aggressively coming after me. I needed to stay focused on fighting my transfer and Langan's day-to-day harassment.

Although I had urged colleagues and supporters to avoid any petitions or public display over my transfer, many came to the school board meeting at Cherry for the Level Two hearing. My grievance was the last item on the agenda, so we sat and waited through the entire meeting. Everyone was surprised when chairman Larry Anderson announced his resignation from the board, effective as soon as a replacement could be appointed.

To make certain I did not overlook any of Langan's red herrings or smoke screens, I wrote a three page written summary of the issues to the board. I read my summary and gave them copies. The packets of information I gave them included the recent letter from the state, clarifying the license issue once and for all.

I concluded with, "I want to state that I don't believe the stated reasons for my involuntary transfer were the real reasons. I believe I was transferred against my wishes in retaliation for my complaint to the EEOC and my complaints on the hiring of unlicensed Abrahamson to supervise the Cook School. I believe the transfer was another attempt to intimidate me into retiring early. However, the timing of my retirement is my decision and mine alone. I will continue to speak out if I believe that the policies or procedures of the district are in violation of law or contract or the best interests of students and communities."

It was late before my grievance was heard, but one young father from Nett Lake stuck it out and insisted on speaking. He told the board about attending the Orr School when he was a student and how much distrust and animosity there had been between Indian parents and students and the Orr School. He talked about the positive changes I had brought to the Orr School and he said trusted me with his daughter. He asked the board to keep me in Orr.

Langan responded. The September 16 *Cook News Herald* quoted Langan's comments. "He said there were three reasons he decided to transfer Pearson to T-S. One was because of the racial diversity of T-S and Pearson's record in dealing with this issue. He also spoke of her success in small schools and her ability to complete jobs. He said that Tower-Soudan definitely needs an expert administrator."

The race card had replaced the license justification and was Langan's current, politically correct camouflage. What a conniver!

There was a motion, a second, no discussion, no questions, and my grievance was denied unanimously. Unbelievable.

They ignored the evidence of Langan's deceptive license rationale, the logic of the geography for both Reznicek and me, and the input from the Nett Lake School Board, which paid tuition for 40% of Orr's students in grades 7–12. If they were so concerned about the issues of racial diversity, you'd think Langan or the board would at least have acknowledged the concerns of the Nett Lake community. They made no reference to the letter and the Nett Lake school board never received a response.

But this was the school board defending itself against my EEOC complaint and its recent determination in my favor. I'm sure they were told they had to keep a united front.

The board then went into a closed meeting with their attorney to discuss pending litigation, most likely, the EEOC conciliation proposal. The newly elected board member from Cherry, Liz Johnson, told me months later, that when they were discussing my transfer grievance before the Cherry meeting, she had said she thought I should stay in Orr. Langan and the other board members jumped all over her, filled her in on my original lawsuit, my current complaint and urged her to just go along.

The next day, I completed and sent a new EEOC complaint on the involuntary transfer to the EEOC. However, Langan had won the first round on my transfer. The school board had reinforced his retaliation. The next round on my transfer battle would be months or years away. I would not be going back to Orr.

The effect was devastating. Not so much for me, I had already committed to working on the new challenges at Tower. It was the school district itself that paid for my failure to prevail on the transfer grievance. My tenure and service was widely known throughout the district and the region. If he could get away with transferring me, he could do it to anyone. No one would challenge or speak up. The chilling silence would become pervasive.

I got e-mail that next day from a teacher in the district I hardly knew. She wrote, "I wasn't able to speak to you last night after your presentation. I thought you did a fabulous job and made all of the necessary points. It would seem the 'other side' either doesn't understand kids and communities or is so caught up in power games that they choose to put their own interests and needs first. It seems to me that these people make a difficult job virtually impossible to do in this district."

Everything would have to be fought the hard way and in the public eye. All the local newspapers weighed in, pro and con. The September 17 issue of *The Tower News* read, "Although we are really glad to have Judy Pearson take over the helm of the Tower-Soudan Schools we feel her grievance against Independent School District #2142 has serious merit. Yes, as Dr. Langan said, Tower-Soudan is in need of an expert administrator and it is universally recognized throughout the local community that Mrs. Pearson fills this requirement nicely. We are really glad to have her on our team! However, that does not change the fact that the school board could have better handled the transfers of principals."

The September 18 *Timberjay* reported on the board's rejection of my grievance, citing much of the Nett Lake letter in the article. The article was followed by a highlighted article in bold titled, "EEOC finds for Pearson." This was the first public news of the favorable EEOC determination. When the reporters called, I said as little as possible, referred them to Prebich. Neither of us wanted to fight the battle in the press.

The next issue of the *Cook News Herald* left no doubt where editor Gary Albertson stood on the issue. Of course, he never called Prebich or me for comment on the EEOC determination, as all the other papers had. His September 18 regular editorial read, "The time has come when we get rid of all the frivolous lawsuits in this country. A lot of people will file seemingly ridiculous lawsuits knowing that the insurance companies will pay off $10 to $15,000, just to get rid of it."

But the regular editorial wasn't enough, so he wrote a separate, highlighted editorial titled, "I Screwed Up!" In an amateurish attempt at irony, he wrote, "I just might have screwed up. I can remember looking for jobs and not getting them. I can remember thinking I would get promoted and not getting it. I could have taken the easy way out. If I didn't get the job, I could have gotten a lawyer and claimed I was being discriminated against. When I didn't get the promotion, I could have claimed discrimination. We have too many people who don't want to work for things they want, they want gifts."

If he thinks a lawsuit is the easy way out or a gift, he has no idea what he's talking about, I fumed. The pounding publicity was back, like blaring, brass riffs in the plaintiff blues.

Albertson's editorial diatribes on lawsuits never mentioned me by name, but they always appeared in the same issue as a news story on my lawsuit or complaint. He never grasped that it's not "frivolous" when the judge and jury or the EEOC find that discrimination took place. When his editorials appeared, friends and neighbors would alert me. "Albertson's after you again, better get a copy of the paper."

My battles with the district soon became more difficult and complicated. In November, I received a most depressing letter from the EEOC.

In August, I had agreed to the conciliation proposal, based on their determination of reasonable cause. This November 1999 EEOC letter read, "The Commission has determined that its efforts to conciliate this charge as required by Title VII of the Civil Rights Act of 1964, have been unsuccessful. The charge file will now be referred to the U. S. Department of Justice for review to determine whether the U. S. government will file suit on your behalf. If the Department of Justice decides not to file suit, it will issue to you a "Notice of Right to Sue" which would enable you to file suit in federal district court if you wish to pursue the matter further. If you receive such a Notice of Right to Sue, you must file suit within 90 days of your receipt of it.

"We regret that we have been unable to resolve this matter, but thank you for your cooperation throughout this process."

Queries to the EEOC indicated that the Justice Department review process could again take years and because only one complainant was involved, it was unlikely the Justice Department would elect to litigate on my behalf.

I was demoralized. The school district was getting away with simply refusing to conciliate—after a finding of probable cause! There would be no resolution, no justice unless I took the initiative and risked everything all over again. I just couldn't believe it. Something's wrong with this picture. They broke the laws but I'm the one who has to pay over and over. It was most depressing.

"I don't know what to do," I told Rick that evening. "It's hard to believe the district wants this to continue after that EEOC finding. Don't they realize that a tough determination like that is rare, that we've already crossed a pretty high threshold of proof with a finding like this?"

"I wouldn't give the jerks credit for realizing anything," Rick said. "Go ahead and get the Right to Sue. You can't let them get away with this crap."

"I know, but do we want to risk a lawsuit again?"

"Forgot about how bad that was. Those legal bills could have wiped us out, but this time we not risking the house. We've got enough equity built up. If you want to go ahead, do it! We're in this together, babe."

"It's not just about the money either. I just don't know about going through the whole process again. It's already ugly enough working with Langan, watching my back all the time. I can't imagine what it'll be like once the lawsuit is filed."

"I'm with you either way, whatever you decide," Rick said. "But I hate to think of them getting away with this crap."

"We're 100% on that issue."

If the prospects of another lawsuit weren't bad enough, life took another nasty turn for us. The daily drive to and from Tower was stressful, partly because of the continuing frustration over the transfer and partly because the road was so bad. A new, direct route from Cook to Tower was under construction and would not be completed for a year or more. I had to drive several miles south of Cook before turning east and heading to Tower. The road was full of hills and curves and narrow shoulders. As winter approached, it was clear the road would stay icy and treacherous for most of the six winter months.

When Max had left in August to fly back to France, he had insisted that I drive his car to Tower. We were storing his car for him while he was stationed overseas. He had a zippy little VW Jetta with far fewer miles that I had on my old Toyota. I finally agreed because his car also had a tape player. I spent hours copying my favorite tunes on tape. Elvis, Tennessee Ernie Ford, the Everly Brothers, Patsy Cline, Ricky Nelson, Joan Baez, the Kingston Trio, and the United States Air Force Academy Chorale helped me get to work everyday.

Max had auditioned and made the Chorale his first year at the Academy. The old, familiar patriotic tunes were better than any drug for lifting depression and creating a happier state of mind. If I was especially down, I'd just crank up the volume. I'm sure they heard me coming miles away.

One of my favorites was the USAFA Chorale's "God Bless the USA." The lyrics made me feel better about standing my ground. "And I'm proud to be an American where at least I know I'm free; and I won't forget the men who died who gave that right to me; and I'll gladly stand up next to you and defend her still today, cuz there ain't no doubt I love this land, God Bless The USA." I kept telling myself that I had to stand up and defend my rights. They're precious and worth fighting for.

We didn't want to add too many miles on Max's car, so after work on Friday, November 5, Rick and I drove to Virginia and bought a new car. Actually it was a used car, but it had low miles, a tape deck, and six cylinders. Max's Jetta and my old Toyota were both four cylinders and produced little heat. I froze everyday driving to work. The arthritis in my hands got worse all the time.

However, this car was a fancy Toyota Avalon and it had more buttons and power gadgets than we'd ever seen. It was our first automatic transmission. The owner's manual was like an encyclopedia. As we drove home with our new car, it was too dark to read the manual and the interior lights were a mystery. One button on the dash read ECT and the one next to it read PWR. We had no clue what they meant and no intention of trying them until we could read the manual.

All I wanted to do was crack my window so I could have a cigarette. Before we figured how to work my power window, Rick had all the windows down, the sunroof open and the trunk had popped open. We almost froze to death. The door locks clicked and some warning buzzer went off. We had no idea what that meant. We must have looked like a couple of drunks driving down the road. We felt like a couple of old fogies. We pulled over, laughed until we cried and had a leisurely smoke. A good laugh is always a healthy thing.

Apparently not healthy enough.

The next day, Saturday, November 6, was the first day of deer hunting season. For the first time in years Rick and I had not gone out. I was tired and Rick had web work to do.

After dinner, I was reading a novel at the table, while he worked in his office. I sensed a heaviness in my chest. My left arm ached in a strange way. I shook it off, but the feelings persisted. The heaviness and aching increased and I could no longer ignore it. I took an aspirin and told Rick I thought we'd better go to the hospital.

There was no crushing pain across my chest, but I knew something was wrong. These were sensations I'd never experienced before. By the time we got to the hospital, eight miles away, the heaviness and aching had increased to the point of discomfort. The doctor gave me a nitro pill, hooked up an IV, took an EKG and blood work. A couple of nitros had no effect and the discomfort increased. The enzyme tests and EKG were normal, but he wanted me to stay overnight for observation. The discomfort made it difficult to sleep. Late that night, the doctor ordered a nitro IV. Within a minute or two, the discomfort was gone.

That's one of those simultaneous good news, bad news contradictions. Good news, nitro worked, pain is gone. Bad news, nitro worked, there's a blockage.

The next morning, the doctor was concerned because the nitro IV had eliminated the discomfort. He ordered more tests and by that afternoon, the enzyme tests indicated that I'd had a heart attack. He made arrangements for me to be taken by ambulance to cardiac specialists in Duluth first thing Monday morning. It was scary. I remember reminding Rick where all the critical paperwork was at home, including the life insurance policies. He was scared as well.

He followed the ambulance to Duluth.

By 3:00 p.m. Monday afternoon, I was in and out of the cardiac cath lab, with two stents to open blocked arteries. I had been awake the entire time. The experience was remarkable. The cardiologist suggested I take some time off work and sent me home Tuesday morning. We got to Cook in time for a hair appointment I'd had for weeks. At Rick's insistence, I took the rest of that week off and cut back on the long days and evening duties for the next couple of weeks. I felt fine. This was nothing like the horror stories of heart attacks I had heard. It was deceptively easy considering the severity of the problem.

Nothing else was easy, though. I had filed a new EEOC complaint on the transfer after the school board denied my grievance. On December 21, 1999, I got a copy of Langan's school attorney Colosimo's response to the EEOC on my transfer complaint. The descriptions of the Tower situation and position were incredible. According to Colosimo's response, Gary Friedlieb had lots of problems at Tower during the past year and that's why he requested the transfer to Cherry.

Yet just months before in January, Langan had given Friedlieb the highest written evaluation of all the principals. Colosimo went on to describe the Tower school as a difficult administrative assignment, presenting unique challenges. Then he described, "the experience, certain unique qualities and special skills" I possessed to address and remediate the problems in Tower. *Interesting, because there was nothing about any 'unique qualities and special skills" in the written evaluation I got in January,* I thought to myself, *only sedition.*

It got better yet. After lauding my unique qualities and special skills, Colosimo argued that I should have taken the transfer as a compliment, a positive instead of a negative. *What an ingrate I was.*

The response concluded, "It is important for the investigator to know and understand that Ms. Pearson has frequently used the threat of a discrimination complaint any time she disagrees with a decision made by the superintendent or other administrators which may involve her. It makes it difficult to run a school district when you have to walk on eggshells when every time you assert a management right, you are threatened with a discrimination complaint or retaliation. It makes it difficult for a well intentioned superintendent to provide oversight to his school district and to otherwise do his job when you have a key administrative employee who is incorrigible and who feels that she can do whatever she pleases…with impunity." *Isn't this the old "attack the victim" fallacy?*

Now I am flattered! I chuckled. To suggest I made Langan walk on eggshells and warranted such powerful terms like impunity, incorrigible, and seditious from guys like these were the highest forms of flattery.

Meanwhile, my day job was back up to 60 hours a week and climbing. Basketball season was upon us. The nights filled up with supervisory duties. With boys' basketball games on Tuesdays and Fridays and girls' basketball games on Mondays and Thursdays, Rick joked that Wednesdays were his. After the heart attack, the Tower teaching staff was great about their supervisory assignments and I could often sneak out early, before the game was over. I'd actually be home by 10:00 p.m. on a good night.

While I had chuckled at the insults in Colosimo's response, there was some truth to the description of problems at Tower. Langan used these issues as pretextual explanations for my transfer. However, in truth, there were serious problems in Tower and as long as I was in there, I needed to address them.

Student discipline demanded more time than it had it Orr. The Tower building was old and reflected several different bond issues. There were outside doors everywhere. Although the school district had mandated a closed campus for all the schools at noon, the Orr School had an open campus when I arrived and I had been able to keep it open for high school students. Some went home at noon; most went downtown after eating in the cafeteria. There were always a few who would misbehave and there were occasional complaints. But by directing consequences to those few students who misbehaved, I had been able to keep the Orr campus open for the rest of the students.

It was clear to me that the closed campus in Tower was part of the problem. There were so many doors for kids to exit, it was impossible to enforce the closed campus rule. The doors could not be locked or blocked for safety reasons. In addition, on the schedule I inherited for 1999–2000, both gyms were scheduled during the elementary and secondary noon hours. On rainy or bitter cold days, the elementary students had to stay inside during their lunch period, but there was no place for them to go.

There was no supervised place for the high school students to stay inside either. They snuck out or roamed all over the building, disrupting the elementary classes that were in session during the high school lunch period. There was not enough supervision available to cover the entire building if the teachers were going to have the duty-free lunch period required in their contract. With inadequate supervision, there were constant problems from fights to locker theft to smoking in the building.

It was a mess. To sum it up, there was no space or place for any of the students to be supervised after they finished eating. They couldn't be contained in the cafeteria because it had to be cleaned and set up for the next lunch period. I took two steps to begin addressing the problem. It's almost impossible to completely change a K–12 building schedule in mid-year. I juggled and tinkered as much as I could with supervisory aid time and rescheduled the swimming pool and swimming instruction to free some gym time for elementary students to stay inside on bad days. I vowed that the following year, both gyms would be blocked off and left unscheduled during the lunch periods, as I had always done in Orr.

The second action was even more complicated. I explained the dilemma of the closed campus to Langan and asked to open the campus for grades 9-12, as it had been in Orr. Before I made the request, I queried several of the businesses downtown and community leaders. I received no objections from them. Most of them were surprised to hear it was a closed campus because the kids were down there everyday anyway.

Langan raised so many objections I almost folded the project. However, it hurt the kids and the school in many ways to have an unenforceable rule. Any unenforceable rule undermines general authority. This one rewarded the sneakiest and cleverest of the students who got away with leaving at noon regularly and often punished the conscientious students the first time they broke the rule.

So I kept at it. First Langan required me to survey the students, parents, and community. Then I had to have eligible students bring in signed parent permission slips. Finally, I had to present all the data at a school board meeting. After jumping through all his hoops, Langan recommended that the board take Tower's open campus under advisement.

I was exasperated. *Is he deliberately making it difficult for me to do my job?* I wondered. These kinds of obstacles had never been imposed on Orr and they still had an open campus. Three months after I started, the campus was finally open for high school students during their lunch period. There was a noticeable change in the lunch period atmosphere. Everyone benefited.

The high school students had more freedom. They could come and go during their lunch period without lying. The teachers had more freedom. I could ease up on assignments for noon supervision and allow some rotation. The unenforceable rule that had created an artificial tension between staff and students was gone. When dishonesty and deception are a pervasive part of the operating order, the institutional integrity suffers.

This brings me back to Langan.

With all his transfer rhetoric about the problems in Tower and my experience and special skills, one would assume he would support my recommendations to address the problems. To justify the transfer he called me "an expert administrator," but now he ignored my input. Instead, he erected one obstacle after another, making every initiative more difficult. Instead of administrative support, I got stalling and resistance. It was also clear that I'd have to waste precious time and effort covering my backside. He was watching for any opportunity to force me out.

In January 2000, following the failure of the EEOC's conciliation attempts, I received the Notice of Right to Sue from the U. S. Department of Justice on the assistant, interim, and superintendent

positions from 1997. After discussing it with Rick and consulting with
Prebich, we decided to request a second Notice of Right to Sue on
the transfer complaint, rather than wait two more years for another
investigation to be completed. Once we had both Notices, we could
consider filing a consolidated lawsuit on the whole works. It didn't
make sense to duplicate all the required filings and steps in an already
complicated process.

On January 12, 2000, the principals got another view of just how
far Langan would go to get rid of administrators who did not kowtow
to him. We had a principals' meeting that morning. Gary Friedlieb
and John Metsa were scheduled to meet with Langan after lunch for
another negotiations meeting on our 1999–2001 contract. Between
the two meetings, the principals grabbed lunch.

Albrook Principal Lisa Nelson had been on our negotiating team as
well, but she was leaving the district at the end of the month. She had
taken an administrative position with an independent charter school
that was much closer to her home. I declined the negotiating work
this time around because I suspected my adversarial relationship with
Langan and the board would hurt our group. I continued to construct
our proposals and do the statistical analysis for the negotiating team
behind the scenes.

"Langan told me that if Judy replaced me on the negotiating team,
it would cost the principals at least two percent on the contract,"
Nelson told us over lunch, confirming my suspicions. That didn't
surprise me, but the others were upset. Fischer wanted me to step in
for her anyway, because I had the most negotiating experience.

"They don't get to pick who negotiates for our side," Fischer said
angrily.

We hadn't arrived at the restaurant until 1:30 and at 2:00. Friedlieb
and Metsa had to leave for their negotiating meeting with Langan
before we were served. The rest of us stayed to finish lunch and wish
Nelson well. Before we left Virginia, we headed back to the central
office to collect district mail and see how the negotiating was going.
Friedlieb met us outside and said he was just coming to get us.

"Langan's given us a proposal you've got to see," he exclaimed.

Walt Fischer, Steve Reznicek, and I followed Friedlieb inside to find Metsa. The current and previous principals' contracts provided that all K–12 principals were paid the same salary. We had tried several times to get a step system, like the teachers had, that recognized experience. The district had always refused to discuss the issue.

"Langan's proposed a step schedule," Metsa announced.

He showed us his scratch notes from the meeting. Our existing annual salary was $64,927. Langan proposed a four-step schedule, from $67,686 for a principal with 0-1 years in the district, to $70,190 for 2-3 years, $72,787 for 4-6 years and $75,480 for 7 or more years in the district. A quick calculation indicated that those increases were between 4% on the bottom and 16% at the top. Langan's numbers were even higher than our opening proposal!

It looked too good to be true.

It was.

"There's one condition," Metsa continued. "This proposal is for this year only and it is depends on Judy declaring her intent to retire at the end of this year. Otherwise it's off the table."

There was stunned silence among the five of us and then everyone seemed to talk at once.

"That's not fair," said Walt.

"They can't do this, can they?" asked Steve.

"Isn't this an unfair labor practice?" asked Gary.

"You need to go back in there and reject this proposal in the strongest terms," said Walt.

They were all ready to reject the proposal on the spot. But I was thinking about it.

It had so much to offer for everyone. The heart attack had me thinking about early retirement anyway and Langan was no prize to work with. The salary increases were huge for everyone. In Langan's carefully calculated proposal, I was the only one qualifying for the top step. However, Walt would get the 12% increase and most of the others would get 8%. We had tried for years to get a step schedule and this was a foot in that door. We all realized that this was a divide and conquer tactic by Langan to force me out. Langan would get what he wanted, but maybe it could work for us as well.

What neither the group or Langan knew was that, as a result of the heart attack, I had already scheduled retirement meetings in March with the Minnesota State Teachers Retirement Association. I informed the group and asked them not to reject the offer on the spot and give me some time to check out my options. If there was any way I could go at the end of the year without jeopardizing my pension benefits, we might have a deal. They agreed to go back in and tell Langan and the board negotiators that we'd get back to them on the proposal.

The next day, Friedlieb sent us all e-mail outlining Langan's four-step contract proposal. He added a note to me. "On a personal note, I think it totally sucks that someone like you with 32+ years of dedicated, conscientious, productive, and valuable service in education can be put in the position of being strong-armed into early retirement, while the district holds your colleagues contractual hostages as you are forced to decide. Until things are precisely how you need them to be, don't worry about the rest of us, we'll support you however we can."

No doubt, everyone knew the score. Over the next two weeks I talked repeatedly to retirement specialists with both the state and Duluth retirement associations, where I had pension funds invested. Due to a provision in state law that applied to a small number of teachers working in 1968–1989, my state pension benefit would be determined by the greater of two different calculations. No matter how we crunched the numbers comparing my two options, I would lose between $1,200 and $1,400 per month in pension benefits if I retired at the end of the 1999–2000 school year. That's income for the rest of my life. I just couldn't do it at that cost.

I explained the numbers and told the group I couldn't afford to retire this year. By February, the step proposal and the big increases were gone. The salary for 1999–2000 finally settled at $67,848. Fischer lost $4,939; Friedlieb and Metsa each lost $2,342 because I wouldn't retire. Langan may have divided the numbers, but he hadn't divided or conquered our group. I never heard another word about those lost salary increases or steps from the group. At the tail end of the negotiating, Langan stuck in an additional memorandum we had not requested. The memorandum read:

"It is agreed that the $6,000 mentorship notice shall be waived for Judy Pearson for a period of 45 days following school board ratification of this agreement, February 28, 2000. Should the district receive written notice of Judy Pearson's retirement, effective June 30, 2000, within this 45 calendar day window, Judy Pearson would be granted a $6,000 mentorship stipend for the 1999–2000 school year." The original mentorship stipend in the contract required a two-year notice of intent to retire.

Langan really wanted me gone, sooner rather than later. He suggested that this memorandum was a favor to me, but we all knew better. I had already made it clear that I couldn't qualify for the Rule of 90 until at least November 2001. That was 16 months after the deadline in his memorandum. This was just another attempt to get rid of me at the end of the year. *Or did it imply a threat to deny me the mentorship stipend if I waited a year to retire?* I worried.

The heart attack, the additional time on the road, and the increasing stress of working with Langan had convinced Rick and I that I should go as soon as the pension numbers worked out. So on April 11, 2000, with Langan's arbitrary 45-day window in mind, I sent the district an advance notice of my intent to retire sometime after the 2000–2001 school year, depending on the pension calculations. It was a year later than Langan had stipulated in his contract memorandum, but if he had really inserted the memorandum for my benefit as he suggested, then he would allow the additional year.

At the end of January 2000, I had received several phone calls from Bob Eckhart with a group called Alternative Dispute Resolutions. Apparently the EEOC had contracted with their organization to try again to negotiate a settlement with the school district. I agreed to participate, but on March 21, Eckhart called to say that the district had refused to participate.

By the end of March, we had received the second Notice of Right to Sue on the transfer complaint. Prebich had prepared a complaint to file in Federal District Court.

"So, you really want to do this?" Rick asked late on March 27.

"I tried everything, I gave them every chance to settle this thing," I responded. "I don't know what else to do except drop the whole thing."

"Maybe that's the best thing to do. Just put in your time and get the hell out of this district."

"The truth is, that sounds pretty good to me," I said. "The problem is, I'm not sure I can live with the frustration of them getting off scot-free. It'll just fester and haunt me if I don't do something. This is the only option left."

"Let's do it then, sue them all and let the judge sort it out."

Prebich filed the lawsuit in Federal court the next day, combining both my Notices of Right to Sue. *Damn, no way but the hard way*, I guess.

Meanwhile, the problems I'd inherited in Tower continued to puzzle me. Like the Orr School, the Tower-Soudan School had a significant Indian student population. The biracial similarity ended there. I observed several differences that I could not explain. In the Orr School, there was interracial dating. There was none in Tower. In fact, a couple instances of interracial flirting had resulted in explosive conflicts. In Orr, most Indian students graduated. No Indian student had graduated from the Tower-Soudan School in decades.

In Orr, Indian students participated in all the school activities, including all athletics, band and choir, honor society, and homecoming royalty. There were no Indian students involved in any extra-curricular high school activities in Tower. I studied these patterns and I questioned whomever or whenever appropriate. I listened. There were no simple or easy explanations.

There were more Indian students in Orr than in Tower. That might have been part of the explanation. In the Orr High School, the Indian population was almost 50%; in Tower the K–12 Indian population averaged only 20%. Indian students in Tower were a numerical as well as a racial minority. I was also hearing more overtly racist comments than I had encountered in Orr, from students and parents on both sides of the racial divide. There was more racial tension in Tower.

Those tensions erupted on May 2, 2000.

A misunderstanding between two high school boys, one Indian and one white, led to a fight one morning. The conflict escalated like wildfire and by noon, most of the high school student body formed up on one side or the other. I pulled the six students—three Indian and three white (four boys and two girls)—who had actually thrown punches into my office. I brought the counselor, the mental health worker, and the school social worker into our meeting. Racial epithets and slurs from both sides had fueled the fire.

I learned long ago that the harshest, cruelest, most intolerant harassment between students takes place below the radar of supervisory eyes and ears. It happens in the unstructured times and unsupervised places, including washrooms, hallways, locker rooms, playgrounds, parking lots, buses, and cafeterias. Too often it never comes to the attention of teachers, aides, or drivers. No one tells. No kid wants to be called a crybaby, tattletale, snitch, or narc. This "below the radar" behavior surfaced repeatedly as we discussed the tensions that led up to the day's fights.

The kids apologized to one another for their poor behavior and seemed almost relieved to take their suspensions. Although the conflicts were resolved between the participants, I was concerned about the overall tension lingering in the school. All six students agreed to join me on stage to explain and apologize to the entire high school student body. I scheduled the assembly for the end of the day, so we could all leave on a positive note. It was tough for them, but they did a great job.

When I left for home late that day, I felt that the tensions had eased. I was wrong. At 9:15 p.m. that night a student called me at home. He had been hanging out with his buddies downtown and told me there was talk that the Indians were bringing guns to school the next day. His buddies were talking about what weapons they were going to bring to school in response.

I asked him where the talk had started. He said his mom had heard it at the beauty shop. Minutes later, the local police officer called. He had gotten several calls from Tower parents concerned about

fights and violence the next day. He asked me to consider closing
school the next day. I described the student assembly that afternoon
and indicated I felt the tensions had eased. I made no decision on
closing but told him I'd contact his callers and my own contacts on
the reservation before making any decision.

I made eight or ten phone calls in the next two hours, to parents
and students, both in Tower and on the reservation. One call led to
another, as I tried to find out what was going on. One source seemed
to be the beauty shop, but the owner was unconcerned, dismissing
the conversations as just gossip and rumors. The Indian parents and
contacts I talked to had not heard anything and said nothing was
happening on the reservation.

I called the police officer back and indicated that my best
information was that it was just rumors, that nothing serious was in
the wind. I indicated that I did not intend to close school, but would
be in the office early in the morning to monitor the situation.

"We got problems," Priscilla said as I walked into the office early
the next morning. "The phone's ringing off the hook and parents are
keeping their kids home. They're coming in to get their kids when
they get off the bus. Some are even stopping the buses on the road
and taking their kids off."

"What are they saying," I asked. "What have they heard?"

"They got phone calls this morning about trouble with the Indians,"
she replied. "They're scared and Indian parents are starting to come
in for their kids too."

By 10:00 a.m., we only had 35% of the K–12 student enrollment in
attendance. I meet with both Indian and white parents all morning,
explaining what I knew and assuring them there was nothing brewing
but rumors. After it settled, I spent the rest of the day and evening on
the phone, with Langan, Simonson, parents, and community leaders
in Tower and on the Vermilion reservation.

What I heard in these conversations was extremely troubling. The
rumors had taken off like a flash fire. The incidents at school the
day before had been blown entirely out of proportion. People heard
one student had been taken to the hospital with broken bones and

another beaten unconscious. Three others heard downtown that I had confiscated a gun from one of the Indian girl's backpacks and found it loaded with five bullets. One father told me, "The Indians were all drunk on the rez last night and they're bringing guns to school today."

The most frequent and troubling comments referred to Columbine. The shootings at Columbine had happened a year earlier, on April 20, 1999. Two weeks earlier, the media had covered that anniversary extensively. They replayed the Columbine horror incessantly along with every other school shooting in their archives. It was fresh again in everyone's mind. Everyone saw schools as dangerous places.

Local newspapers and TV stations called about the incident, often asking if I thought it could become another Columbine. FDR said in reference to the depression, "The only thing we have to fear is fear itself." It was so apt. I urged reporters and editors to downplay the incident and just refer to non-specific rumors.

My calls and meeting with parents paid off and the next day we were at close to full attendance. However, we needed to address the depth of fear, emotion, and racial prejudice underlying the incident. A week later, after a sense of normalcy settled in, we held a large public meeting in the school library. Sixty-five people attended, from both Tower and the Vermilion reservation. Langan moderated so I could listen and take notes.

The most common complaints from Tower parents were that the Indian kids were always in the hallways during class, that they had their own special room for socializing and they got too much extra help with schoolwork that other kids did not get. Indian parents and students voiced few complaints at the meeting, but brought up the names they were called, like "squaw" and "timber nigger." They also complained that teachers were always sending their kids out of class.

We explained why students were in the halls during classes. The Indian Education facility and support staff were mandated and funded by separate and dedicated Federal funding. We took time to explain that most students with learning disabilities, Indian or non-Indian, had IEP's (Individual Educational Plan) that specified they go to the special education teachers when they needed help. None of the explanations made any difference. The perception was that Indians got special treatment and the resentment was palpable. Perceptions often trump reality.

There were suggestions that a volunteer parents' group be formed to patrol the halls during the school day or that a uniform policeman be stationed in the school. Given the prejudiced and stereotypic comments I had been hearing, I could just imagine the kinds of confrontations that could result. The images gave me nightmares! I had to figure out a response that would work and not create additional problems.

As I wrestled with the events and comments of the past week, I came to a couple of conclusions. The Indian Education and the EBD (Emotional/Behavior Disorder) rooms were located next to each other, right inside the most frequently used public entrance to the school. This door was at the opposite end of the building from my office. Everyone who came to the school during the day used that door, passed those two rooms and walked the long, main hallway to get to the office.

Although the small communities of Tower and the Vermilion Reservation were only a few miles apart, there was little interaction between members of the two communities. I suspected that the most contact Tower folks had with Indian kids or parents was right inside that school door.

By definition, the EBD classroom served students who had behavior or emotional problems. Student misbehavior too often greeted parents when they came into the school. The proximity of the two rooms connected the misbehavior with the Indian Education room, regardless of which students were out of line at the time. It was guilt by association. It was crystal clear to me that I had to move the Indian Education and EBD classrooms out of the public eye. I also wanted them closer to my office.

I spent the rest of the school year and most of the summer negotiating to accomplish those changes. This was more difficult than it sounds. I first met the Tower Indian Education Coordinator before school started in the fall. Her first words to me were, "You better not take the Indian Ed room away from us and try to stick us in the basement or you'll have a fight on your hands."

"Others tried before and failed," she warned.

This does not bode well, I thought at the time.

By May, she and I had established a more trusting relationship. I explained my observations about the public door and the flow of traffic in the main hallway, stressing the public misperceptions that led to the parent pullout in early May. I proposed changes in facilities for the school counselor, the Indian Education staff, and the special education staff. No program would be stuck in the basement and every program would have larger facilities.

No one was eager to move, but I kept at it, explaining my thinking again and again. Finally, they were all on board, even the Indian Ed coordinator. It would have been quicker and more efficient to just order the changes. Tricky changes are more likely to be successful in the long run if time is taken to bring others along, to share ownership. Arbitrary or unnecessary exercise of authority can leave lingering animosity, producing stealthy submariners who lay in wait to torpedo the project. There's undoubtedly a correlation between the amount of resistance to a proposed change and the time and/or effort required to build a consensus for that change.

The improved atmosphere in the Tower-Soudan School the next school year was beyond all my expectations. The combination of the open campus, the available gym space during the lunch periods, and the room changes worked wonders. It was a like a new school, like a cool rain had fallen on a simmering fire. The number of discipline incidents dropped dramatically. The halls were relatively quiet and the relocated staff all agreed it had worked out exceptionally well.

While I was busy that first spring trying to get a handle on Tower and putting out the daily brush fires, the lawsuit we had filed in March hit the fan.

The newspapers picked it up soon after it was filed. The April 14 issue of *The Tower News* headlined, "Principal Sues School District for

Sex Discrimination." The article contained a brief summary of the issues in my complaint to the Federal court. The April 15 *Timberjay*, headlined, "School District Slapped With $2 Million Suit. Pearson Lawsuit Alleges Sex Discrimination, Retaliation, and Closed Hiring Practices." That same issue of the *Timberjay* ran an editorial titled, "No Way To Run A School District." It read in part:

"Top officials with the St. Louis County school district have got some explaining to do. The lawsuit filed last week by School Principal Judy Pearson is a devastating indictment of the hiring practices of the school district as well as the treatment of those employees who raise objections to arbitrary and possibly illegal decision-making.

"Some of the allegations in the complaint are simply stunning – and none more so that the charge that Superintendent Don Langan offered all of the district's principals a sizable salary increase this year, but made it contingent on Pearson's resignation. If true, the school board should demand Langan's immediate resignation, since such a bizarre proposal could only be intended to undermine support for Pearson from the other principals, further adding to the hostility of Pearson's work environment.

"What's more, the district has had the opportunity to settle this case before it hit the court room, but has shown no willingness to do so. School officials rejected a conciliation proposal from the EEOC and later ignored the offer of a federally funded mediator.

"Is this any way to run a school district? Is the culture of the St. Louis County schools really that backward that a woman can still lose out to a less qualified man for a top administrative post? Can retaliation still be so blatantly employed by district administrators, when such actions have been prohibited for decades?

"The answer is yes – but only when district employees refuse to stand up for their fights. That is what Pearson is doing in this case."

I was impressed with the editorial. They had actually read my full complaint and understood the broader issues. On the other hand, Albertson took his customary shot at me in the April 20 *Cook News Herald*. On the front page, he simply duplicated the headline and article on the lawsuit from *The Tower News*. He saved the vitriolic rhetoric for his editorial.

"The first thing they (school boards, city councils, etc.) have to worry about is whether they could be sued. Did they dot all the I's, cross all the T's, notify everyone, post everything, comb their hair right, smile, bow and whatever. After all those precautions are taken, then they can decide if the action they are taking is for the good of the school district, city, etc.

"If you want to make some easy dollars, file a lawsuit. Most insurance companies will be quick to give you $10 to $15,000 if you'll settle. It will cost them more for attorneys otherwise.

"We definitely need some reforms in the tort system. Frivolous lawsuits should be punished, severely. Losers in lawsuits should automatically have to pay all costs. Attorneys taking frivolous lawsuits should be punished financially."

Nothing in Albertson's polemic surprised me. By this time, I had read most of the same crap many times. Anytime my challenges hit the news, he'd pull some variety of the same stuff out of his word processor and slap it in his editorial. He'd been doing it since 1986.

Once the news of the lawsuit hit the papers, my telephone rang off the hook. Teachers called to tell me that some teacher had sued Langan for discrimination up in Grand Marais. Fischer called to tell me the same thing. Marconett, now back in the classroom, told me that one time she was in the central office, she had seen a check made out to Kevin Abrahamson for a $1,800 reimbursement for tuition. After telling me these little tidbits, most admonished me not to tell anyone where I heard it.

Marconett also complained that Reznicek, who took my place in Orr, had never been to the Cook School. In his convoluted principal assignment memo for 1999–2000, Langan had assigned Reznicek to Orr with the additional assignment as the Elementary Principal for Cook. Langan had done the same thing with Marconett during the 1998–1999 school year. Both assignments were made to cover for Abrahamson's lack of any administrative license. She was upset because Reznicek was getting paid $4500 each semester, the year was almost over and he had not been there once. *Wasn't this the same windfall license bonus she received last year?* I wondered to myself.

It is interesting to point out that the Abrahamson hiring cost the school board quite a chunk. They paid full principal's salary for an unlicensed person. Then they paid for his tuition and expenses to get licensed. Then they paid other principals—Marconett, Reznicek, Metsa, and Fischer—to use their licenses to provide paper cover for Abrahamson's lack of license—and as part of his convoluted camouflage for my retaliatory transfer (see assignment letter p. 251). Not one board member questioned these additional expenditures.

The publicity about the lawsuit also brought e-mails and letters of support, even from former high school teachers and college instructors. But day-to-day, face-to-face, I heard very little. Support came only in private communication or passing whispers, just like the first lawsuit. However, those quiet, almost surreptitious contacts occasionally brought some useful information, even if it was accompanied with the caveat, "don't tell anyone I told you."

I called Prebich and asked him to check out the information about a discrimination lawsuit pending against Langan from his last superintendent's position in Grand Marais. He checked it out but was unable to find a lead.

In the next issue of the *Timberjay*, Colosimo responded to my lawsuit. He referred to my charges as "blatantly spurious." In reference to Langan's salary proposal offering significant increases to the principals contingent upon my resignation, he said, "That's a blatantly spurious claim and charge as far as Dr. Langan is concerned. That offer did not exist and would not happen."

The *Timberjay* quoted Prebich in response. He said that the other principals were witnesses to the unusual offer by Langan. "We'll be deposing those principals. Their testimony will support our contention."

Colosimo told the *Timberjay* that the job of defending the district was being turned over to Twin Cities attorney John Roszack, who specialized in school district defense work. *The same John Roszack that told two different stories in the first lawsuit.* Colosimo also confirmed that school officials expected the district's insurance carrier to pick up the costs of any judgment. Colosimo went on to give an astonishing explanation for the district's refusal to conciliate or settle.

"Colosimo also said that had the district agreed to the EEOC settlement, the damages would have to be paid from district funds. He said the cost of court damages would likely be picked up by the district's insurance carrier."

Incredible. He was just shy of saying they expected to lose their defense. According to Colosimo it was just a matter of determining who was going to pay the damages. The damages would include my legal costs, which were starting to climb. I had started paying Prebich $500 every month in November 1999, but the balance kept climbing. I resented the district's intransigence and Colosimo's games every time I wrote the check.

On Monday, April 17, two days after the articles and editorials on my lawsuit, John Metsa called from Babbitt in the morning. I was at a collaborative committee meeting in Virginia but got the message when I got back to Tower. The call back message read, "Great article! Call me." I called him back later in the afternoon. He asked me if I thought the principals' group should issue a statement saying that our principals' organization was not a part of the lawsuit. I said that I didn't think it was necessary; none of the articles had associated the lawsuit with the group. It didn't feel like a "great article" conversation. *Wonder what changed?*

I called Walt Fischer at Cotton right after talking to Metsa. Metsa had called him earlier and suggested that the principals' group should issue a statement. Walt had said "no way" in no uncertain terms. I called Friedlieb at Cherry and he had also gotten a call from Metsa a short time ago. He told Metsa he didn't think it was necessary to issue any statement about my lawsuit. I called Reznicek in Orr and he said he had not heard from Metsa but he would not support issuing any statement.

The next day, Fischer called a principals' meeting for April 19, following the district-wide "bump night" for teachers. We met in Friedlieb's office at Cherry.

"After thinking about it, I think we're better off to say nothing about Judy's lawsuit," Metsa started out.

"Langan called me yesterday and said that the four step contract proposal was reported wrong in the papers. It was never meant to pressure Judy to retire," Friedlieb added.

"I was right there and it was clearly taken as pressure on Judy to retire by everyone there," Reznicek insisted. "That's what I'd have to say under oath."

"But weren't we just waiting for Judy to find out about her pension?" Metsa asked.

"No way," Fischer responded heatedly. "The rest of us wanted to reject it right away, but she wanted us to wait until she could check and see if she could go this year. Remember, she said that we'd worked so hard to get the steps, maybe she could make it work."

"Hey, if that was not intended to pressure Judy, only to assist her as Langan says, why wasn't I included in the deal? I'm older than Judy and I'll reach the Rule of 90 about the same time," Fischer insisted, angrier by the minute.

"I'll tell you something else," he said. "Sid stopped in Cotton yesterday and told me that the principals could get shuffled around for next year or replaced with Deans of Students. Do you think this threat has anything to do with whether or not we issue a statement?" he asked sarcastically.

"I told my board member Arlette Krog and she called Langan and told him that she wouldn't tolerate it because if they put a Dean in Cotton, the community would see it as the first step in closing the school."

Metsa finally explained to us that Langan and Fowler (Babbitt board member) had been in his office most of the afternoon before he made the calls suggesting issuing a statement. Fowler was upset about the heat he was getting after the newspaper articles. Now we understood where the pressure for the group to make a statement about my lawsuit had come from. The group decided unanimously not to issue any statement about the lawsuit or any of the newspaper articles.

No surprise, the next day we received another Principal

Performance Assessment for our teachers to fill out. E-mails flew between the principals. Fischer wrote, "Here comes the retaliation. Same thing as last year, when he was mad, it was time to evaluate us." Friedlieb wrote, "Hey, how 'bout the principals evaluation we have to distribute. Ain't that neat? Hope nobody rips me on it so I don't end up in Albrook!" Fear of retaliatory transfers was heavy in the air.

However, by now Langan's tactics were widely known throughout the district. Later that day, leadership for the teachers union sent the following e-mail: "Please send out to all building reps: The union position is that no union member shall participate in the evaluation of a building principal or site administrator." One more time, the threatened evaluation was dropped. But one more time, Langan had flexed his authority and intimidated the troops.

I was never so glad to finish a school year and head out fishing. That first year in Tower had been extremely stressful. Bitterness over the retaliatory transfer dictated that I go to work and just bide my time. However, if there's an on/off switch for the work ethic, I never found it. The challenges in Tower had hooked me. A lot had been accomplished in spite of the awful way the year had started.

I worked the child study process as hard in Tower as I had in Orr. It makes a statement by example when the principal attends the weekly meetings. Early interventions for failing or troubled students began to make a difference in Tower just like they had in Orr. On May 31, 2000, several Indian students graduated from the Tower-Soudan High School. They were the first Indian students to graduate from the Tower School in decades. By mid-June, the room changes were complete. Things were looking up in Tower. The next year would start on a much more positive note.

Chapter 12

2001

CIRCUMSTANTIAL EVIDENCE

"Direct evidence of retaliation is rare."
EEOC Compliance Manual

ON JUNE 28, 2000, the Pretrial Notice and Orders from the Federal Court interrupted our summer fishing and vacation. The order set a Pretrial Conference for July 17. The attorneys were ordered to meet at least fourteen (14) days prior to that conference to discuss parameters for discovery and process deadlines. The order continued in underlined, bold capital letters: "*COUNSEL ARE EXPRESSLY DIRECTED TO SERIOUSLY DISCUSS SETTLEMENT AT THE TIME OF THE 'MEET AND CONFER.' THE RESULTS OF THAT DISCUSSION SHALL BE REPORTED TO THE COURT AT THE TIME OF THE INITIAL PRETRIAL CONFERENCE.*"

I was encouraged by the Judge's emphasis on settlement. The situation was looking good for a settlement. Langan's lawyer Colosimo was off the case, replaced by Margaret Skelton, an associate in Roszak's firm. The August 1999 EEOC conciliation proposal, which I had already accepted, was a good starting point. With this pressure from the court, I hoped we could get a settlement relatively soon. Having been through the litigation process once before, I did not want to go there again.

I should never have been so naïve.

Shortly after receiving the order, the dates were extended to August. There was never any settlement discussion or proposal from the district. Colosimo was gone, but the district remained intransigent. Any lingering optimism I had was quickly being replaced with bitterness and cynicism.

I had warned the school board that my transfer to Tower and Reznicek's assignment to Orr would result in additional principal turnovers for Orr. I was right. The July 22, 2000, *Timberjay*, headlined, "Orr School gets new principal." The article continued, "In a move to improve their personal logistics, the principals of the Orr and Babbitt Schools will be trading places. Orr principal Steve Reznicek, who has to commute from his home in Aurora, will now have a shorter drive to Babbitt. His drive to and from home (to Orr) was a grueling 170 mile round-trip." The article failed to mention the fact that Langan had approved the two transfers.

Although I was happy for my two colleagues, I resented the reality that Langan's principal assignments could be so rewarding for some and so punishing for others. *Wonder if there were any quid pro quos involved in these favorable transfers?* Nothing that overt, I was certain. While I never suspected Reznicek or Metsa of having cut deals with Langan at my expense, there were rewards for going along with Langan's agendas.

I learned later that both Reznicek and Metsa had gotten the $4500 per semester during the previous 1999–2000 school year. This was for the additional licensure assignments Langan had manipulated into his Notice of Assignment that included my transfer. Reznicek got it for elementary supervision of Cook (to cover Abrahamson who had no license) and Metsa got it for elementary supervision of Tower (to cover my lack of an elementary license).

Metsa's additional assignment was cover for Langan's license justification for my transfer. However, the state letter clarifying that my license was appropriate for a K–12 school came before the start of school in August 1999. That made the extra compensation Langan paid Metsa for that school year all the more intriguing.

Reznicek also told me both he and Metsa were given an additional

10 days of pay when they started with the district. This had not been done before, was not provided in our contract, and to my knowledge, it was done without board approval. Out of curiosity, I asked Lisa Nelson and Kim Juntunen (the principal hired to replace Lisa Nelson at Albrook in July 2000) if they had also gotten the extra 10 days of pay when they started. They both said they had requested it, but Langan denied them both. Men got it, women didn't!

Interesting what a guy can get away with when no one challenges.

Rick and I needed a break from the tensions of the past year and some renewal of spirit to face the battles ahead. We scheduled a fishing trip to Alaska at the end of July. We flew into Anchorage, rented a car and drove to Valdez. It was a spectacular drive, with mountains, canyons, raging rivers, and glaciers around every curve in the road. We rented a small fishing boat and spent three glorious days fishing for silver salmon in the Valdez Arm of Prince William Sound.

The 12 silver salmon we caught each day weighed between 14 and 17 pounds each. But that's only half the story. They fought like no fish we had caught before. You would set the hook and reel it into the boat, only to have the fish turn and run. They grey-hounded away at lightning speed, peeling line out so fast the reel smoked. In addition to the exciting fishing, the views were breathtaking. Out on the astonishing aqua water, mountains, glaciers, and countless waterfalls surrounded us. Eagles soared above us while harbor seals and sea otters kept us company on the water. We scooped up floating chunks of glacial ice to keep our fish cool.

There are not enough synonyms for "spectacular" in the thesaurus to describe Alaska. The vast scale of everything Alaskan literally transported us out of our daily trials and tensions. Everything and everyone seemed so insignificant by comparison. The wonderment of it all restored a sense of balance and perspective. We vowed it would be an annual retreat.

I was back to work in Tower the day after we got back from Alaska. As always, the teachers began coming in to prepare on their own time before school started. On August 15, one of the teachers told me she heard that Langan had a discrimination suit against him from Grand Marais, in the Cook County School District. I had heard that before, but we were unable to track it down.

This time was different, however.

She gave me the name of someone to contact.

After following several leads, I finally reached Jaye Clearwater Day on the telephone. She was more than willing to provide information and shared a deep dislike and distrust for Langan. She was an Indian teacher who had three suits pending against Langan and his former school district. The issues were harassment, discrimination, and violation of Minnesota's Open Meeting Law.

It was dismaying to talk to Jaye Clearwater Day.

In my plaintiff-induced state of self-absorption, I thought I had experienced the worst of Langan's tyranny. Her story was worse. She had been harassed, transferred, and then, forced to resign. She was a single parent with few of the resources and support Rick gave me to fight back. Yet she was staying the course with her lawsuits, often acting *pro se*. *Pro se* refers to a legal action where one represents oneself, without the aide of counsel. She had my admiration and support.

I asked Day for the names of people in Grand Marais I could contact to get more information on Langan. She gave me the names of several teachers and former board members who had similar trouble with Langan. I shared all this information with Prebich. He was going to check the state and federal court calendars to find out the status of Jaye Day's civil actions. Day's complaints were filed in the mid–90s and would probably be resolved before we got into court. Decisions in her suits could benefit us.

In the meantime, we received a new Pretrial Schedule from the court. I no longer paid much attention to procedural dates because they'd all be extended again. In this Order, dispositive motions (summary judgment) would be heard by May 1, 2001 and the trial could begin on June 1, 2001. The only pressure these dates put on me was to heighten my desire to retire as soon as possible.

I wanted to get out of Langan's crosshairs. Besides, working with him had destroyed my joy and enthusiasm for the job. I could not imagine going through a long trial while working under his authority. I immediately called the state teachers retirement association and scheduled my final retirement conference as soon as I could. The soonest appointment I could get was January 24, 2001.

Aside from the deadlines, I was worried about the rest of the Pretrial Order. The judge had severely limited the scope of discovery. The limits of 50 interrogatories and admissions didn't bother me. My experience was that those questions and answer documents seldom revealed new information. The attorneys would carefully construct the district's answers to those questions. They would be full of the same deceptions and distractions we'd already heard. Their only use might be as possible contradictions to other discovery documents.

But the judge's limits of 25 document requests and 10 depositions from witnesses bothered me. After all, it was discrepancies between the documents and depositions that had provided the big breaks in the first lawsuit.

This lawsuit was vastly more complicated than the first one. The first lawsuit only dealt with discrimination and a single board action. This one involved both discrimination and retaliation and five separate board actions. The retaliation complaint took us back fourteen years to 1986. Most of the relevant people and positions had changed several times, including superintendents, principals, and board members. The school district itself had consolidated, changed boundaries, board structure, and legal designation. These discovery limits would make our job, our burden of proof, very difficult.

We discussed these limits several times with Prebich. We finally decided not to challenge the pretrial orders. Prebich worried that any motions to amend the limits could alienate the judge and make matters worse. By December, the court had issued another amended Pretrial Schedule, moving the close of discovery to April 15 and summary judgment to June 15. Both sides had filed their original document requests back in August.

We provided the documents they requested of us in compliance with the deadline. It was a huge stack, including court documents from the original lawsuit, newspaper articles, board minutes, my anecdotal notes, e-mails, evaluations, notices related to the transfer, grievance documents, and medical records. They wanted copies of any documents we were using to make our case.

Naturally, the district did not provide the documents we requested in the same timely manner. We had received nothing by the end of October. We had requested board minutes, agendas, and memos related to the first and second round superintendent selections in May 1997 and October 1997, assistant and interim superintendent selections in June 1997, including closed meetings and study sessions. We requested telephone records for that period of time, board member expense vouchers, and any calendars kept by the defendants during that period of time. We also requested copies of board documents related to my transfer, including all the principal evaluations from January 1999, so we could compare the ratings.

We were looking for any documentary evidence or witness testimony that would confirm what we thought we knew and that would answer remaining questions about the closed selection processes and my transfer.

For comparative purposes, we requested the credentials of all candidates for the two rounds of superintendent selection and any interview notes or ranking documents used by board members in the selection processes. The district refused to provide the credentials, insisting they were protected under the Minnesota Government Data Practices Act. At the end of December, the district filed and received a protective order from the court stipulating that the candidate credentials we requested would be considered confidential and could only be used for trial preparation. We had no problem with this order, but it signaled trouble ahead.

These legal maneuvers and obstructive tactics made our case much more difficult. That's their intent. We got a similar stall on Langan's January 1999 principal evaluations. We needed them to compare with mine and with the rationale for my transfer. By the time they finished their legal maneuvers, we had to get waivers signed by every individual. Pretrial deadlines dictated that we had to start depositions without most of the documents we had requested. I remembered a similar frustration with first lawsuit. The calendar almost always works against the plaintiff.

We were already at a distinct disadvantage. Prebich was a sole practitioner, with one legal secretary. We were up against a huge law firm, with 18 attorneys and dozens of paralegal and secretarial employees. They had the deep pockets of the insurance company as well as the procedural and grunt work advantage. There would be thousands of pages of documents to read. Because I paid per page for copies of every document they requested, we sent just the documents they requested. They, on the other hand, would likely apply the "needle in the haystack" strategy. They'd send mountains of material for us to plow through. They had many eyes to analyze our few documents. We had far fewer eyes to search for the needle in their haystack.

Rick and I still felt we had made the right choice with Prebich. After having struggled with Williams and his large Minneapolis law firm in the original lawsuit, we were much more comfortable working with Prebich. There was none of the arrogance we had encountered with Williams. Prebich was a local, he knew the area, he listened, and he answered our questions.

We needed to hire an expert witness to evaluate the district's hiring practices for the three positions being challenged. The expert would also compare the credentials of all the candidates. We were fortunate to hire Dr. Clifford Hooker again as our expert witness. He had been our expert witness in the original trial and had done a thorough job. He had years of experience and credentials in the superintendent selection business. He was the most popular consultant of school districts for their administrative searches.

By this time, the mounting costs were beginning to pinch. I paid all the bills as they came in. The monthly payments towards our fees for Prebich were nothing compared to Hooker's costs. He charged $125/hour and that included reading time for all the documents and depositions. His bills would total over $8,000 by the time his preliminary analysis was finished. We had already paid all the printing and duplicating bills for the document exchanges, totaling over $1,000.

Our depositions began in December. The bills from the court reporter for time and transcripts were due as they came in. A short deposition of two hours could cost over $300 and longer depositions could go as high as $600. Our deposition costs were several thousand dollars before we finished. We also paid a process server to deliver the subpoenas for the depositions. We were going further into debt as the case wore on.

Our savings were gone and the credit cards were maxed out. Rick's truck was in tough shape, but we could not afford to replace it. Instead we paid to keep fixing a vehicle that had out-lived its worth. We often joked when paying the bills that creditors better be careful not to tick us off or we wouldn't even put their names in the hat.

The calendar continued to work against us. The Pretrial Orders required the plaintiff to submit all reports or affidavits from expert witnesses in February. That meant that Hooker would not see most of the depositions and many of the documents before his work had to be submitted. Frustrations continued to rise.

In the meantime, my retirement appointment in January 2001 had convinced me that I had to retire at the end of the year. The comparison of my benefits under the two state plans left no doubt. The IMP formula was set higher than ever before and was not likely to be repeated the following year. The difference was over $1,800 per month for the rest of my life. To qualify for that benefit, I had to retire by June 15, 2001.

Rick and I agreed this was a no-brainer. I had some misgivings, but Rick was ecstatic that I'd be out of the district. When we got back from our appointments, I sent my retirement letter to the district with mixed feelings. I was young and not ready to quit working. However, it was an immediate relief to know that my days with Langan were numbered. The sooner I got out the better.

Our 10 depositions took from December 2000 to April 2001 to complete. Just scheduling them was a nightmare, because all parties, including attorneys, had to agree on the dates. I couldn't attend them all because I had a limited amount of leave time available and the district wasn't eager to extend my options. I spent hours preparing questions for Prebich to consider when he conducted the depositions.

That's not as easy as it sounds. Most of the witnesses we deposed were defendants and were reluctant to give us any more information than they had to. It meant finding the right question to get at the information you think they might have. Ask the wrong question or ask it in the wrong way and you give them wiggle room for unresponsive answers.

The district had consistently maintained that the 1991 court decision had nothing to do with my not being considered for the top administrative positions. The district's response to my EEOC retaliation complaint on the administrative positions stated, "There is no temporal connection between Ms. Pearson's action of previously filling a charge and the 'adverse' employment action by ISD No. 2142. There are only two board members on the current board at the time of Mrs. Pearson's prior charge. Generally, as they were not involved, the remaining board members only have vague, second hand knowledge about the prior charge. She has provided absolutely no evidence, direct or indirect, that her prior charge was in any way related to these decisions."

In his deposition, Chet Larson denied several times that he had any resentment toward me as a result of the previous lawsuit. He denied that there were any discussions of my previous lawsuit amongst board members. He gave an unambiguous "No" to that specific question. However, Larry Salmela (Cook board member elected in 1995) was not on the board during the previous lawsuit or my court ordered 1992 hire at Orr. He contradicted Chet in his deposition. In reference to my application for the superintendent's position:

"During your tenure on the board from 1995, do you recall any conversations with the board members regarding Judy's litigation with the district?" asked Prebich.

"That topic would come up from time to time. Obviously that is one of the ways with which I became familiar with what had happened in the first litigation," Salmela responded.

"Do you recall who those conversations were with?"

"I can say that the more experienced board members were the people who offered the history. Tone or tenor would be described as very serious."

"What was Chet Larson's attitude toward Mrs. Pearson's previous litigation?" Prebich continued.

"Obviously the board in its earlier experience went through a–let's describe it as a painful experience, painful being measured in terms of the financial penalty; therefore it was a serious event in the past."

"So you did have conversations with Mr. Larson about that issue, correct?"

"That's correct."

When asked about discussions of my lawsuit during the selection process, from January 1997 through November 1997, Salmela replied,

"Now with the specific time frame defined in the question, obviously the past litigation was brought up during that time frame."

Arlette Krog (Cotton board member elected in 1997) reinforced Salmela's testimony. She indicated that she had been told about my previous lawsuit against the district after she came on the board in July 1997. Fowler (Babbitt board member, came into district with 1993 consolidation) also admitted he had been told about my 1986 lawsuit.

Three board members contradicted Chet Larson about board discussions of my previous lawsuit.

When I applied for the superintendent's position in the spring of 1997, I knew I did not meet the five-year superintendent experience requirement. When the more experienced finalists were announced in early May, I was not surprised or upset. My only concern at that time was the illegal board meeting documented in the Duluth newspapers on May 21 and May 22. There were no official records of that meeting, no posting, no agenda, and no minutes.

However, that five-year minimum experience issue surfaced as a major factor from the depositions. In his deposition Chet Larson said that Superintendent Mobilia had given the board a checklist with a point system to evaluate applicants. According to Chet, the five-year requirement was on Mobilia's form and was his suggestion.

"Why wasn't Ms. Pearson a finalist in the first round?" Prebich asked Larson.

"Lack of years of experience was enough point totals to keep her from getting up there with the top ones," Chet responded.

However, in his deposition, Mobilia contradicted Chet. Mobilia said that there was significant disagreement on the years of experience to be required.

"The minimum years of experience was not a recommendation made by you?" asked Prebich.

"No, no," Mobilia responded adamantly. "I let them know that they better not push their luck, knowing what I knew about the lack of candidates in the state, and knowing what I knew already when Virginia just tried to fill a position, that they had to go out twice to solicit applicants. So I knew that if they made the criteria too rigid and too tough, they are not going to get very many candidates."

"Do you recall any conversations about what's Judy's experience level was as superintendent when they were setting the minimum criteria?"

"At that time, we only—or, I should say, the board only set those minimum requirements and the only thing I can remember in that discussion is warning them that you're not going to have a whole bunch of candidates."

Dave Clement (Board member from Cherry 1984–1990, reelected 1996–1999) was more specific about the five-year minimum discussion. He said Chairman Chet Larson was adamant about the five-year requirement even though Mobilia warned them the five years might narrow the field. *Did Chet insist on the five-year minimum, against Mobilia's recommendation, just to eliminate me?*

They may have differed about who insisted on the five-year minimum requirement, but there was total agreement that I hadn't met it. Chet Larson, Larry Anderson, Dave Clement, Rolland Fowler (Board member from Babbitt, came into St. Louis County with 1993 consolidation), and Larry Salmela were clear and specific in their depositions. They all pounced on the five-year minimum and insisted it had eliminated me from consideration for the superintendency.

By February 2001, we had received Dr. Hooker's preliminary assessment of the district's superintendent selection process. He wrote, "The experience criterion requirement in both Superintendent searches was not gender neutral. The ISD 2142 experience requirement discriminates against women because an employment pool described in this fashion is limited primarily to male candidates.

"The entry position for the superintendency in small districts is the high school principalship. In 1997, forty-three of the 450 high school principals in Minnesota were women. The Superintendent selection criteria for ISD 2142 excluded all of these female principals. In 1997, fewer than six per cent of Minnesota school superintendents were women. The experience requirement posted by the St. Louis County School Board was not a bona fide occupational qualification (BFOQ)."

A BFOQ is defined as a requirement that relates to an essential job duty and is considered reasonably necessary to the operation of a particular business. Hooker continued, "Moreover, I cite numerous school boards in Minnesota that have hired superintendents with no prior experience; Minneapolis, St. Paul, Duluth, St. Cloud, Bloomington, Roseville, Mankato, Proctor, Moose Lake, Cass Lake, Sartell, and Fosston, to show that such experience is not essential to the operation of a school district."

The quickness and unanimity of the board members' responses about the five-year minimum were significant in light of Hooker's opinion. The clarity of their memory that the five-year requirement had eliminated me was in stark contrast to their fuzzy and equivocating answers to other deposition questions. Larry Anderson (Albrook board member elected in 1985) was elected chairman after Chet Larson left the board in July 1997. His deposition was particularly frustrating. He was a college administrator with a Master's Degree.

His deposition was important because he served as chairman of the board from the second superintendent selection in October 1997 through my transfer grievance September 1999. His deposition lasted only 50 minutes. In spite of his administrative position and training, he responded with, "I can't remember, I don't recall, I don't know" over 20 times. He concluded with, "I'm getting confused on the dates." And "I'm getting a little—goofy from these questions."

That's a college administrator? It was always my fear that the more time passed in this process, the more it provided an excuse for these kinds of memory lapses.

"I don't recall" sent my blood pressure to the moon because these dates and events were burned in my memory. Ironically, the only thing Larry Anderson remembered clearly was that I did not meet the five-year minimum requirement for the superintendency.

On the other hand, Chet Larson's responses were often absolute, just one word.

"Did you suggest to Superintendent Mobilia that he arrange for Langan to meet Simonson and discuss the assistant superintendent position?" Prebich asked.

"No."

"Did you meet with Sid Simonson at Ludlow's to discuss the interim superintendency?"

"No."

"Do you recall talking to Lee Bloomquist from the *Duluth News Tribune* and telling him that Simonson would be named interim superintendent?"

"No."

"After Dan Mobilia left Ludlow's, did you announce that Sid was going to be named interim superintendent?"

"No."

"Were there any discussions at the June 16 Special Board meeting at Cherry when Sid was hired an interim about making him the permanent superintendent?"

"No."

Several other depositions contradicted Chet Larson item for item.

"Do you recall when it was that Mr. Simonson was first offered the assistant superintendency?" Prebich quizzed Mobilia.

"Chet Larson talked to me, and he was pretty much in favor of feeling out Sid Simonson to see if he would be – I don't know if I want to say willing, but at least willing to talk about the assistant's job, and try to make an arrangement with Don Langan and him to meet and talk, and I did that," Mobilia responded.

"I did the arranging and Don came up. I sat in on that meeting for a short time and then I had to leave. They talked a little bit and then I came back. Langan told me he was very comfortable with Sid Simonson as the assistant, I know that."

Other contradictions surfaced about this meeting between Langan and Simonson. When asked about this meeting Mobilia set up between the two, Langan denied it happened. He said he'd only been briefly introduced to Simonson.

"My best recollection there would be that the entire interaction probably lasted less than a minute," Langan lied. However, both Mobilia and Simonson confirmed that it was in fact a meeting. Mobilia stepped out for awhile and then offered Simonson the assistant superintendent position when the meeting concluded.

Chairman Chet Larson denied he met with Simonson at Ludlow's. But Mobilia testified, "I know Chet had a conversation with Sid because Jim Techar (former Babbitt superintendent and colleague of Mobilia's, became Babbitt principal with 1993 consolidation) called from Ludlow's to tell me that. He heard the conversations between Chet and Sid."

Chairman Chet Larson denied that he told the *Duluth News Tribune* reporter Lee Bloomquist that Sid would be named interim superintendent. Mobilia contradicted, "I specifically went to Ludlow's (June 11) to talk to Chet, because that day I got a phone call from Lee Bloomquist from the paper and Mr. Bloomquist asked me about some details of the decision of the board to hire Sid Simonson as the interim superintendent and I said, 'I don't know anything about that.' He told me he had discussed this with Chet Larson that morning or the day before and Chet told him that's what the board is going to do."

"And what did Chet tell you that day?" Prebich followed up.

"That was his opinion, what he felt should happen. I told him that may be his opinion, but he overextended his authority for speaking for other board members. You could assume he had already met with Andy Larson and Rolland Fowler (two other board members in attendance at Ludlow's). It sure wasn't their right to have a closed meeting under my watch. My concern was that we were going to be—it is going to be viewed as a closed meeting." What's the missing word,—*sued?*

Chairman Chet Larson denied that he had announced Sid Simonson as interim superintendent at the Ludlow's conference. But Walt Fischer (Tower principal 1994–1997, Cotton principal 1997–2003) was in attendance and contradicted, "We were in a big room, I think the whole group was together and Mr. Larson was to my right and he made this announcement to the whole group, that Sid was going to be the interim superintendent."

Chairman Chet Larson denied there was any discussion about making Simonson permanent superintendent at the June 16 Cherry board meeting when Sid was officially hired as interim. But the conversation was reported in the *Mesabi Daily News* on June 18. Mobilia testified that it was discussed at Cherry, that "wheels were set in motion" to make Sid permanent superintendent. Chet was "pushing it," according to Mobilia.

If Chairman Chet Larson were to be believed, then Mobilia, Fischer, Techar, Clement, Salmela, Krog, and two newspapers were wrong or lying. No one had said or written specifically that Chet and/or the board had eliminated me from the three administrative positions in June 1997 in retaliation for my lawsuit. But the contradictory testimonies were strong circumstantial evidence. Two additional deposition testimonies highlighted Chet Larson's ability to take me out.

Salmela described Chet Larson as, "a board chairman who would control the process very carefully." Mobilia's comments about Chet were most revealing. "Anybody that knew Chet knew that he pretty much knew how to run the board, to get what he wanted."

Although we were still struggling to get the documents we

requested from the district as late as April 2001, by January 2001, we had received the district's first batch of responses. Included were the board members' notes from their interviews of the first round superintendent finalists. On Salmela's notes of the May 6 interview with Don Langan, he wrote that two board members in Grand Marais had resigned while Langan was superintendent. Copies of his vouchers indicated that a week later, on May 14, he and Fowler traveled to Grand Marais for the background check on Langan.

According to their depositions, Salmela and Fowler never tried to talk to the two board members that had resigned. School board resignations are rare and two with the same superintendent should have been a warning flag. Instead, they allowed Langan to make all the arrangements for their interviews of staff and board members while they were in Grand Marais. Not exactly due diligence.

Frustrated with the board's failure to check out any negative lead, Prebich recommended we hire a private investigator to follow up. We had known nothing about these board resignations until we reviewed the documents and found the Salmela's interview notes. That's what discovery is all about. We found a needle in their haystack. In March 2001, we hired Ron Taggert, a private investigator, to check out the status of the pending lawsuits against Langan and find out why two board members had resigned.

We could only take 10 depositions and needed to get most of the board members and top administrators on the record. However, Walt Fischer was the one principal who had been present at all major events. On April 10, his was our tenth and final deposition. He was at the board meetings when Simonson and Langan were hired, Ludlow's retreat, the principals' negotiation meetings, and other attempts to intimidate the group or me. I thought we had shared most of it, but his deposition contained a disillusioning revelation.

Fischer's testimony finally explained how Simonson's licensure report from the State had come to light and what the "emergency board meeting" had been about on August 29, 1997. Although a colleague had alerted me to problems in Simonson's past right after he was hired for Assistant Superintendent in June 1997, I first heard about a specific licensure report on Simonson from Fischer in 1999. He wouldn't tell me who told him about it. In the deposition, Prebich asked Fischer how he first heard about Simonson's license problems.

"Do I have to answer that question? Because the person who told it to me told it to me in confidence," Fischer replied.

"Well, sadly enough, I think you do have to answer it." Prebich insisted.

"It was after a principals' meeting. Cindy Jindra told me she had gotten this call from someone saying something about Mr. Simonson's licensure problems, and that she should check with the state department. So she called and they stuck it in the fax machine and up comes this whole thing about something that had gone on in the Glenwood school system."

"Do you know anything about the emergency meeting of the board that was held at Scott Neff's office in August 1997?" asked Prebich,

"She was horrified with what she was reading. 'What do I do with this?' So she went and took it to the school district attorney and gave it to them."

"What month was this conversation that you had with Ms. Jindra?" Prebich asked.

"Oh, this was April, a long time after Ludlow's conference."

Apparently the Associated Press had picked up the news of Simonson's hire as Interim Superintendent at the Cherry School on June 16, 1997. When it appeared in the Twin Cities papers, one of the women from Simonson's previous district read it. She was upset and called the Cherry School, the location given in the AP story. She told Cindy Jindra about Simonson's history. Jindra called the state department and was faxed a copy of the report. This happened within days of the June 16 meeting. She decided to remove all evidence that she had received it and took it to the school district attorney. This produced the August 29, 1997, emergency board meeting in Neff's office.

Defense lawyers argued all along that I gave Simonson's license report to the school board in 1997. Not true. I never saw it until 1999.

According to his deposition, Fischer knew about it a year before he told me. Another principal colleague told me years later that she also knew all about Simonson's licensure report back in 1997. Jindra had told her about it at the time. So initially two and later three principals in the district knew how Simonson's license surfaced in our district and no one told me. From Fischer's deposition on April 10, 2001—almost four years after the fact—I finally heard the whole story.

The disillusionment following Fischer's testimony was not about Simonson. It was the silence of my colleagues. They privately gave me support throughout my struggles, but held back critical information. They never hesitated to call me when they had problems or concerns, saying, "Judy, someone's got to do something about this." They asked me to negotiate several contracts and to act as their grievance representative.

For four years, the two women had known about the license report. Fischer had known for many months and said nothing. Why not? My guess is that they were afraid of what I'd do with the information. They knew I would use Simonson's report, not bury it. They were afraid their names would surface and retaliation would follow. Consequently, I did not learn who knew what, when, until the discovery deadline—too late to respond with additional depositions or discovery.

They used my willingness to speak up, when the issues affected them. That way they took no risks. Since this issue only affected me, so I was more on my own than ever. Taking a stand was a solo performance in the plaintiff blues.

I've wrestled with feelings of betrayal throughout this process. So many had so much to tell me, as long as I didn't use their names. In their defense, I don't believe my colleagues ever intended to make things more difficult for me. I believe they were sincere when they privately wished me well or provided other information. These are good folks who are generous with their time and talents. But taking a public stand or being associated with someone who does is another issue. Most people will avoid such public exposure at all costs. They were simply doing what most people do, taking care of number one.

The EEOC Compliance manual provided insight into why people

kept quiet. "Retaliation has a 'chilling affect' on the willingness of individuals to speak out against employment discrimination or to participate in an investigation." Langan's retaliatory bent was well known. My transfer was clearly retaliation and everyone in the district knew it. I had failed to reverse it through the grievance process. If I eventually prevailed, it would be years after the fact. As far as my colleagues, the school district, and general public knew, Langan got away with the retaliation. He could act with impunity. They wanted no part of crossing him.

Salmela's deposition revealed more startling information about Simonson's background. The pieces were beginning to come together. The board got Jindra's fax on Simonson—with all identifying names and numbers erased—in August and had an emergency meeting with their attorney, Scott Neff, on August 29, 1997. Depositions from both Salmela and Krog confirmed that they read the full report at that time. In spite of the report, the board announced Simonson as a finalist in the second round selection for the superintendent's position on September 9.

Vouchers and depositions from Salmela and Krog indicate they traveled to Glenwood on October 9 and 10, 1997, to finally do a background check on Simonson. According to Salmela, they met with the chief of police in Starbuck, Minnesota. When asked about the public record regarding Simonson, the chief read from several documents, referring to an assault charge by a woman. Salmela and Krog also met in Glenwood with a former board member who referred to Simonson's "character issues." They then met with six or seven women employees of the school district, each of whom told their own story about Simonson exposing himself to her.

According to their depositions, by the time they headed home, both Salmela and Krog had concluded that they could not hire Simonson for the superintendency. Salmela testified:

"I being very upset at that testimony received, it was clear to me that such reported incidents were very offensive to many people in the community, and I hate to use the word 'politically,' but that's the word that came to my own mind, that politically, Sid Simonson's appointment as superintendent would be untenable."

"We had a meeting in Cotton shortly thereafter. Either before or after the open meeting, there was a closed session; I told the other board members as a group about our findings in Starbuck and Glenwood."

"What transpired at that board meeting in Cotton regarding the superintendency search?" Prebich pressed Salmela.

"Prior to that meeting, when I had called every board member the day after I got back about our findings, I was struck by Chairman Larry Anderson's reaction. His reaction, after a long period of silence, 'I wonder if Don Langan's still available.'"

Aha! Salmela's testimony finally explained how Don Langan got back into the second round of superintendent selection at the last minute. Salmela's deposition was also an admission of another violation of Minnesota's Open Meeting Law. The relevant section of the law deals with any "meetings" by a quorum of the public body. A quorum consists of that number of the public body capable of exercising decision-making powers. The courts have determined that serial communication through telephone conversations with the intent to avoid a public hearing or to come to an agreement on an issue relating to official business violates the law. Salmela's testimony that he "called every board member the day after I got back," certainly fit the law's definition of serial communication about official business.

Sid and I were the two finalists for the position. With Sid out, you'd think I would have been a shoo-in, right? Chairman Larry Anderson, who had also been on the board I sued in 1986, never considered me and reached in desperation for Langan. *Why was I named as a finalist if never to be considered? Just for appearance and legal cover?*

According to Fischer, the principal in attendance at Cotton for that October 27 board meeting, the board hired Langan following a long, closed meeting from which everyone else was excluded. Fischer testified,

"Larry Anderson, the then board chairman, had indicated that he had contacted Langan and had brought him into the picture in the last week. Then somebody made a motion to hire Langan, and that was it, he was hired." *Again no discussion because the decision was made earlier behind the closed doors of a study session.*

The discovery evidence was also blatantly contradictory in relation to my 1999 transfer to Tower. Langan's deposition contradicted his own memoranda about when and where I would be transferred.

"And when did you personally reach that conclusion that you were going to move her to Tower?" Prebich asked in deposition about the timing of the decision.

"I made that professional decision very early in June, if not the end of May 1999," answered Langan.

Yet a confidential memo from Langan to board members was dated July 7, 1999, and read, "Mr. Friedlieb requested a transfer to the Cherry School. I responded to his request and informed him that I would not be approving his request for transfer at this time. Regarding assignments for the 1999–2000 school year—it is my intention to leave Walt Fischer, John Metsa, Gary Friedlieb, and Lisa Nelson in their current position. Judy Pearson will be assigned Cherry School and Mr. Reznicek would be assigned to Orr School. I would encourage the school board from any action regarding these assignments and leave them simply as my responsibility as superintendent."

He's actually warning his board to stay out of it.

When Prebich asked about the contradictions in the memo, Lagan responded that if he had written the memo (it's dated and signed by him) then it had to be a "flat out error in name." However, that "error in name" appeared in several places in the memo in relation to both Friedlieb and myself.

"Why was Pearson transferred to Tower?" Prebich asked Langan. His answer was simply incredible considering his written comments in both my and Friedlieb's earlier evaluations. Friedlieb got the highest rating; mine was one of the lowest.

"With the administrative situation that I had in '00, preceding the '99-2000 school year, without reservation, Judy had the strongest set of talents, experiences, and resources to meet the needs of the Tower situation."

"Suffice it to say, if I can, I was experiencing in Tower a very significant—a very significant amount of staff unrest, and to a certain extent, I was—the organization was experiencing some student unrest, to the point of being, let me just say, very significant. The history I was able to determine and my own observation of Judy's work in Orr said that—led me to conclude that in terms of dealing with those two types of issues, Judy Pearson by far was my most resourceful and effective administrator; that is why she was transferred to Tower," Langan continued.

Other depositions contained similar contradictions. Assistant Superintendent Simonson was asked about the problems in Tower and my transfer.

"There were student-related problems in Tower. I don't know how I could specifically describe it other than it appeared as though maybe things were getting out of control," Simonson replied.

"What discussion do you recall with Dr. Langan in that regard?" Prebich asked.

"The only thing that I can think of was that because of the prior difficulties that they had in Tower, they needed somebody with experience in working with the Indian population, and Judy was that person."

Board members echoed the same theme to questions about my transfer in their depositions.

"There had been concerns the year prior to that when Mr. Friedlieb was there with regards to the discipline and so forth with regards to the particular entity, and knowing Judy Pearson had engaged in some of those same kinds of challenges at the Orr school, it was felt that assignment would be appropriate and that she could very well do a nice job there," Krog replied.

"Well, we had had problems in Tower with the Native Americans, for one thing. Judy, of course, being at Orr, where there is a large portion of Native American students, we felt probably had the best knowledge of how to deal with that. Gary Friedlieb had problems there and we thought that Judy would be—because of her experience dealing with these folks could probably handle the situation a little better," Fowler replied. *Seems to me they've all been coached about using the race card.*

Salmela responded similarly. "The Tower school was known to have some issues especially with the Indian reservation being a significant contributor of population to the Tower school. Ms. Pearson having had served at Orr had dealt with similar issues there. Ms. Pearson was also a very experienced principal, extensive experience in our district. Ms. Pearson from those viewpoints was a logical candidate. Judy Pearson had superior—a superior credential in that she had much longer experience in our district. There was clearly no question about that."

Yet when Prebich asked Salmela why I was never considered for any of the administrative positions, he said I did not survive the first round superintendent selection process because, "At a minimum, she didn't have the experience. I concluded that no further review was necessary." *Apparently experience cuts both ways, depending on the hidden agenda.*

When comparing their depositions on my transfer to their depositions on my not being considered for the superintendency, their depositions were incredibly contradictory about my disciplinary skills. According to Chet Larson, "Her discipline was poor; the staff was leaving early or coming late."

Salmela testified that he had heard from former board members, superintendent Mobilia, and current members, "Allegations about inadequate discipline in the school, extending to both employees and to students. I was left with the impression that Ms. Pearson was not one of our top performing principals, and therefore would not make a top candidate for superintendent."

Salmela's testimony on this issue was intriguing because former superintendent Mobilia had written in an evaluation of my performance, "Judy promotes positive expectations for student behavior. This is one area I would rate her at the extreme top of the scale. Judy makes all of her decisions based on this very premise, which sometimes is viewed as weakness by some. However, those who believe this are wrong."

So I've got poor discipline of staff and students when you don't want to promote me, but I'm the most effective administrator for discipline problems when you need to justify my transfer. *They're so desperate to camouflage their real agendas, they can't keep track of their own contradictions,* I fumed to myself.

Fischer's deposition shed additional light on several of the main issues in my complaint. In reference to the board's surprise hire of Simonson for assistant superintendent, Fischer said, "Mobilia told the board that Langan wanted Sid Simonson."

"Were you upset when they hired him?" Prebich asked Fischer.

"I was shocked. All of sudden this fellow who just came into the district less than a year ago and who didn't even apply for the assistant superintendency in January, all of sudden is now the assistant superintendent. I was flabbergasted."

Regarding Langan's four-step salary proposal contingent on my retirement, Fischer clearly contradicted Langan. Langan had testified adamantly, "That did not happen."

Prebich asked Fischer about the discussion amongst the principals after receiving Langan's proposal.

"I was quite shocked about that and I said to the group, you know, this is wonderful—you know, it is a big pile of money for us, especially me and especially Judy, but I said this just isn't—I'm chairman of the group. This isn't going to happen. We are not going to ask any principal to retire prior to when they want to—the rest of them agreed with me."

"What was Judy's response to what had happened?" asked Prebich.

"Oh, she was kind of feeling bad and decided that, you know—like she was holding up the group, holding up a raise for the rest of us and so she was feeling kind of guilty, feeling bad, and actually said she would look into the option of retiring."

"After Judy decided that she could not retire that year, did that four-step proposal stay on the table?"

"No. It was gone. That was the contingency there, that Judy was going to have to retire by June 30, 2000."

Langan was all over the board on the issue of my retirement. When asked about his "conversation that didn't happen" with me in May 1999, he admitted offering me extras if I retired that same year. He said he had heard "rumors" that I might retire. "I needed to know from Judy if there was something that the organization could do in an accommodation."

In contrast, district documents included a July 13, 1999, memo from Langan to the two school board members on the negotiating committee for the principals' contract. This was just weeks after his offers to me. "If they come in with a package that has a heavy emphasis on retirement benefits, we as a board will be less than compassionate." *"Accommodation" on the one hand, "less than compassionate?" on the other. How many times can they have it both ways?*

By the time we finished depositions in April, my retirement was official and just two months away. I began the process of filing my final paperwork and determining my benefits from the district. On April 16, I e-mailed the bookkeeper in the district office responsible for benefits and insurances. I asked when I would have to start paying my health insurance premiums. She indicated that the district coverage would go through June 30. After checking contract language, I e-mailed back and indicated that the contract provided 12 months of coverage each year I worked. I had begun in August 1992, so I assumed that I would have district coverage through August or September, depending on what month my coverage had started.

She e-mailed back later that day. "Hi Judy, you are right. You will have coverage through the end of August 2001. You will start paying your own premiums by the 1st of September 2001."

Four days later I received a summary of district retirement benefits from the Personnel/Payroll Coordinator. The health insurance date was back to June 30 and there were problems with the severance calculations as well. Severance was based on the number of days of accumulated sick leave, multiplied by our daily salary (capped at $50,000). Our severance calculations differed by $5,226. When I called the Business Manager to try to resolve the differences, she abruptly cut me off.

"The decision is final," she said. "You'll have to grieve it if you don't agree."

Just what I needed, another battle to fight! Wonder if that's the strategy? Keep me so embattled I can't keep it all straight.

Even as we were finishing the depositions in April 2001, contradictory testimonies, closed meetings, and illegal straw votes continued. The school board had a regularly scheduled meeting on at 5:00 p.m. on Monday, April 9. All the building principals were directed to meet with the school board in a study session at 3:00 p.m., before the regular meeting. I had casually mentioned the study session to a reporter from the *Timberjay* that morning when she stopped in to discuss the impact of the pending teacher cuts on Tower. The editor showed up at the 3:00 p.m. study session.

During the study session, there was discussion of the controversial budget cuts and teacher layoffs. They were the major agenda items for the evening's regular school board meeting. However, it was the minor item of school calendar adoption for the following year that was most revealing.

Following a heated discussion of the calendar issue, Chairman Salmela conducted an illegal straw vote on the school calendar. Langan had proposed a significantly different calendar from previous years. This one included a long spring break and extended the school year two weeks into June. The issue was contentious because the extension into June had significant impacts on the northern schools in tourism country. Those northern communities depended on high school students for summer help at the area resorts.

When the calendar adoption failed on the four-three "straw vote," it was removed from the agenda of the regular meeting. I was stunned. I couldn't believe it when Salmela actually referred to a "straw vote" and called on each board member to vote. A straw vote is an unofficial or informal method to gage the opinions of a group. But in this instance, they had voted and acted on that vote at an unposted, illegal meeting. I was sitting right there in the front row at the time and this was one of my major complaints in the lawsuit against the district.

It was a blatant violation of the Open Meeting Law. The board had abused study sessions and the closed meeting provisions of the law throughout the administrative hiring process, from May 1997 through the hiring of Kevin Abrahamson in 1998. When I left the meeting that day, I felt the board had just handed me a victory in the lawsuit. There were lots of witnesses this time.

The day after that study session and straw vote, we took our last two discovery depositions, Arlette Krog and Walt Fischer.

"Did you attend the study session of the board yesterday?" Prebich asked Fischer.

"Yes, I was there."

"Do you recall any type of a straw vote having been taken during that meeting?"

"There was a straw vote taken as to how people were going to react to the calendar," Fischer responded.

"Describe for me what you mean by a straw vote." Prebich requested.

"The term straw vote was used by Larry Salmela."

"And did you actually observe board members voting?"

"Yes. It was a four to three vote, I think."

Prebich asked Arlette Krog the same questions in her deposition about the study session the day before.

"This school district continues to use study sessions?" Prebich asked.

"Correct."

"And at study sessions are there straw votes that are sometimes taken?"

"No."

When I heard her answer I was shocked. We had both been at the meeting just the day before. Chairman Salmela had used the term "straw vote" more than once. I had watched him call on each board member for their vote. The vote of four to three was announced to all of us present and then the item was removed from the agenda for the public meeting that night. *How could Krog sit there across the table from me, under oath, and deny the straw vote we had both witnessed less than 24 hours before?*

The April 14, 2001, issue of the *Timberjay* headlined, "School District Violates Open Meeting Law." The article explained, "Neither the notice, nor the agenda, nor minutes from the previous school board meeting contained any mention of the 3:00 p.m. study session." The article concluded, "In other study session action, the board rejected the proposed 2001–2002 school calendar on a 4-3 straw vote."

The article quoted Minnesota Newspaper Association attorney Mark Anfinson, an expert on the state's open meeting statutes. "That's pretty appalling. At a minimum, it seems clear that the Open Meeting Law was violated by their failure to provide notice," he said.

"According to Anfinson, study sessions qualify as special meetings, which are clearly covered by the provisions of the state law. That law is intended to prevent government bodies from operating in secret."

In a separate editorial, the *Timberjay* complained, "Once again, parents, residents, and students in the St. Louis County school district are feeling blindsided by a plan for significant teacher cutbacks throughout the district. Unfortunately, some district administrators seem to prefer to work in secret and the school board, in general, is far too subservient to challenge that tendency. The alternative is growing distrust on the part of parents, teachers, and students in the district. There may be good reasons for all of this (teacher cutbacks). Unfortunately, in a district that operates largely in secret, the public simply had no way of knowing."

On April 13, 2001, I picked up a box of audiotapes we had finally received from the school district. A year earlier, we had requested the tapes the school board was required to keep of all closed meetings. Most of the tapes we requested were missing. Correspondence from Margaret Skelton, the school district's attorney, said, "During the District's move from one administration office to another one, the tapes of the closed meetings were misplaced and staff have been looking for them."

On April 12, she warned, "The District has been unable to locate any closed meeting tapes from 1997 when Dan Mobilia was the superintendent." There were no tapes of the closed meetings or "study sessions" held just prior to the three administrative hires being challenged. *How convenient!*

The district's failure to produce material they are required by law to have was another violation of the Open Meeting Law. I spent hours checking the few tapes that were provided. They were 90 percent blank or inaudible. In particular, the tape of a closed meeting held on January 10, 2000, was missing over 100 minutes. That was the closed board meeting on negotiating strategy immediately before Langan presented principals with the four-step salary proposal that was contingent on my retiring.

Deadlines left us no time to hire another expert to examine the tapes, even if I had the money. This round went to them. If there was a smoking gun anywhere in the tapes, it had been erased. *There was perjury in the depositions and now there were erased tapes. Weren't presidents impeached for those offenses?*

Later in April, Margaret Skelton, attorney for the school district, requested yet another extension of the discovery deadlines. It was too late to allow our expert Hooker to review the rest of the depositions and documents and revise his preliminary report, but this time the extension worked in our favor. We were still missing documents we had re-requested several times.

So far the documents and depositions had not produced direct evidence of discrimination or retaliation. The EEOC defines direct evidence of retaliation as any written or verbal statement by a respondent official that s/he took the challenged action because the charging party engaged in protected activity. But the EEOC Manual on retaliation warns, "Direct evidence of retaliation is rare."

None of the board members were going to give us direct evidence, by writing or saying that I did not get hired for any of the administrative positions in retaliation for my lawsuit. Langan was not going to write or say that he transferred me to Tower in retaliation either.

According to the EEOC, "The most common method of proving that retaliation was the reason for an adverse action is through circumstantial evidence. A violation is established if there is circumstantial evidence raising an inference of retaliation and if the respondent fails to produce evidence of a legitimate, nonretaliatory reason for the challenged action, or if the reason advanced by the respondent is a pretext to hide the retaliatory motive. " Circumstantial evidence is defined as indirect or secondary evidence from which facts may be reasonably inferred.

"Typically pretext is proved through evidence that the respondent treated the complainant differently from similarly situated employees or that the respondent's explanation for the adverse action is not believable." We could show that I had been treated differently than other principals in several instances and we had mountains of contradictory evidence that made their explanations unbelievable. It seemed to me we had a solid case.

Retirement was now just a month away. The teachers at Tower hosted a retirement dinner for me on Wednesday, May 16, 2001. I had discouraged the dinner partly because I was focused exclusively on the lawsuit and current retirement battles and also because I felt like I was leaving the district under a cloud of sorts.

Of course they went ahead anyway. I hadn't said anything about the dinner to anyone, so I was stunned to see the number of people present when I got there. They had even notified my parents and family. Former colleagues and teachers came from Mt. Iron-Buhl and Orr. Reluctant as I had been, we had a great time in the roast and toast tradition.

I was amazed at the amount of planning that went into the thing. I never picked up on any of it during the preceding days at school. One of the roasting activities required me to sit on a stool up in front of the gathering and pass a "quiz" that was projected up on a large screen for every one to read. A lot of thought and creativity had gone into this multiple-choice quiz. The questions dealing with the central office, student discipline, teacher supervision, transfers, and other job frustrations were hilarious.

The question that drew the most laughter was, "What is the world's most complex language? a. Hebrew, b. Chinese, c. Greek, d. Langanese." After what seemed like hours of side splitting laughter, it was determined by a rather raucous consensus that I had passed the quiz. I was given the prize—the going away gifts—which included a huge basket full of gardening tools and a fabulous new spinning rod and reel, far more expensive than any I had owned before.

I was also presented with a beautiful, bound booklet that included copies of the overheads used in the quiz and the following poem:

"Here's to our leader – a principal named Judy.
Who is "turning in her keys," relieved of her duty.
You've taken on the roles of principal, mother, and wife.
It's now time to retire, Go out and GET A LIFE!
Forget the hassles and confrontations. And you might just as well,
Forget the mediations, conferences, and the ringing of the bell.
Sleep in, enjoy life – have a drink or two.
Don't think of your job or you'll have quite a few!
And so, with great fondness, we wish you the best,
Go hunting and fishing, and gets lots of rest.
Selectively forget those who made problems in the past.
Concentrate on the good times, and may THOSE memories last."

Marilyn Dimberio and her daughter, a professional photographer, were also there and weeks later presented me with a photo album full of candid pictures of the event and everyone present. It turned out to be a terrific evening and a huge boost to my morale. My only regret was that Erik and Max couldn't be there. Erik was out of the state on a consulting project that week and Max was just completing his fellowship in France. Like Rick, they had shared most of the triumphs and tribulations over the years and had earned a share of the celebration.

About that same time, the private investigator we had hired to go to Grand Marais to check out Langan's previous superintendency reported back. His preliminary reports on Langan were astounding!

He struck gold for us.

Chapter 13

2001

SUMMARY JUDGMENT

"Defendants' Motion for Summary Judgment is Granted"
Paul Magnuson, United States District Court Judge, August
22, 2001

B Y EARLY APRIL 2001, Ron Taggert filed the first reports
on his investigation in Grand Marais.

His investigation took him to the high school and district offices
for the Cook County School District, which were located in Grand
Marais. He interviewed Jaye Clearwater Day, the two school board
members who had resigned while Langan was the superintendent,
and two other teachers in the district. The information confirmed
what we had heard about Langan's previous superintendency. I was
stunned by how much he got away with.

Taggert's information established that the St. Louis County School
Board had not done a thorough background check on Langan before
they hired him. My initial assumption that his years of experience and
Ph.D. made him the more qualified candidate was wrong. What good
are years of experience if those years have been dreadful? Apparently
the experience and the doctorate simply meant that Langan had
more practice at being vindictive and dishonest. He was very good
at both.

Our problem was that we had used all of our allowed 10 depositions and we were running out of time to meet the discovery deadlines. Our only option was to get notarized affidavits from the witnesses in Grand Marais. Affidavits are written statements made under oath. We could then submit these affidavits to the court for the pending Summary Judgment hearing.

Jaye Clearwater Day's affidavit told a grim story. She taught elementary school in Grand Marais for several years. She was well liked and respected, and elected Teacher of the Year by the local PTA organization. She was one of ten finalists for the state honor. However, during the 1992–1993 school year, Day went through a bitter divorce that made it difficult to manage day care for her children and get to school on time. Langan was her superintendent and wrote her up for tardiness. She filed a grievance on the reprimand.

Langan suggested they meet over lunch to discuss the grievance. Instead of meeting in the school lunchroom, he picked her up in his truck and took her to the hotel for lunch. After spending the time discussing his life and his divorces, Langan said, "This has been a pleasant luncheon. Let's make an evening of this."

Day was affronted by this and told him, "No, I don't to want to make an evening of this."

According to Day's affidavit, "I returned to the school after the lunch and within a half hour or less, my grievance was denied by Dr. Langan and it moved on to the next step in the process. Dr. Langan saw to it that it went then to arbitration and bypassed the School Board." In a July 26, 1993, memo from Langan to Day, he threatened to transfer her if she did not drop her grievances.

Later, there was a school board meeting to discuss disciplinary action against Jaye Day. "I wanted the meeting left open to the public so that I could get support from other teachers and people in the community. Langan refused and called the meeting behind closed doors." There were many supporters at the meeting when Day objected to it being closed.

According to the affidavit of another teacher who was present at the meeting, "She had many supporters there, including me. Many of the parents were there to tell the school board that Jaye was really a quality teacher. However, the Board decided to have this be a closed meeting. Jaye protested in front of everyone and on videotape. The Board closed the meeting anyway over Jaye's protest and the protests of her supporters. The video tape of the meeting was 'conveniently lost' by the time Jaye made her decision to litigate." *Apparently Langan habitually lost tapes.*

The "lost" videotape was confirmed in the affidavit of one of the former board members. The board member also stated, "I thought at first it was a professional dispute between Langan and Jaye, but I soon found out it was not and that it had taken on the complexion of vengeance of the part of Langan."

Langan's harassment of Day increased. According to an affidavit of a teacher who worked with Day, "Dr. Langan was 'out to nail her.'" Langan had a time clock placed in her classroom. He proposed other agreements to her that she was coerced into signing. He told her that she would be terminated if she didn't sign them and comply with his wishes. A teacher and a former board member both said they knew that Langan had the district bus drivers watching Day's home.

"Finally, Dr. Langan made it so difficult for me to work there that I was forced to resign," said Day.

Jaye Day wasn't the only one subjected to Langan's retaliation.

It got worse.

After tracking several leads, the investigator was successful in interviewing both of the women who had resigned from the Cook County School Board in protest over Langan's tactics. One had left the district since resigning. According to both former board members, the St. Louis County school board never contacted them before hiring Langan.

This was significant to us because the St. Louis County board knew about the two resignations before Salmela and Fowler drove to Grand Marais to conduct the background check. They knew about the resignations but made no effort to check them out. In their affidavits, both women said it was unfortunate they were not contacted because they would have provided lots of negative information on Langan.

One of the former board members stated, "I wish that someone from the St. Louis County Board would have contacted me because I feel I have a lot to say. Dr. Langan was bad both for the district and for the Board." The other said, "Dr. Langan is not a truthful person and he spent a good deal of the school's money, more than he should have."

They said Langan was a micromanager, a total manipulator. One said, "If you crossed Langan as we did, he would publicly chastise and criticize you. It was a totally dysfunctional school board, we were just yes men for Langan."

When the two women objected to one of Langan's building projects because of cost, he brought in a "consultant" from the Twin Cities to help get a consensus on the project from all board members. The board members all went to a retreat where the consultant chastised the two of them during the entire retreat as not being "team players." Following the retreat, Langan held meetings when the two of them couldn't attend.

One of their affidavits stated, "He would isolate the two of us and brief us on things and budgets and then expect our vote separate from the other board members. I am sure this was done to separate the dissenters from the others so there was no chance to convince the others of the folly of the building project and other problems."

Both former board members referred to a DWI that Langan received. The board chairman called each board member and said there was a "gag order" on them; they were not to discuss it with anyone. Everyone had heard about it, but board members were told that if anyone called from the press, only the chairman or Langan could answer questions.

Finally, both women had enough and resigned from the school board.

In their affidavits, Jaye Day and a second teacher referred to another incident that was revealing about Langan. He had the principal call all the women teachers to a meeting. They were told that it was now school policy that they could not use sick leave when their children were ill. The teacher knew this was discriminatory and illegal. She called the state teachers' association to challenge the policy. After her successful challenge, Langan refused several times to approve her transfer requests.

In her affidavit, the teacher described her frustration over her district's hiring of Langan. Teachers in Grand Marais had heard negative stories about Langan from Mesabi East, his previous district. They heard he was arrogant and micromanaging. They sent an interview team to Mesabi East. The team came back with fairly positive comments. She called a Mesabi East teacher back after the visit and asked about the contradictory messages. She was told that they wanted to get rid of Langan and thus told the Grand Marais people good things about him. *Guess that explains how a guy like this survives.*

The Pre-Trial deadline for expert disclosures had forced our expert witness, Dr. Cliff Hooker, to conclude his report in February. At that time, without the information from Grand Marais, he wrote, "The Board made superficial background checks of male candidates to the detriment of Judy Pearson. A more thorough and professional background check of Simonson and Zitterkopf would have revealed unfavorable information on these candidates and elevated Ms. Pearson's rank among the candidates."

"The St. Louis County Board of Education did not know, but should have known of Sidney Simonson's alleged sexual misconduct while employed by the Star-Buck-Glenwood Board of Education. Zitterkopf's background of 'job hopping' from one position to another in several states raises questions about his performance and stability as an employee. Don Langan received a DUI (Driving Under the Influence) citation in 1993."

"If the St. Louis County Board of Education had done thorough background checks on these three candidates, it would have discovered these 'red flags.' Instances of sexual misconduct, job hopping, and DUIs have arisen in most of the 100+ Superintendent searches that I have conducted. I cannot recall a single school board that knowingly employed a candidate with a blemish of this sort."

Wonder what he would have written if he'd seen the affidavits from Grand Marais?

In his written reports, our investigator indicated that many of the witnesses interviewed in Grand Marais had provided names of additional people who could also add stories and details of Langan's tenure in Grand Marais, including names of other women who had left or been forced out because of Langan's behavior. But we were out of time. By the time the Grand Marais affidavits were prepared for notarized signatures, we had only three days left to get our response to defendant's Motion for Summary Judgment in the mail.

Rick and I raced up to Grand Marais on Friday, June 8 to get the affidavits signed and notarized. It was great to meet Jaye Day for the first time and give her a hug of support. She was a stunningly attractive woman with a personality to match. On the way home, Rick said he was sure that every student in her class must have fallen in love with her.

On June 9, Jaye Clearwater Day faxed me a copy of the United States District Court decision she had just received June 4th on her case. Langan and his former district had been denied Summary Judgment on her Title VII claim of unlawful reprisal. She had argued her case on her own, "pro se" because she could no longer afford an attorney. The judge wrote, "Not withstanding the Plaintiff's procedural misstep, we allowed her to participate in oral argument, and submit documentary materials, because of her status as *pro se* litigant."

This seemed like a great for Jaye Day and good for us as well. Another judge had determined that she would get her day in court on Langan's retaliatory tactics. However, it was not to be. By October, she had lost on appeal and everything was over for her. To my knowledge she never got her teaching position back. In the court's final decision, the summary of the facts and arguments sounded like they were taken right out of Langan's playbook and bore no resemblance to our witness affidavits from the former board members and teachers who worked with Jaye.

Jaye had also faxed me some of the documents she had used in court. One was a 1993 letter from Langan to his lawyer buddy Colosimo—the same Colosimo he brought along to our district. He wrote in reference to Jaye Day, "I'm convinced that if and when the

pin is pulled on this lady there will be a law suit. So, I would hope you
will be planning for a rather long haul on this one. See you soon, and
did you forget to send me the purchase agreement on *Das Boat,* or
did you change your mind?" *No wonder Langan got rid of Neff as school
attorney and brought in Colosimo. They had a long-standing and mutually
beneficial relationship.*

After returning from Grand Marais, we spent that entire weekend
in Prebich's office photocopying and collating the mountains of
documents that had to be mailed out on June 11 to make the court's
deadline. It was a huge job. Just condensing the complexities of our
case to fit within the court's limits on our written response to their
Summary Judgment motion was a huge challenge.

Our response plus the supporting documents or exhibits made
a stack of paper eight inches high. Our attached exhibits included
the 1991 Court decision, EEOC documents, depositions, board
minutes and agendas, license reports, evaluations, contracts, e-mails,
newspaper articles, medical records, expert testimony, and affidavits.
There were 95 exhibits in all.

We were required to provide both the court and the defendants
with multiple copies of our response. It was a hot and humid weekend.
The copy machines got overheated and kept jamming. We used every
available fan to keep them cool enough to keep running. By the time
we finished late Sunday night, after stacking and collating on tables,
chairs and the hallway floors, we were exhausted.

Meanwhile, I was battling Langan on another front. I still had no
response from the district to my concerns about retirement benefits.
I was just days away from my last day of service. I had been told I'd
have to grieve the district's calculations on my benefits. Before filing
a grievance, I asked Langan one last time to resolve the differences.
From April 24 through June 14, I sent six e-mails or memos to Langan
outlining the issues and requesting a response. He took weeks to
respond to each. He forced the principals' organization to get
involved and created several hoops for us to jump through. After all
that, he denied my requests on June 11.

As a result, I filed a grievance on the retirement issues on June 14.

June 15 was my last day of service, but my struggles with Langan would continue on even after I was out from under his authority.

Langan denied my grievance at Level One by e-mail the same day I filed it. He concluded his June 14 denial, "The next school board meeting is scheduled for June 25, 2001 at 6:00 p.m. in the District Administration Office. Your grievance will be placed on the agenda to be heard."

I arrived early for the board meeting to prepare. It was a damn good thing I did. The meeting started at 5:00, not 6:00 p.m., and my grievance was nowhere on the agenda. Was the wrong time stated in my letter deliberate or just a typo? Two typos, I suppose, because my grievance wasn't on the agenda either.

"We don't like to change the agenda at the last minute like this," Langan resisted. "A board committee will look over your documents and make the Level II decision."

"I respectfully reject that suggestion. I have a copy of your June 14 e-mail with me. It specifically states a date and time that my grievance would be on the agenda. Any last minute variation would clearly be an unfair labor practice."

The guy was so full of last minute games and changes to the rules of the games, it was difficult to keep up with him.

I was determined to at least have my say in public, which is probably what he wanted to prevent in the first place. The newspapers were there, so the board had little choice but to place my grievance on the agenda. It made no difference; the board followed Langan's recommendation as usual and denied my grievance.

Although I was exhausted from fighting on so many fronts, I decided to take the grievance to Level Three, mediation. In his deposition, Langan had stated that he "needed to know from Judy if there was something that the organization could do in an accommodation" in reference to his retirement proposals—buy-out deal—to me in May 1999. Things had certainly changed. Instead of "accommodation," I got the stingiest possible interpretation and calculation of our contract provisions for health insurance coverage and severance.

I hadn't retired when he wanted me to in 1999. The carrots he dangled as incentive, $80,000 in family health insurance (paid in full until age 65) and months of extra salary, were long gone. Instead, I paid my first full family health insurance premium of $797/month on July 1, 2001. I don't think any other principal or teacher had gotten stuck with full health insurance premiums two weeks after they retired in a long time.

I couldn't let him get away with it. I filed a petition with the State Bureau of Mediation Services on July 6, 2001. Mediation was scheduled for September 14, 2001.

Just three weeks after I retired, Langan made it evident that he was not going to hire a principal to replace me at the Tower School. Although he had posted my Tower position for a K–12 Principal, he was going to assign a Dean of Students. The headline in the July 13, 2001, *The Tower News* read, "Who's in Charge? Parents seek answers about Tower school leadership."

The article continued, "Judy Pearson, according to one teacher, stood up for the school. She knew school law, understood the rules, and was not afraid to fight for the Tower-Soudan School. This person wondered if a dean, hand-selected by the Superintendent, would have the fortitude to stand up to his boss." A parent wondered, "If a parent has a question about what is happening with his/her child at school—whom do you call? A Dean of Students cannot legally redress a member of the licensed staff–the teachers at the school."

The July 21 *Timberjay* editorial zeroed in on the critical questions. "What a difference two years makes—apparently. Back in 1999, when St. Louis County School Superintendent Don Langan announced the transfer of Principal Judy Pearson to the Tower-Soudan School, the official line from the district was that Pearson's extensive administrative experience was needed in Tower to help address a number of outstanding problems at the school. Yet with Pearson's retirement this year, and with the district looking to save money, things are apparently coming up roses at Tower-Soudan. No longer is there a need for administrative experience–in fact, says the superintendent, there's no need for a principal in the building at all. Instead, Pearson will be replaced by a so-called Dean of Students with virtually no administrative experience and no legal ability to instruct or address issues related to teachers."

The editorial continued, "The problem, once again, is the closed and secretive manner in which the decisions are rendered in this district. When questioned about those decisions, Langan offers up only vague and often condescending answers to legitimate questions that go to the heart of the district's credibility.

"It was no different two years ago, when district officials cited Pearson's experience as the reason for her transfer to Tower—an explanation that few people really accepted. Now, just two years later, district administrators have a new official line that says experience is no longer an issue in Tower. It leaves an obvious credibility gap."

While I was glad others were finally figuring Langan out, I was concerned about the lack of a licensed principal in the school. A Dean could patrol the hallways and maintain student discipline as well as a principal. Perhaps better because that was the only task assigned. But who would make the tactful interventions on behalf of students with teachers? Who would advise and correct new teachers as needed, often on a daily basis? Who would provide the curriculum and staff development leadership that's responsive to shifting state and federal mandates as well as local concerns? Who would carry local concerns to the central administration? Who would provide the leadership in child study and early interventions? Who could address high failure rates, low test scores, or rising dropout rates?

In spite of community concerns, Langan just plowed ahead. Since the first dean of students was assigned to Tower in 2001, deans have replaced licensed principals at all three of the district's small schools; Orr, Tower, and Cotton. In addition, full-time counselors have been cut back to half time. Most of their remaining time is involved in testing, registration, and scheduling. There is little time left for individual work with students who are struggling or failing.

In the years since I retired, I've heard that the dropout rates have risen and the graduation rates have fallen in those smaller schools. This is very difficult to document because no one is keeping or publishing the numbers. However, the Minnesota Department of

Education has a section on its web site that at least lists the previous year's attendance and graduation rates by school. In 2005, Orr Secondary had an attendance rate of 88% and Tower Secondary's was 89%. In nine years at those two schools I never saw an attendance rate less than 92%.

In 2005, the Orr Secondary graduation rate was 93% and Tower's was an abysmal 75%. From 1992–1999, we had a graduation rate at Orr of 98–100%. The two years I was assigned to Tower, our graduation rate was 94% or better, including the first Indian students to graduate from that school in decades. Drop out rates are not published. Apparently no one's interested in keeping those statistics. Even if they were, accuracy is a big question.

Schools or districts can code or categorize students who leave the school in several ways that can camouflage dropouts. For example, a student who is absent for 15 days can be coded as a transfer or an alternative placement, rather than a drop out. Worst of all, these disturbing trends almost always involve those students at the bottom of the socioeconomic ladder who seldom have assertive parents or advocates.

Much as the change to a dean at Tower concerned me at the time, I was retired and there was nothing I could do. I was relieved to be able to focus on the lawsuit without looking over my shoulder all the time. Rick and I drove to St. Paul for the hearing on defendant's motions for Summary Judgment, held at 2:00 p.m. on Friday, August 17.

Prebich met us at the Federal Courthouse. He was uptight and worried. Most of the recent summary judgment decisions had gone against the plaintiffs. He also knew that Judge Magnuson was a conservative Reagan appointee to the Federal bench. I was confident however, that the 1999 EEOC investigation and finding of probable cause would be a huge factor in our favor.

When we walked into the courtroom, my confidence wavered. The courtroom in Duluth had been intimidating in 1991. This one was bigger, grander, and even more intimidating. The ceiling seemed a mile high and the courtroom was like an auditorium. Whispers echoed like canons. The judge's bench was elevated on a high pedestal. The setting did little for my sense of empowerment in asserting my civil rights.

Margaret Skelton, whom we had worked with on all the depositions and preceding motions, was not present to argue the district's motions. Another lawyer in her firm, Scott Anderson, would present the defendants' oral argument for Summary Judgment, asking the court to dismiss the case.

The clerk of court came in shortly after we were all seated and informed both sides that there would be a strict limit of 20 minutes for each side to make their argument. According to the clerk, the judge was leaving right afterward for a weekend trip to his cabin in northern Minnesota.

My father was a judge, so I was well aware that judges are people who have lives outside the courtroom. But I was still put off by the announcement that the judge's weekend plans dictated the length of the oral arguments. Our case contained several complaints, spanned 14 years, involved over a dozen depositions and affidavits, and 95 exhibits. It would be difficult to condense these facts and arguments into 20 minutes on the spur of the moment. However, Prebich did a great job given the last minute warning on the unexpectedly short time limit. He hammered home the "wouldn't/couldn't" dilemma facing the board in October 1997, when they brought Langan back in at the last minute.

I left the court that day feeling very confident.

After all, we already had a ruling of probable cause on both discrimination and retaliation by the EEOC following an on-sight investigation. Hooker was a preeminent expert and his testimony was strongly in our favor. There were numerous contradictions in the district's explanations for their behavior. These contradictions were ample circumstantial evidence that their explanations for their actions against me were unbelievable and therefore a pretextual cover for their retaliatory motives. I thought we were in good shape.

I was wrong.

On August 22, 2001, just two full working days after our hearing,

Prebich called.

"You're not going to believe this, Judy, but we lost on all counts," he said.

"You're kidding of course," I said.

"I wish I was," he said. "I've read it once quickly and I just can't believe it."

He had just been faxed Magnuson's decision. He was angry and frustrated. I felt as if I'd been socked in the gut. We couldn't believe the speed at which such a complicated case had been dismissed. My immediate response was, "OK, so we'll appeal." Prebich said he'd fax the decision to me to read. Then we'd decide what to do.

Reading Judge Magnuson's decision was infuriating. In the first place, the Judge said that we did not claim retaliation stemming from my first lawsuit. It was the entire basis for our original federal complaint filed in March 2000. It was first mentioned on page one of our summary judgment argument and referred to many times throughout that document. The 1991 Court Decision was the second exhibit we submitted. Retaliation for the first lawsuit was the basis of my first EEOC complaint in 1998, which was validated by the EEOC, after an on-sight investigation, with a finding of reasonable cause and a generous conciliation proposal.

Then the Judge wrote, "In any event, Pearson's earlier lawsuit is too remote in time from the allegedly retaliatory actions she complains of to have any connection to those actions." However, the EEOC did not consider the issue too remote in time when they concluded that there was reasonable cause to believe retaliation had occurred. The EEOC guidelines on retaliation stated, "An inference of retaliation may arise even if the time period between the protected activity and the adverse action was long, if there is other evidence that raises an inference of retaliation."

In 1997, the EEOC supported another plaintiff's retaliation claim even though the adverse action came much later than the protected activity. "Absence of immediacy does not disprove causation," asserted the EEOC. Don't federal judges pay any attention to the rules and procedures of their federal agencies? In fact, Judge Magnuson never mentioned the EEOC findings in his decision, although we referred to it several times and included the decision in our exhibits.

The words, "No evidence," dominated the text throughout Magnuson's decision. Granted there was no "smoking gun" direct evidence. But he ignored all the circumstantial and contradictory evidence we provided, in spite of the EEOC admonitions, "Direct evidence of retaliation is rare" and "The most common method of proving that retaliation was the reason for an adverse action is through circumstantial evidence."

On the issue of retaliation regarding my involuntary transfer, Magnuson concluded that I failed to show that the transfer was an adverse employment action. "Mere inconvenience or unhappiness on the part of the employee will not lead to a finding of actionable adverse employment action. An adverse employment action is that which materially alters the terms or conditions of the plaintiff's employment. She did not experience a cut in pay or benefits and she had the same job title she had previously."

In the huge geography of our school district, transfer was the big threat. No loss of money, benefits, or title, but every principal quaked with fear at the thought. We provided several documents documenting the fear all principals had of screwing up or angering the boss and then being targeted for transfer.

Magnuson completely missed the whole point of the Title VII prohibition of retaliation against those who complain about discrimination. It's not about the money; it's about the "chilling effect" of retaliation on anyone who asserts their rights and on all of their coworkers. Enforcement of the laws against discrimination depends solely on people's willingness to assert their rights. There are numerous ways to retaliate without affecting an employee's compensation or benefits. This essential concept is clearly defined in the EEOC's Compliance Manual on Retaliation, found at www. eeoc.gov/policy/docs/retal.html.

The single most infuriating statement in Magnuson's decision was his conclusion. "Once again, the Court comes to the end of its discussion drained of energy and patience." *Isn't that your job? Aren't*

I paying you big bucks out of my tax dollars to have energy and patience?
Assuming he went to his cabin up north for the weekend immediately
after we concluded our oral arguments, he had spent little time
becoming "drained of energy and patience."

Magnuson continued, "In an effort to stem a disturbing trend in
employment litigation, the Court feels compelled to express again
its dissatisfaction with the presentation of this lawsuit. A 'shotgun'
approach to litigation cannot and will not be tolerated by this Court."
If you are frustrated with my attorney's presentation, why take it out on me?

I read and reread his conclusion. It was clear to me that I did not
matter. My rights did not matter. Whatever happened to my Seventh
Amendment rights, which read, "In suits at common law, where the
value in controversy shall exceed twenty dollars, the right of trial by
jury shall be preserved?" This amendment applies to civil cases heard
in federal courts. *Mine was a civil case in federal court and involved a lot
more than twenty dollars. Why didn't the amendment and the Bill of Rights
apply to me?*

Magnuson was upset with the way Prebich had presented our
claims. Prebich acknowledged from the beginning that he had not
had extensive experience in federal courts. Should that preclude me
from working with an attorney I trust and can afford? Does that mean
that the only successful access to the federal justice system is through
the doors of a few huge, experienced, and expensive law firms? Is the
federal justice system only for the big guys?

Why weren't these issues brought to our attention earlier during
all the pre-trial procedures so we could have adjusted course? Why
wait and summarily throw me out, deny me my right to a trial by jury,
because you are "drained of patience?"

After reading the judge's decision several times, I called Prebich
and told him I wanted to appeal. He agreed, but felt we should consult
with an additional attorney, experienced at the appeals level of the
federal judicial system. I understood his position, particularly after the
judge's scathing conclusion. Prebich said he'd search for an attorney
we could work with. We had 30 days to file an appeal. That's not much
time to find another attorney, who would need time to read all the

documents, decide whether to accept the case, and still file the appeal within the 30 days.

But then, even that 30–day window was blown away. On 4:30 p.m. on August 27, five days after the judge entered his summary judgment decision, the school district's attorneys faxed a letter to Prebich. The letter concluded that the since the judge apparently felt my lawsuit was "frivolous, unreasonable, and without foundation," they had been given the go ahead by the district to seek their fees and costs from me. Their fees and costs already totaled over $90,000. The letter referred to the "collection of a judgment against any property" we owned and to the "garnishment or attachment procedures" that might ensue.

If they were successful, Rick and I would lose everything. And of course, we still had Prebich's bill to pay.

Their letter continued. We had until 4:00 p.m. on September 5, 2001, to indicate in writing my agreement to waive any and all rights to appeal or they would file a claim for attorney's fees and costs. Thirty days had shrunk to less than 10 days. It was a calculatedly short window for decision. In addition to the compressed deadline, disbelief, despair, disillusion, rage, frustration, fury, and fear make a great recipe for bad decision-making.

While Prebich and Rick hashed over their ultimatum and our options, I said little. I felt paralyzed. I didn't want to decide anything. I resented being squeezed into a quick decision. Maybe I was still in shock. After the toughest sleepless night I ever put in, I finally decided to discuss an appeal with a large firm in the Twin Cities. We still had a week to respond.

Prebich found an attorney experienced in federal appeals work to look over our case and our prospects for an appeal. The catch was the firm required an $8,000 retainer just to look over the documents. I sent the check and signed the retainer agreement on August 29. The hourly rate for this legal assistance was $270. If associates were needed, the hourly rate would increase accordingly.

The stress of waiting for the consulting attorney to evaluate our chances for an appeal was relieved briefly by one of the most bizarre incidents I ever experienced.

Another rumor surfaced.

The Tower School secretary called one afternoon at the end of August. Rick took the call while we were visiting at the kitchen table.

"I'm so sorry about Judy," she said tearfully. "I just heard about it."

"What about Judy?" Rick asked her. "Hold on a second, she's sitting right here, I'll hand her the phone."

After she stopped crying and calmed down, she explained. The local funeral service had just called the school to find out which mortuary would be handling my funeral. They had received several calls of inquiry.

"The story is that you had a heart attack in the bathtub and drowned," she explained.

The three of us laughed until we cried about the small town rumor mill. She was very relieved and said she'd try to get more information in Tower about how this rumor got started. Rick and I were even more relieved that it was just a rumor!

Late that evening, I got a call from a colleague who was downtown at a local tavern.

"Judy, you'll never believe what I just heard!" he exclaimed.

"Don't tell me, I had a heart attack and drowned in my bathtub, right?"

"You heard, right? Everyone's talking about it!"

"Well, did you want me to confirm or deny the rumor?" I chuckled as we laughed about the joys of small town living.

The next day, my brother called. His wife had called from work and wanted to know why they hadn't heard I had died. She had heard it from a teacher in Tower. After assuring him it was just a rumor, we laughed so hard it hurt over the story he heard. Apparently when the teacher told her husband, who we had grown up with, he said,

"No way that happened, can't be true! I know her family and they don't take baths, they take saunas in the summer."

The Tower School secretary called the following week and we pieced together how the rumor had started. Although school had not begun yet, practice for the fall sports had started two weeks earlier. Apparently, driving into practice, one of the volleyball players had heard on her car radio that a Judith Peterson had drowned. She brought the news into practice.

At the Orr School and later at Tower, students and staff just called me "Mrs. P." I suppose it was easier than differentiating between Pierce, Peterson or Pearson. Take that misunderstood news report, mix in my heart attack of the previous year, fold it into a small town and voila, I'm dead!

The rest of the story appeared in the September 1, 2001, *Timberjay*. It headlined, "Reports of Pearson's Death Greatly Exaggerated." Unfortunately there was an actual drowning that precipitated the rumor and tempered our light-hearted response.

The comic relief provided by the rumor was short-lived in any event.

At the very last minute, 2:25 p.m. on September 5, the attorney we consulted faxed an analysis of our appeal prospects. Although the analysis indicated that an appeal would not be frivolous and that I did have sufficient grounds for appeal, the rest of the news was not good. Without direct evidence, it would be very difficult to obtain a reversal of the court decision. Hooker's expert opinion and the EEOC findings were cited as sufficient grounds to file an appeal and to defend against defendants' motion for fees. The firm agreed to represent me on appeal and to defend me against the district's motion for fees if we decided to proceed.

We had less than two hours to decide whether or not to appeal. I did not trust we'd be given a minute beyond their 4:00 p.m. deadline. Rick and I talked it over. We talked to Prebich. We talked twice to the consulting attorney, firing off questions as they popped up. She estimated that the cost of the appeal alone, if we got all the way to the appeals court, would be over $200,000. This did not include the cost of defending against their motion for fees.

When I asked her to estimate how long the appeal process would take, it was one of her casual asides that became the deciding factor. The Court of Appeals could refuse to hear the appeal at any time in the process. One month or one year and thousands of dollars into the appeal process, the appeals court panel of judges could arbitrarily dismiss our appeal and refuse to hear it. We had the right to file an appeal, but we had no right to a completed appeal process, to a final ruling. It was all at the judges' discretion and they could exercise it at any time in the process.

After an intense hour on the telephone with the attorneys, Rick and I took a look at the numbers. The answer was clear. Our financial liability would be huge, far beyond our ability to pay. That was just for our legal fees, to say nothing of the possible loss on the school district's threatened claim for their legal fees. If their references to collecting on a judgment against us, including garnishments and attachments, were intended to scare us off, they succeeded. Garnishment and attachment are legal procedures to take someone's property. The risks were too big.

I called Prebich at 3:40 p.m. and told him to fax a response to the school district's attorneys before 4:00 p.m., waiving all rights to an appeal.

It was over.

It was like a sudden death. For four years, this fight was part of who I was. It had been with me everyday, whether at work or at play. I felt like an amputee, like a major part of me had been cut off. The colors were gone, my days resembled leeched out black and white photographs. When I moved at all, it was in a daze, hollowed out and numbed to the core. I couldn't even cry. Sleep had been my nemesis for years. Now all I wanted to do was sleep. I had no idea what I'd do with myself. All my energy and planning had revolved around the lawsuit and gearing up for the pending trial.

Losing was the ultimate dissonance in my plaintiff blues.

The experts say the grief process occurs whenever a death or horrific event occurs. The process has several stages including shock, denial, anger, depression, and acceptance. For me, the first four stages swept in simultaneously. There was so much emotion I just shut down. I have no memory of those next several days. My notes indicate I called the Bureau of Mediation Services and dropped my retirement grievance. I didn't want to think about it or the district. Rick said he was worried because I never cried or swore or paced in anger. I didn't want to talk about it. He feared it would become a permanent elephant in the living room.

Rick was actually relieved to see some sign of life when I blew up over the bill we received from the consulting attorney. I had sent a check for $8,000 on August 29. By September 5, the consultation had cost me $5,540. The bill showed 20 hours of time, for which I received a two-page analysis. It was shocking to realize that the consulting attorney could have cost me over $40,000 a month if I had proceeded, on top of Prebich's fees. It confirmed my decision to drop the case, but it didn't make it any easier to accept. I never considered us poor, but apparently you have to be really rich to access the federal justice system.

In retrospect, three events saved me from whatever combination of depression and rage that might have followed. Six days after I decided not to appeal was September 11. The county tax assessor stopped in about 2:00 that afternoon. He noticed that our TV was not on and asked us if we had seen the news. We had been working outside and knew nothing. He told us about the Twin Towers. We turned the set on.

Nothing I was going through could compare to the horror we saw unfolding in New York, Washington, and Pennsylvania. Those events blew my troubles away.

I became consumed with the events of 9/11. I read everything I could to help explain the horror of those attacks, to try to understand how and why something like that could happen. I reviewed the history and geography of the Middle East. I read books about Islam. I read online newspapers and analyses and was obsessed with the news. I say obsessed because I desperately needed a distraction.

The events of 9/11 shocked me out of my misery and provided an intellectual focus other than my own loss, which seemed petty in comparison.

Our family was indirectly affected by the terrorist attacks shortly after September 11. Max was serving in the Air Force and had been stationed in Korea since August. His fiancé, Julie, was studying veterinary surgery in Lyon, France, at the time. Julie planned to fly to Korea to see Max whenever she had a break in her studies.

However, the attacks had forced tightened security at all levels of the military. It seemed unlikely that Max and Julie could see one another while he was stationed in Korea. Julie was a "foreign national" and they weren't married. They did not have the privileges afforded to married couples in the service.

Max had a leave scheduled for December and called to ask if my father, who was a retired judge, would marry them at our house when he came home for Christmas. Julie would fly in from France. Once they were married, she would be able to visit Max in Korea when such visits might otherwise have been prohibited as new uncertainties prevailed and security tightened.

Of course, my dad agreed and I set about making the arrangements. I kept very busy, with the complicated marriage license details between two countries, cleaning house for the festivities, and planning our first wedding. Granted it was a quick, small, and relatively informal ceremony for just the immediate family, but it focused my energy and attention.

Rick and I had flown to Paris to spend time with Max and Julie in the spring of 1999. While Julie attended classes, Max was a magnificent tour guide. He introduced us to the wonderful fresh pastries, crepes, and paninis sold by sidewalk vendors as he walked us through what seemed like the entire city of Paris. We visited the Pantheon and the Luxembourg gardens, both close to Max's apartment. We toured Les Invalides and Napoleon's Tomb, walked the Champs-Elysees, and climbed to the top of the Arc d' Triomphe. We were awed by Notre Dame and countless other ancient churches and cathedrals. He gave us a running account of the history and culture as we walked and walked and then walked some more. We vowed to be in better shape when we visited again.

One lesson I learned while visiting Paris. There are so few public washrooms in Paris that men rather routinely and inconspicuously step around a corner. Women's plumbing makes us either much more conspicuous or much more miserable. Plan accordingly. Who says you can't learn from your kids?

Julie's family, the Baldovinis, treated us to a traditional dinner at a marvelous French restaurant. It was a five course, four hour affair unlike anything we had experienced. The food was terrific, with a different and wonderful wine with each course. Max had warned us to drink a glass of water for every glass of wine we drank and it was good advice. We thoroughly enjoyed the evening and their company. The following year, Erik joined Rick and I for our second trip to Paris to visit Max and Julie. We took a train south to Julie's home in Hyds and spent time with the Baldovini family. We felt bad that current events and circumstances meant Julie's family was not able to come over to the states for her wedding on New Year's Eve.

However, Rick and Erik had a plan. We took many digital pictures of the festivities on December 31, 2001. Max and Julie were married by 4:00 p.m. Rick quickly put the pictures up on the web and the Baldovinis were looking at them shortly afterward, by midnight their time. Rick had bought digital cameras for the family a year earlier, so we had been digitally sharing our travels for a while. Sharing a wedding in almost real time between rural northern Minnesota and rural France seemed amazing at the time.

The wedding pictures were a study in contrasts, from French champagne chilling in the snow outside to forced hyacinths filling the table with the fragrance of the Luxemburg gardens, from French foie gras to Slovenian potica and Scandinavian pickled fish.

It was a great night for us. In addition to Max's wedding, Erik brought his girlfriend Jill with him and they witnessed the ceremony for Max and Julie. Erik had met Jill that summer and we thought she was as perfect a match for Erik as Julie was for Max. I told Erik at that time if he didn't ask Jill to join the family soon, I would. He promptly but politely informed me that it was probably their decision to make.

Max and Julie told me I could begin planning for their next wedding in the fall when Max got back from Korea. They wanted to have a more traditional ceremony when the Baldovinis could be here.

Double weddings were not uncommon in the military. Max teased that it was the perfect task for a retired administrator, to plan a wedding ceremony 250 miles from home, at a hotel by the airport in the Twin Cities and coordinate it over three continents and two oceans—Max in Korea, Julie and Baldovinis in France, and Rick and I in the U. S. It was a challenge I couldn't refuse. On August 3, 2002, Max and Julie had a formal ceremony at the Airport Hilton in Bloomington, followed by a wonderful dinner and dance for 90 guests.

The Twin Cities' airport location was critical for the August ceremony because many of Max's Air Force friends had to fly in and out on short leaves. Julie's family—father Jean-Paul, mother Lysiane, and brothers Laurent and Pierre—came for this second wedding. It was their first trip to the states. They spent two weeks here in Minnesota, most of it visiting with us at the lake.

We introduced them to saunas, water skiing, fishing, and all the wild fish and game Rick and I so enjoyed. They had shared so much wonderful French wine, food, and tradition with us when we visited them in France, that it felt great to return the hospitality.

The day before the ceremony at the Hilton, Erik and Jill helped us with final preparations. In a casual moment, they mentioned that if they decided to get married, they would probably elope to Hawaii. Neither of them wanted a big ceremony. What did we think? Would it be okay with us?

Rick and I spontaneously said it was a fantastic idea. Not because we wanted to avoid more expense or festivity, but because we were excited to have Jill join Julie as a member of the family. What parents really want most for their kids is for them to find their partner for life. We were pretty impressed with the partners our kids had chosen.

Erik and Jill were concerned that people might feel cheated out of the wedding ceremony if they eloped.

"I can think of a few who might feel bad about it," I commented, "but Dad and I think it's a great idea, the sooner the better!"

"Besides, Ma's had lots of practice and can throw you a great reception when you get back," Rick chimed in.

"Don't go jumping the gun here, there's no plans yet, but we wanted to let you know we're thinking about it and wanted to make sure you guys and Jill's folks were okay with the idea." Erik said. "I think my friends and family who really know me will understand that I'm not comfortable with the pomp of a big ceremony." *He is a bit more shy than Max,* I thought to myself.

Right after Christmas 2002, Rick and I, and Erik and Jill flew to Germany to tie up with Max and Julie. Max was now stationed in Germany and had rented a house that easily accommodated all of us. We spent a marvelous ten days with Max and Julie as our guides. The memorable night of the trip was New Year's Eve 2002. We drove from Max's home in Germany to Julie's family home in Hyds. That evening was the first anniversary of their first wedding. The Baldovinis hosted a marvelous celebration.

Dinner was absolutely a gourmet feast. Lysiane served her fabulous foie gras, which Jean-Paul paired with champagne from his incredible wine cellar. Dinner progressed with every course accompanied by another great wine from Jean-Paul's wine cellar. We joked about Jean-Paul being "the greatest sommelier" in the world. That dinner proved it was no joke!

Other guests that evening included Julie's Uncle Pierre and his wife Francoise and close family friends, Pierre and Marie Genest and their daughter Celine. Marie had made a heavenly tiramisu for dessert and we all made room, even after we decimated the traditional cheese tray.

Laurent and Pierre had helped decorate their large attic for a dance following dinner and even had a disco ball to match the music. We rang in the New Year in real style and partied well into the early morning. We loved every minute of it.

On April 26, 2003, Erik and Jill were married in Hawaii. We worked long distance with Max to mail order a gift basket, a bottle of the best French champagne, and two flutes to be delivered to their hotel room the night they were married. Erik, of course, is the tech wiz of the family, so he blogged their wedding and honeymoon pictures to us in almost real time.

I didn't even have to exercise my latent administrative skills for a reception when they got back. Erik, Jill, and Jill's family—parents Pat and Kathy Suer and her sister Charmin—did a fabulous job of decorating and recreating a Hawaiian atmosphere for a reception held in the front yard of their new home in Eden Prairie on August 30, 2003. Max and Julie were able to fly in for the party as well and we met Jill's brother Aaron and his wife Amanda for the first time. It was a terrific warm, sunny day to have a party outdoors. We drank pina coladas in our leis and Hawaiian shirts and had a great time.

About all Rick and I got to help with was clean up afterwards. Even on that task we had great family fun, including Jill's aunt and uncle, Pat and Judy Corrigan.

For Rick and I, the circle was complete. Our sons had partners to share the joys and sorrows that life would bring.

Back in November 2001, while I was busy cleaning and planning for Max's first wedding, I got two calls that took care of the rest of my time that first winter as a retiree and summarily dismissed plaintiff. Two administrative colleagues of mine had scheduled to teach college classes as adjunct instructors that winter. One was teaching for St. Mary's University and the other was teaching for Bemidji State University. They both called because other plans were interfering with their adjunct teaching. They asked me to take their classes for the winter and spring quarters, beginning in January 2002.

One position involved teaching graduate level administrative classes on the principalship to teachers working on their administrative licensure. These classes were taught on weeknights or weekends on the Range or in Duluth. The second involved teaching an undergraduate human relations class one evening a week in Hibbing to students working on a teaching degree.

Both of the adjunct positions involved a lot of driving, between 50 and 80 miles. I hated the winter driving, but I loved the teaching. I always had. That winter and spring I taught two sections of the course on the principalship, with about a dozen students in each section. I taught one section of the human relations course that lasted three months and included 35 students.

Once again, teaching helped me through a brutal period. The

graduate courses on the principalship were particularly stimulating. Preparing for them forced me to analyze and evaluate the essential lessons I had learned over the 16 years as high school, junior high school, and K–12 principal. In doing so, I developed a summary document I called the Principal's Principles. It contained many of the little nuggets I had gleaned over the years. Use as little authority as possible to accomplish your goal, keep the number of absolutes to a minimum, use all the common sense you can muster, catch them doing something good, beware simple solutions to complex problems, remember humor is power, take notes, and keep the coffee brewing—to mention just a few.

The human relations class was a real eye opener for me. Over two-thirds of the class were adult students, many with children or grandchildren. They knew so little about the racial and diversity issues I took for granted that I seemed to be starting from scratch. The Arab-Muslim issue was difficult to address with perspective because it was so close to 9/11.

We reached a quick consensus that we all had a lot to learn about the Middle East. What does the term Arab refer to in historical, geographical, and cultural terms? Iran is a Muslim country in the Middle East, but is Persian, not Arab? How far back would we need to go to understand the Israeli-Palestinian conflict? What are the basic teachings of the Muslim religion? How do we begin to understand the anti-American feelings in the Arab world if we can't answer any of those questions?

The class knew next to nothing about the history and current realities for American Indians. They had never heard of Sand Creek or the history of Wounded Knee. Slavery was history they knew, but not its current impacts on black life. Of course, none saw themselves as racist, but none wanted their daughters dating a black man.

Most had not studied the holocaust in school and other than recognizing the name Auschwitz, they had not thought or discussed how that appalling genocide could have occurred. I met little resistance in introducing these topics of tolerance and diversity until I brought in staff and students from a GLBT (Gay, Lesbian,

Bisexual, Transgender) youth group to discuss their experiences with harassment and violence in the public schools. The class was polite to the guests, but the tension was palpable. Over the next couple of weeks, the arguments between class members were heated and bitter. Was homosexuality about nature (genetics) or nurture (choice)?

These were adult students studying to become teachers. I reminded them many times, regardless of their personal feelings about homosexuality, they were obligated under Minnesota law to protect all students from harassment and intimidation. When the course ended, I realized once again that my students had taught me as much as I taught them. I had a much better grasp of the resistance to tolerance and acceptance of diversity.

By the spring of 2002, I had pretty well put the school district and court battles behind me. Between planning weddings, and preparing and teaching the college courses, I stayed busy enough after losing the lawsuit to avoid thinking about it. I had to settle for knowing I was right. I knew absolutely that chairmen Chet Larson and Larry Anderson had kept me out of the administrative positions in retaliation for the first lawsuit. I knew absolutely that Langan had retaliated against me for speaking up and filing complaints when he tried to buy me out, transferred me, negotiated against me in our contract, and minimized my retirement benefits.

I firmly believed a trial would have surfaced their contradictory and pretextual explanations for those actions and I would have prevailed. However, I'd have to be content to trust the concept, "as you sow, so shall you reap." I believe that people who exercise authority from such shallow and vindictive motivations eventually have to pay their dues. What goes around comes around.

However, events during the summer of 2002 brought the school district battles back up on my radar screen. The May 25 *Timberjay* headlined, "Principal May Be Forced Out." At a board meeting in Babbitt, Walt Fischer, the remaining senior district principal at Cotton told board members, "He was being 'bullied' into retirement by the district administrators. Following the meeting, Fischer said he believed district administrators were angry at him for his testimony in support of a recent lawsuit by Judy Pearson."

Fischer had requested that the school board rescind their approval of his letter of intent to retire sent earlier. He had decided to work another year or two. Langan recommended against Fischer's request and the board took no action, even though the same request had been granted for several other employees in the past.

The article went on to state, "Langan's four-year tenure with the St. Louis County district has been a difficult one for principals hired prior to the superintendent. Fischer said most of those principals were pressured by one means or another to leave."

Then the June 29 *Timberjay* headlined, "Fischer won't be back in Cotton this fall." Langan had now eliminated the principal's position in Cotton and assigned the administrative duties to the Albrook principal he had hired in 2000. The article explained that although the board had finally voted on June 10 to rescind Fischer's letter of intent to retire, Fischer would be assigned elsewhere in the district for the coming year.

Fischer complained to me that there was discussion that he would be assigned a social studies teaching position at Babbitt. That was the school farthest from his home, over 100 miles one-way. The huge district had a long history of using such transfers to get rid of people. When asked about this possibility, board chairman Salmela was quoted, "The superintendent has the right of assignment. Mr. Fischer could be assigned to any of the schools."

In July, Langan changed course. Parents and staff had signed petitions in support of Fischer. *Perhaps I shouldn't have been so quick to shut down those petitions against my transfer in 1999?* The July 20 *Timberjay* headlined, "Fischer to return to Cotton after all." Langan said he was unable to find another suitable position for Fischer.

Larry Salmela, the Cook school board member, was up for reelection in November 2002. As chairman, Salmela had been the ultimate "yes man" for Langan. That fact plus Fischer's troubles, particularly if they were on my account, convinced me to file for Salmela's position. I wanted to put the board and Langan on notice. The retaliation had to stop. I hoped my filing would be sufficient to send the message. I never campaigned or worked to get elected. I wasn't anxious to win because I knew it would be stressful to work with the other board members whom I had sued. They just blindly followed Langan's recommendations, without question. Any input or insight I had would be automatically discounted.

But it was interesting to read the *Cook News Herald* as the election approached. The October 24 issue headlined on the front page, "ISD 2142 has become a model district with Salmela as board chair." In the next issue, Albertson endorsed the incumbents in his editorial. No surprise. Salmela and his supporters did a lot of campaigning and advertising. He won reelection in November, but with only a slim plurality. The two of us running against him got more votes combined then he did. I hoped the days of apathetic electorates and automatic incumbencies were over for our school board.

Rick and I had a terrific fall in 2003. We made our annual fishing trip to Alaska and added a couple of duck and goose hunting trips to Canada. It is thrilling to watch thousands and thousands of geese appear on the horizon and then fly right over your head, even if they're mostly out of range. But then a small flock comes off the horizon lower than the rest. When they set their wings, lower their landing gear and drop into your decoys, it's a spectacular sight. Learning to prepare Canadian geese was another fascinating challenge, fraught with trial and lots of "tough" error.

By the winter of 2003, I was emotionally strong enough to begin organizing my files and documents from my years of work in the school district and my years of struggle as a plaintiff. The newspaper clippings alone took weeks to organize.

I used to joke with friends that someday I'd probably be ready to begin thinking about the possibility of starting to organize materials and might contemplate writing about my experiences. Two years had finally given me the distance and perspective I needed. I was ready. I could revisit the experiences without reliving the pain.

Chapter 14

2002–2005

WHAT GOES AROUND
COMES AROUND

"We hold that direct evidence is not required."
Justice Thomas in Desert Palace v. Costa, June 9, 2003.

S UPERINTENDENT LANGAN HAD BEEN forced to
back down on Walt Fischer's transfer from Cotton in July 2002.
Fischer remained the Cotton principal for the 2002–2003 school year.
It was a big win for Fischer and a small blow against Langan. However,
it was the beginning of a change in the board's typically rubber-stamp
support for Superintendent Langan.

In October 2002, the tide began turn for Langan.

On October 5, 2002, the front page of the *Timberjay* headlined,
"Questions Raised on Superintendent Contract Changes." The
article continued, "Superintendent Don Langan, who already earns
more that most of his counterparts at other Iron Range schools, has
asked for changes in salary and benefits that would boost his pay by
thousands of dollars." The newspaper did a great job of catching some
of the subtle contract language changes Langan proposed in unused

sick leave accumulation, daily pay calculation, and severance. Those proposed changes would have increased his benefit package by close to $25,000. That was in addition to the three-year salary increase of over $10,000 he requested.

The *Timberjay* editorial continued the analysis. "Perk-filled supt's contract sets wrong tone for district," headlined the editorial. The editor reported that Langan's salary was the third highest of 16 area school districts. "At a time when most teacher's salaries and other benefits are being held in check by area school districts due to budget constraints, school boards can't afford to hold superintendents to a different standard," concluded the editorial.

I followed these challenges to Langan's contract from the distance of retirement. Then on January 5, 2003, Walt Fischer dragged me directly back into district business. He complained that ever since he'd been allowed to stay at Cotton, he had been getting constant grief from the superintendent and central office. He had trouble with supply requisitions and his recommendations for hiring Cotton staff.

"I went in to see Langan the first day back from Christmas vacation. I told him I was upset and unhappy with the way things were going," Walt explained to me.

"How did he respond?" I asked.

"He asked me if I wanted to resign, what would it take for me to retire? I told him I'd want the two-year early notice waived so I could get the $12,000 early retirement incentive."

"You'll need health insurance won't you?" Langan asked Walt.

"I said yes, so Langan offered an extra year of paid family health insurance. I was surprised, because I hadn't asked for it and it's over and above what the contract provides," Walt continued.

The January 23 *Cook News Herald* carried the official minutes of the January 13, 2003, School Board meeting. "Motion and seconded to accept Walter Fischer's letter of retirement/resignation as principal at the Cotton School, effective January 15, 2003 and to provide Mr. Fischer with an additional year of family health insurance." Langan's stick tactic of the threatened transfer to force Walt out in the fall had failed, so now he used the carrot of health insurance. *Just like he did with me, only I didn't buy it,* I thought.

This extra perk was great for Walt, but it just rubbed salt in all my old district wounds. After I retired, I had to pay my full family health insurance premium the first month. I had filed a grievance on the retirement issues, but dropped it after I lost in summary judgment. Walt's extra health insurance meant the principal that retired before me and the principal that retired after me, both men, got significant health insurance benefits denied to me. I was furious, again.

There seemed little I could do about it. I had retired a year and a half earlier, far beyond the timelines for filing a complaint under the laws I was familiar with. Nevertheless, I began searching the web sites and laws to find any possibility of challenging.

I read the federal Equal Pay Act (EPA). It prohibits pay discrimination between men and women performing substantially equal work in the same establishment. It defines pay as all forms of compensation, including fringe benefits and retirement benefits. The EPA timelines for filing a complaint were two years from the alleged unlawful compensation practice or three years if it was a willful violation.

Voila! I had found legal grounds and timelines that would allow me to file a complaint. I was determined not to let them get away easily with the same old crap. I knew it was a long shot. I had been out of the district for 18 months and had no access to the documents or information to support my challenge.

I was unable to reach Fischer until January 27. He had been out of town since his retirement. I told him I was going to file a complaint on the retirement health insurance issue under the EPA provisions. I asked him to send me the board agenda items from the January 13 meeting when the board approved his retirement and gave him the extra health insurance. He agreed to, but was clearly worried that my filing would "screw up his deal."

By the beginning of February, 2003, I had not received the documents from him. I called Metsa at the Orr School and asked him to send the documents. He agreed, but I never got them from him either. I couldn't blame the guys. My transfer and loss in summary judgment made it seem like there was no limit to Langan's retaliatory reach.

However, I had the published minutes that documented the extra health insurance, so I hustled to file the complaint anyway. I couldn't wait any longer to get the documents. I had a very small window to meet the EPA timelines.

My complaint would fall within the EPA timelines, but those timelines were different than any I had worked with before. The filing of an EPA charge does not extend the timeline for going to court. That means that any EEOC investigation had to be completed in time to file a suit, all within the two-year limit. The two-year limit was absolute. In this case, there were only four months left before the time limit expired. The clock began ticking with the alleged compensation discrimination on June 15, 2001, the date I retired.

In March I received several interesting phone calls related to Langan. The first was from John Metsa, the Orr Principal. He indicated that several board members, including Zelda Bruns from Orr and Liz Johnson from Cherry, were upset with Langan. A discrepancy of $600,000 in the district audit and staff unrest in the central office were the big issues. A few days later I got a call from Mike Zupetz, a former principal from the Mesabi East school district. He said Langan was retaliating against the special education director of the cooperative Zupetz was currently working with. He was looking for information to fight Langan.

The third call was the most interesting. It was from Liz Johnson, the Cherry board member elected in 1999. She was also concerned about Langan's actions against the special education cooperative, her current employer. In addition, she wanted to prevent Langan from getting a renewal of his contract with the district. She was looking for any information I might have she could use against Langan. I indicated that I had nothing current to help them with, but referred her to the board members and teachers in Grand Marais. I warned her about how Langan had used the board chairman in his previous district to isolate and discredit board members who challenged him.

In the course of the conversation, she volunteered that when my transfer grievance came to the board in September 1999, she had wanted to support me. But she had only been on the board for a few months. When she spoke in support my remaining in Orr, the other board members had jumped all over her. They filled her in on my first lawsuit and my current challenge on the administrative positions. At the time she thought, "Boy, the board really doesn't like this lady."

Like so much of the information I was given during my battles with the district, her revelations were too late to do me any good. Had we been able to depose her, her testimony on those conversations would have been the "direct evidence" I needed to survive summary judgment.

I advised her to keep careful notes of any actions Langan or the board chair took against her. Document everything. I also suggested that she keep other board members aware of any harassment that came her way. I recommended that if necessary, she use her board position to take any retaliation public. It didn't seem appropriate so I never mentioned my pending EPA complaint during that conversation. She never referred to it. I wondered later if Langan had even made the board aware of it.

On April 21, 2003, I received the district's response to my EEOC complaint filed under the EPA. The response was amazing. It read, "Importantly, Ms. Pearson never requested any benefits over and above those in which she was entitled pursuant to the master agreement be accorded to her upon her retirement."

The next paragraph continued with more of the same. "It is notable that Ms. Pearson did not make any request for retirement benefits beyond those accorded to her by the negotiated master agreement and the memorandum of understanding which were in effect at the time of her retirement as mentioned above."

In other words, I didn't get any extra benefits because I didn't ask for them? According to Fischer, he hadn't asked for them either. Langan offered them to him to sweeten the incentives for him to retire. What about the grievance I filed on severance and health insurance? I specifically requested the three additional months of paid health insurance I believed I was due under the contract.

Their response included the argument that since Fischer retired in the middle of the school year, it enabled the district to eliminate the Cotton principal's position and save a half-year's principal salary. What about the fact that they also eliminated the Tower principal's position immediately after I retired and saved much more the entire following year? The district argued that Jurkovich's health insurance benefit came because he had a lawsuit pending and it was a part of a negotiated settlement in return for his retirement. *But I also had a lawsuit pending at the time of my retirement and the district refused every opportunity to conciliate or negotiate a settlement with me.*

I sent the EEOC my response to the district's defense on April 30, 2003. I included all the relevant documents I had and listed all the witnesses that might provide information. But I also warned them retaliation was the operating system in the district and many employees who had information might be reluctant to cooperate.

Fischer had been promised extra benefits when he retired in January. In early April, 2003, I e-mailed Walt to determine whether he had actually received those benefits or whether my filing would put his benefits at risk. He didn't respond until April 28, when his e-mail response said, "So far I'm getting everything I agreed to, but I have nothing in writing and am therefore vulnerable." *Interesting how vulnerability prevails even after retirement when Langan's at the helm.* I had listed Fischer as a witness on the EPA complaint, but I knew he would be reluctant to jeopardize his benefits.

On June 10, 2003, I received the EEOC notice that they were unable to conclude there was a violation of the statute. The notice was clear that it did not mean the district was in compliance. The letter included my Right to Sue notice. This was of no use, because the 2-year deadline would be exhausted in five days.

Ironically, the Supreme Court added a bittersweet twist to my story that same day. According to the June 10, 2003, *New York Times*, in *Desert Palace v. Costa*, a unanimous Supreme Court had just made it significantly easier for workers to win discrimination suits against their employers. Justice Thomas wrote, "We hold that direct evidence is not required."

Back in 1989, the Court had ruled that a plaintiff must prove by direct, not circumstantial, evidence that discrimination had been a motivating factor in an employer's action. In 1991, Congress amended the Civil Rights Act of 1964 to make it easier for plaintiffs from protected categories to bring an action against an employer. Although Congress did not require direct evidence in the 1991 amendments, the lower courts had continued to require it.

With the *Desert Palace* decision, more cases would survive summary judgment and reach a jury. Summary judgments could no longer include "No evidence" as the indiscriminate gatekeeper for the federal courts, as had been the case in the 1990s.

In the June 9 *Desert Palace v. Costa* decision, Justice Thomas explained in reference to the 1991 amendments, "On its face, the statute does not mention, much less require, that a plaintiff make a heightened showing through direct evidence. Circumstantial evidence is not only sufficient, but may also be more certain, satisfying, and persuasive than direct evidence."

The *Times* analysis continued, "Beyond the decision's impact on civil rights litigation, an effect that could be substantial, the case was notable for the court's unanimous rejection of the position argued by the Bush administration. The administration had urged the court to adhere to its direct-evidence requirement." *Wasn't it the first President Bush that had vetoed the original Civil Rights Act of 1991, forcing a congressional override? What is it with the Bushes?*

The *Times* article concluded, "The unanimity of the ruling today, along with the fact that the appeals courts other than the Ninth Circuit were still requiring direct evidence, "illustrates how much more conservative the lower courts are these days than the Supreme Court.""" After my 2001 summary judgment experience with Judge Magnuson, I certainly agreed with that analysis.

Isn't it interesting how justice is relevant to time and place? Had the *Desert Palace* ruling come two years earlier, before my summary judgment hearing, I would have had my day in court. Had I lived and filed in the Ninth Circuit instead of the Eighth, I would have had my day in court. I would pay a lot more attention to federal judicial nominees in the future.

But the Supreme Court had spoken and times were changing. I chose not to dwell on the irony of this decision coming too late to help me. It was healthier to look back to the beginning of women's rights and mark the progress. In its first case on sex discrimination in 1873, the Supreme Court upheld a state law barring women from the practice of law. Justice Bradley wrote in *Bradwell v. Illinois*, "Man is, or should be, woman's protector and defender. The natural and proper timidity and delicacy of the female sex evidently unfits it for many of the occupations of civil life." *We've come a long way, baby!*

A year later, however, the heartening news of *Desert Palace v. Costa* was offset by a study of the Bush administration's record on civil rights. The November 22, 2004, *New York Times* carried the headline, "Enforcement of Civil Rights Law Declined Since '99, Study Finds." A Syracuse University study reported that federal enforcement of civil rights laws dropped sharply since 1999 even though the number of complaints remained constant. The study reported that only 84 charges of civil rights violations were brought by the U.S. Justice Department in 2003. During the same period, the department brought 33,000 illegal drug prosecutions. Priorities change as the political pendulum and appointments swing. Combined with his constant campaign rhetoric against "frivolous lawsuits" in 2004, I knew Bush was no advocate for civil rights enforcement and litigation.

I had never expected much to come from my EPA complaint, but I felt obligated to continue challenging the district on the unfair, retaliatory, and unethical treatment Superintendent Langan dished out to employees. Now I was done. I had done all that I could do. Besides, life was too good to let anger creep back into the living room. If I let that happen, I'd lose more than a battle, I'd lose the whole war.

Finally Madame DeFarge could put away her knitting needles. It had been the worst of times; now it would be the best of times. George Herbert once said, "Living well is the best revenge," and that was revenge I could live with!

Both sons were happily married and doing well. Rick's umbrella website www.lakevermilion.com was getting over 1 million looks a day. His web work was bringing in a good income, which helped to offset the dramatic increases in our health insurance. When I retired in June 2001, my health insurance premiums were $797 per month. In 2005, they were $1,434 per month. That's an 80% increase in 4 years. Health insurance premiums were chewing up more of my pension each year. Premium increases averaged 20% each year, while pension increases averaged only 2% per year.

For me, the events of 9/11 and the substitute teaching I did as college adjunct instructor had redirected my intellectual energy. Time and redirection had created a perspective by 2003 that allowed the writing of this account without rekindling the fires of rage and pain. Moreover, the research and writing brought a kind of cathartic closure. I felt a growing sense of relief and release as I wrote. Putting the experiences and emotions down on the page, out of the suppressed darkness and into the light of day was a lot healthier than keeping them buried where they could continue to fester and burn.

My story would end at this point, except for the rest of the story about Langan and the district. It's not exactly a "happy ending" because the district I had committed so much time and energy to was in serious trouble. However, I must admit to a certain sense of vindication, of the "I told you so" variety, as the following events unfolded.

Apparently a combination of factors had changed Langan's fortunes dramatically. On May 3, 2003, the *Timberjay* reported that his contract was finally approved for three more years. However, the paper stressed that board members wanted to see improvement. Langan's pay and benefits were frozen, in stark contrast to the thousands of dollars in increased salary and benefits he had requested several months earlier.

One board member added, "She was also concerned about employee morale in the district, which she said was being damaged by the perception that Langan was too retaliatory towards employees who raise objections or who talk privately to board members. We've got to get away from the "wrath of Langan,' she said. 'Morale needs to be dealt with.'"

On July 26, 2003, the *Timberjay* ran a long article and an editorial on the operating relationship between the superintendent and the school board. Two women on the board questioned some of Langan's recommendations and argued that he was not providing enough information for them to make decisions. This regarded a recommendation to purchase over $50,000 of new computers. Langan and board chairman Larry Salmela argued that the women were trying to micromanage the district. A Minnesota School Boards Association director contacted by the newspaper sided with the board members, saying that with such large expenditures, the board members need to be involved from the beginning in calling for bids.

The *Timberjay* editorial headline was clear. "County school board members right to ask questions." The editorial continued, "It's appropriate for board members to ask questions and seek more information before signing off on district initiatives. Stifling debate or discouraging research by board members doesn't serve the best interests of either the district or the public."

The tensions between school board members and Superintendent Langan hit the fan at a study session held a few days later on July 28, 2003. School board chairman Salmela had appointed board members to serve on a subcommittee to review Langan's recommendations for central office reorganization. In the process, the committee members discovered that Langan had hired Peterson, a college student, to work on the district's computers more than a year earlier. Neither that new position nor Peterson's hiring had ever come to the board for action. They learned that Peterson was paid $15 per hour, allowed overtime compensation, given the use of a district vehicle, and received insurance benefits. This salary and benefits package exceeded that of comparable district employees.

Langan's first response to questions about the position was that Peterson was hired as casual labor to avoid having to post the position with the union. According to the August 2, 2003, *Timberjay*, Langan changed his explanation at the July 28 study session. "That's when he announced that Peterson was actually fulfilling a student internship through Bemidji State University. But that explanation has raised question of its own. According to Gloria Joy, an official in the BSU career office, the university has no such internship agreement on file." She also added that BSU internships usually last six weeks and pay only $5.50 per hour.

The two women on the subcommittee drew a rebuke from board chairman Larry Salmela, who continued to blindly support the superintendent. Salmela was quoted, "I think the micromanagement line has been crossed here." He went on to say that he was "deeply disturbed" by what had happened. Salmela then summarily dismissed Bruns and Johnson (the two women) from the Non-Licensed Staff Committee.

Zelda Bruns (the most senior school board member) responded that she didn't deserve to be, "reprimanded for asking questions and taking a more active role on the board. Otherwise, you're just a rubber stamp."

The August 2 *Timberjay* editorial was very blunt. The title read, "Langan's Loss of Credibility." The editorial began, "Can the superintendent of the St. Louis County Schools be believed? That is the question following two lengthy board study sessions this past week, during which Superintendent Dr. Don Langan offered evolving, contradictory and, in some cases, apparently false explanations to legitimate questions raised by two board members." Langan has some explaining to do, "But it could well be too late for that now. The damage to Langan's credibility has been done."

There were more fireworks at the next board meeting on August 11. All three local papers covered the meeting. The August 16 *Timberjay* headlined, "Langan Warned on Retaliation."

The August 16, 2003, *Voyageur Sentinel* printed the full text of board member Liz Johnson's statement. "Many of you know that I am an employee of the Northland Special Education Cooperative. The Co-op Board consists of Superintendents from several Districts, including District 2142. Many of you also know that my position and inquiries on several issues has recently caused quite a stir. In, fact, I understand that I am referred to as the 'blankety-blank, agitated

Liz Johnson.' I am not in this to win a popularity contest, but I do bring this to your attention because the State of Minnesota has laws that protect elected officials from retaliation. I would hope that Dr. Langan understands that any attempt to use his influence to either directly or indirectly affect my employment would be considered by me to be retaliatory."

Following Johnson's statement, Orr Board member Bruns added that arrangements were being made for Board members to meet with a representative of the Minnesota School Boards Association sometime in September. While I sympathized with the two women who were challenging Langan, their belated insight into his methods and tactics came too late to do me any good. During my years of struggle with Langan, they had followed his direction in lockstep.

It finally dawned on me that Langan's most effective control tactic was to pay lip service, in obscure Langanese, to the required or ethical course of action and then go ahead to do whatever he wanted. That tactic left victims or critics of his actions the choice of folding or taking a stand. Most fold and he gets away with it most of the time. It takes a long time before people see him for the control freak he is and then build up sufficient outrage and courage to confront him.

I suspect Langan understood this unfortunate aspect of human behavior, either intuitively or from experience and used it to drive his agenda. Everyone wants to give a new superintendent time to get established, so he gets a honeymoon of a year or two. By then, he's created the atmosphere of retaliation and he's home free.

Langan could then get away with almost anything. He could create new positions and fill them without board approval; he could transfer or refuse to transfer teachers according to his agenda, not according to the contract. The teacher's only choice then was to acquiesce or to file a grievance and surface within range of his retaliation. With the cooperation of a compliant chairman, he could harass and isolate critical board members and watch them quit in disgust. It had taken these two women on the board six years to get out ahead of the men and zero in on Langan and they were paying for it. At least they didn't quit.

It was a constant disillusionment for me that the concepts of rights and legal protections only appeal to people when they are affected personally. Few people understand the toughest test of civil rights. Everyone's rights have to be defended, even those of unpopular people or causes, if anyone's rights are to remain secure.

The most powerful expression of this concept I've ever read was Maurice Ogden's poem, *The Hangman*. When the Hangman first came to town, they asked him, "Hangman, who is he for whom you raise the gallows-tree."

"He who serves me best," said he, "shall earn the rope of the gallows-tree." After the hangman has hung everyone else in town, he comes to hang the last one standing, who had spoken up for no one.

"You tricked me," he cries to the Hangman.

"First the alien, then the Jew...I did no more than you let me do," replied the Hangman. "Who has served me more faithfully?"

A more succinct statement of the concept is, "All it needs for evil to prevail is for good people to do nothing."

On a more positive note, I felt my challenges were vindicated by the growing consensus about Langan's vengeful and retaliatory tactics. What had gone around was beginning to come around.

According to the September 25, 2003, *Cook News Herald*, the school board held a four hour study session with a representative from the MSBA to deal with board member's working relations with each other and with the administration. But it was too late to fix things for Langan. The September 27 *Timberjay* headlined, "Investigation finds more troubling inaccuracies from Sup't Langan." Board member Bruns was quoted in bold about computer tech Peterson's salary. **"We were told as a board the district was being reimbursed for part of his salary. That concerns me, because it was just not so."** Bruns went on to say that the amount of money was less important that the fact that the board was misinformed by Langan.

"The district is in desperate need of new leadership." That was the October 11, 2003, editorial in the *Timberjay*. "Employee morale is at rock bottom. Financial errors have dogged the district. Important changes in educational structure have been made haphazardly, without sufficient planning. School infrastructure continues to deteriorate without any credible plan to address the problems. The superintendent's credibility is in serious question and his decisionmaking has become increasingly flawed."

In response to that editorial, the school board decided it should evaluate the superintendent. They discussed contacting the MSBA for assistance in determining which format to use. The October 16 *Cook News Herald* reported on their discussions, including asking principals and staff to participate in the process. It was stipulated that none of the participants would have to sign their names.

The October 16, 2003, *Timberjay* editorial identified other issues related to evaluating the superintendent. "For years, the board has had its understanding of the district's operations filtered almost exclusively through Langan." The editor pointed out that the board would have to take a more active role, to seek out other district personnel willing to talk openly in order to conduct a valid evaluation.

"Finding individuals willing to speak openly could prove a problem in a district that has operated for too long on fear. Over the past couple years, I have personally received dozens of e-mails from individuals within the district, citing Langan's latest act of retaliation, another problem unaddressed, or yet another ulterior motive behind the latest scheme he's offered to the board. Virtually all of them are anonymous or written by individuals who urge me not to use their name for fear they'll be transferred to some district purgatory. The board can't be unaware of Langan's penchant for retaliation, nor his constant scheming against perceived enemies. What some on the board don't seem to be aware of, however, is how destructive Langan's actions have been not only to employee morale, but to the effective functioning of the district."

That's the effect of my failure to reverse my involuntary transfer. That's the chilling effect of retaliation.

Those were powerful editorials that made me proud of my neighborhood. Who would think that such a rural, remote, and sparsely populated region would produce journalism of that caliber.

This was journalism which courageously performed the highest professional calling, to monitor and hold accountable those in public positions of authority and power. It reminded me of Jefferson's statement. "If I had to decide whether we should have a government without newspapers or newspapers without government, I should not hesitate a moment to prefer the latter."

That professionalism is even more remarkable when it occurs in a weekly publication in very small towns. It's easy to understand why the *Timberjay* has not been selected as the official newspaper of any of the local city councils or the school board. Only newspapers that don't bite the hand that feeds them get those contracts.

In 20 years, I've never read an editorial in the *Cook News Herald* criticizing the superintendent or school board. The critical editorials are reserved for those who challenge the school district. Guess who holds the official publishing contract for the school district?

The November 1, 2003, *Timberjay* reported on the process being adopted to evaluate the superintendent. District office staff and principals were being asked to contribute, as well as board members. Langan recommended color-coded response sheets. District staff and principals refused to participate if their responses were put on color-coded forms. They were afraid they could be identified. It was then decided that all responses would be on white paper and anonymous. *That's how cold the chilling effect of retaliation can be.*

On November 15, the *Timberjay* continued its demand for accountability in the superintendent's evaluation. The article and editorial demanded that a summary of the superintendent's evaluation be published and that the summary be detailed. The summary should include the superintendent's identified strengths, weaknesses, plans for improvement, and future goals.

The storm surrounding Langan's superintendency quieted for a few months, but the pressure built again in March, 2004. The March 11 *Cook News Herald* reported that things were a little tense at the March 8 board meeting. This round of trouble began in early March, when two board members, newly elected chairperson Zelda Bruns and Rolland Fowler, attended a regional school board conference on student testing. At that meeting they learned for the first time that Langan had committed the district to a new testing program, above and beyond what the state and federal government required.

The March 13, 2004, *Timberjay* quoted Fowler on the revelation, "We went into the meeting. It was like we'd got hit in the head by a brick wall." Fowler described the shock he felt upon learning that Langan had been working on the proposal since October. "We had known nothing about it."

Then the board learned that there was no estimate of what participation in this new testing program would cost. The *Timberjay* discussed this with the business manager who said that in addition to $9,000 in software already ordered, the testing program required laptop computers for all teachers. In reply to questions about costs, "She wouldn't know the cost of the computer purchase until bids come in next week. It could be $300,000 or it could be $1.3 million." No wonder the board was upset.

Tensions erupted at the March 8 board meeting after chairperson Bruns brought a policy amendment to the board for a first reading. The new policy would severely limit the powers of the superintendent. It had seven provisions. Any new positions, new hires, changes in personnel assignments (including transfers) or job descriptions, or changes in employee wages or benefits had to have prior board approval. Any new programs added at any school site and any change in the district's testing program had to have prior board approval.

Former chairman Larry Salmela objected to the reading of the policy amendments, saying it was not added correctly to the agenda and could be construed as a violation of the Open Meeting Law. He said he would not be a part of it and he walked out of the meeting. I don't remember another time when a board member walked out of a meeting in protest. *Interesting behavior from the former chairman who called for illegal "straw votes" at unposted study sessions, all in violation of the Open Meeting Law.*

The March 13, 2004, *Timberjay* editorial headlined, "School Board Right to Demand Accountability." The article continued, "While Langan wastes time and district resources on pet projects, all of which seem to have ulterior objectives, real needs within the district go unmet." Board member Rolland Fowler was quoted, "We're tying his hands, and justifiably so."

This from Fowler, who had traveled with Salmela to Grand Marais in 1997 to check on Langan and never talked to the board members who had resigned during Langan's superintendency. "Retaliatory," "vindictive," "dishonest," "wants the board to be a rubber-stamp," "destructive," "spends more than he should" were all expressions currently being used to describe Langan's behavior. They could have heard these same comments and had warning about Langan seven years earlier, in 1997, from board members in Grand Marais—if they had only done their job.

Friends, family, and former colleagues commented to me throughout these months of turmoil for Langan. I heard a lot of, "You were right all along," "They should have listened to you when you warned them," "This stuff never would have happened if they'd hired you in the first place." Better late than never, I thought—but not bitterly. Truthfully, it sounded pretty good.

By March 27, 2004, the *Timberjay* reported, "St. Louis County school district superintendent announces he'll retire at the end of the current year." That was inevitable after the board's recent actions to limit his authority. Such limitations would be a nuisance to most, but intolerable to a control freak like Langan. The entire process was long overdue, but what had gone around was finally coming around.

However, the next board meeting was astounding. According to the April 15, 2004, *Cook News Herald,* at their regular meeting on Monday April 12, the board voted to put Langan on paid leave until June 30, *effective the next day.* The board's next motion was to hire former superintendent Dan Mobilia as interim superintendent *effective the next day* through August 30.

A district employee told me that *the next day,* two board members met Langan at the door when he came in to pack his things. They monitored his packing and escorted him out of the central office. This was a first and could have only been precipitated by an immediate and extraordinary failure of trust. *I wonder what caused this drastic action?*

Mobilia's service was intended to be short-term and the school board posted the permanent superintendent's position. The board offered the position to a woman in June, 2004, and in what I consider the ultimate demonstration of progress for women in their ongoing assault on the glass ceiling, she turned it down!

Mobilia agreed to extend his service to the district for another month. By August, the school board had hired another retired superintendent, Russ Johnson, to serve as interim superintendent until another candidate could be selected for the permanent position.

Four months later, the January 15, 2005, *Timberjay* headlined, "Simonson among finalists for superintendent job."

Unbelievable! Several board members had testified in their 2001 depositions that they could not hire Simonson as superintendent in 1997 after what they had learned from their visit to Glenwood.

However, the board did not select Simonson for the permanent position, turning instead to Charles Rick who was currently serving as superintendent in a southern Minnesota school district. He would begin his superintendent service with the county schools in July, 2005.

Meanwhile, another controversy distracted the school board. In the previous November school board elections, there was a close election in the Orr attendance area and the results were challenged. Many absentee voters did not receive their ballots in the mail, so a district court judge ordered a new election. The January 27, 2005, *Voyageur Sentinel* carried a paid political ad from Zelda Bruns, Orr incumbent in the new election. "It is unusual for the elections of School Board representatives in our District to be contested in the manner they were last November. The unusual level of campaign activity against incumbent Board members has clearly been organized and assisted by a few influential supporters of the former superintendent." *More of Langan's vindictiveness.* However, Bruns prevailed in the court-ordered election and continued to serve a chairperson of the school board.

The last chapter in this school district saga came with no warning on May 9, 2005. The *Cook News Herald* reported that at a regular school board meeting, the interim superintendent Russ Johnson abruptly resigned, effective immediately. His resignation statement included, "My comfort level has always, and will always, be aligned with the philosophy of the Minnesota School Boards Association with regard to the school board/superintendent relationship as it relates to the roles and responsibilities of each. In the absence of such a relationship, that comfort level on my part has reached a point where I no longer wish to continue as the interim superintendent of ISD 2142. Hence, I am resigning effective the end of the working day on May 9, 2005." *That same day! And another guy just walks off the job!*

The May 11 *Duluth News Tribune* said that Johnson attributed his resignation to an unsatisfactory relationship with the school board. Assistant superintendent Simonson would serve as interim until Charles Rick took over in July. That same article quoted Assistant Superintendent Simonson, "The district has employed at least seven superintendents during the past nine years."

On June 4, 2005, the *Timberjay* reported that the school board was still struggling to cope with Langan's tenure as superintendent. "We're putting a hold on everything to have a better look at our finances," said board chairman Zelda Bruns. Obviously, in spite of his Ph.D. and his years of experience, Langan was not the most qualified candidate when they hired him. The editorial in that issue discussed the costs of not having had a detail-oriented top administrator. "Lacking such an administrator, the district has been left mostly with chaos."

After I failed to get the Cook principalship in 1986, the Cook School had five principals in 10 years. That high turnover was followed by three years with an unlicensed administrator receiving OJT (on-the-job-training). The superintendency had not fared much better. That kind of administrative turnover compromises continuity and leadership. I hoped for the sake of the students, teachers, and communities that the St. Louis County School District would finally have the leadership it needed with the new superintendent.

Even that hope seemed dashed in early 2006. The March 25, 2006, *Timberjay* reported that the new superintendent, Charles Rick, was one of two finalists for another superintendency in southern Minnesota. The article stated that, "Board Chairwoman Zelda Bruns acknowledged that she was disappointed that Rick even applied for another job after only seven months as the district's superintendent."

Rick said he knew when he was hired that the district faced significant enrollment and financial challenges. "I knew it was not going to be easy." *The district was continuing to pay a high price for Langan's tenure.*

What had gone around had come around for my discriminating and retaliating former colleagues, for both Langan and the school board.

The circle was complete. I had begun my administrative career in 1979 after my predecessor walked off the job as high school principal at Buhl. Over the years, I watched many other men in top administrative positions break their contracts and walk off the job. The Buhl superintendent left abruptly mid-year in 1983. Bangston left the Mt. Iron-Buhl superintendency overnight after his falsified letters of recommendation and mail-order degrees were made public. Neuenfeldt had walked off the job as assistant superintendent in the St. Louis County district in 1996 over disagreements with the superintendent. Zitterkopf disappeared from that same assistant superintendent position in May 1997.

Simonson had been forced to resign from the Glenwood assistant superintendency in 1990 and Langan had been forced to resign from the St. Louis County superintendency. That's eight men, most of whom I had lost positions to, that were either forced to resign from their administrative positions or who walked out on their contracts.

I was proud I had never done that. Make no mistake, I was sorely tempted many times, particularly when Simonson was hired as assistant and interim superintendent in June 1997, when Langan was hired as superintendent behind closed doors in October 1997, and when I was involuntarily transferred to Tower in August 1999. But my dad had always been adamant, whether it was my younger brother who found a morning paper route less rewarding than he expected or myself when a summer job in junior high messed up my social life. "You don't quit something you've started, you see it through, you stick it out." I learned his lessons well.

Maybe those lessons helped determine that when the going got tough and the choice was fight or flight, I chose to stand and fight. I didn't always win, but I fought righteous battles. In retrospect, I'm comfortable with the choices I made. I've nothing to be ashamed of and it seems to me, those men do.

Every time I challenged, filed a formal complaint, or sued against discrimination or retaliation, women won. I don't pretend to take credit for their successes. Their achievements were due to their merit and talents. However, the door has to be pried open for merit and talent to get into the offices and boardrooms. I was simply fighting my own battles. But by asserting my rights, I believe I helped end some discriminatory practices and open a few doors and opportunities for others.

Civil rights works a lot like Adam Smith's capitalism. When individuals selfishly pursue their own rights, an "invisible hand" works to advance the rights of everyone. Following my battles, women gained pay for maternity leave and the first women were hired as high school principals and superintendents in northeast Minnesota. Even after my 2001 loss in summary judgment, changes continued. In 2004, the district finally terminated Superintendent Langan's reign of retaliation, which I had first identified and confronted in 1998–1999.

Sometimes it is better to stand and lose than to never stand at all.

Civil rights will continue to evolve, as evidenced by the 2006 Supreme Court decision in *Burlington Northern Santa Fe Railway v. White.* Linda Greenhouse reported on this case in the April 17, 2006, *New York Times.* This was a case about retaliation against a woman after she had complained about sexual harassment on her railroad job and was then transferred from her position as a forklift operator to the much more arduous track gang. The railroad and the Bush administration argued for a definition of retaliation requiring a "materially adverse change in the terms, conditions, or privileges of employment."

Unfortunately, the original prohibition against retaliation in Title

VII of the Civil Rights Act of 1964 was mute on the definition of what constitutes retaliation. Since 1964, conservative lower courts had made it almost impossible to win a retaliation case unless the retaliation resulted in dismissal. The standard used by the EEOC had been adopted during the Clinton administration and defined retaliation as "any adverse treatment that had a retaliatory motive and was reasonably likely to deter employees from making complaints in the future." Now the Supreme Court would decide and define retaliation.

In June, 2006, the Supreme Court added a final, bittersweet riff to my plaintiff blues. The Court's 9 to 0 decision in *Burlington Northern Santa Fe Railway v. White* was five years too late for me. As Greenhouse reported in the June 23, 2006, *New York Times*, Burlington significantly expanded employee protection against retaliation in the workplace. The decision provided that any materially adverse employment action that might have dissuaded a reasonable worker from complaining about discrimination would count as prohibited retaliation.

"Thus, retaliation can be found in unfavorable evaluations, unwelcome schedule changes, or other actions well short of losing a job." *My experience exactly!*

I lost in summary judgment in 2001 because I had no "direct evidence" and because the retaliation had not resulted in my dismissal. In 2003, the Supreme Court removed the direct evidence hurdle in *Desert Palace v. Costa* and in 2006, the *Burlington* decision significantly broadened employees protection against retaliation. Costa and White stood up and everyone won.

So while my plaintiff blues may have had some poignant riffs and discordant licks along the way, the composition ends on the upbeat, on a positive note.

People have to know and assert their rights or nothing changes for anyone. Martin Luther King wrote, "Injustice anywhere is a threat to justice everywhere." President John F. Kennedy once said, "The rights of every man are diminished when the rights of one man are threatened."

I never doubted that meant me too!